ADVANCED BUSINESS MATHEMATICS

Series editor
Brian Coyle

PASSWORD ADVANCED BUSINESS MATHEMATICS

First edition May 1990

ISBN 1 871824 09 5

Published by
BPP Publishing Ltd
Aldine House, Aldine Place,
142/144 Uxbridge Road, London W12 8AW

Printed by Dotesios Printers Ltd, Trowbridge

A CIP Catalogue reference for this book
is available from the British Library

CONTENTS

PREFACE

Password is a series of multiple choice question books on business and accountancy topics. If you are studying for an examination, or would just like to test your knowledge on one of these topics, Password books have two special features which are designed to help you.

1 They contain about 300 multiple choice questions, with answers provided later in the book. You can get an objective idea of your strengths and weaknesses, and whether your standard is as high as you would like it to be.

2 We explain most solutions in some detail, to show why one answer is correct and the others are wrong. Our comments should help you to learn from any mistakes you have made, and to improve your understanding of the subject.

Objective testing is an increasingly popular method of examination. An answer is right or wrong, and there are no 'grey areas' or 'in-between answers' that are half-right or arguably correct. Multiple choice questions (MCQs) are the form of objective testing that is now most widely used. Professional bodies that have adopted MCQs for some examination papers include the Institute of Chartered Accountants in England and Wales, the Institute of Chartered Accountants of Scotland, the Chartered Institute of Management Accountants and the Chartered Association of Certified Accountants.

MCQs offer much more than exam practice, though. They test your knowledge and understanding. And they help with learning.

- The brevity of the questions, and having to select a correct answer from four choices (A, B, C or D), makes them convenient to use. You can do some on your journey to or from work or college on the train or the bus.

- We know from experience that many people like MCQs, find them fun and enjoy the opportunity to mark their own answers exactly.

- Being short, MCQs are able collectively to cover every aspect of a topic area. They make you realise what you know and what you don't.

If you're looking for the fun and challenge of self-testing, or preparing for an examination - not just a multiple choice exam - Password is designed to help you. You can check your own standard, monitor your progress, spot your own weaknesses, and learn things that you hadn't picked up from your text-book or study manual. Most important, Password books allow you to find out for yourself how good you are at a topic, and how much better you want to be.

Good luck!

Brian Coyle
May 1990

PASSWORD. MULTIPLE CHOICE

HOW TO USE THIS BOOK

Aims of the book

This book is designed:

- to familiarise you with a type of question that you are increasingly likely to face if you are studying for examinations.

- to develop your knowledge of Business Mathematics through repeated practice on questions covering all areas of the subject. There are about 300 questions in this book.

The multiple choice approach

A multiple choice question is in two parts.

- The *stem* sets out the problem or task to be solved. It may be in the form of a question, or it may be an unfinished statement which has to be completed.

- The *options* are the possible responses from which you must choose the one you believe to be correct. There is only one correct option (called the *key*); the other, incorrect, options are called *distractors*.

There are various ways in which you may be asked to indicate your chosen response. If you meet with MCQs in an examination, you should obviously read the instructions carefully. In this book, you will find that the options are identified by the letters A, B, C, D. To indicate your choice, draw a circle round the letter you have chosen.

The notes

In Section 1 of this book each chapter begins with brief notes which are designed to refresh your memory of the subject area and get you thinking along the right lines before you begin to tackle the questions.

The notes are *not* a substitute for a textbook: Password assumes that you are already broadly familiar with the topics covered in the chapter. Nor do they give you answers to all the questions.

- The notes are a *reminder* of the key points in each topic area. If your studies have left you feeling that you can't see the wood for the trees, the notes may help to bring the important issues into focus.

- They provide brief *guidance* on particularly knotty points or areas which often cause problems for students.

The questions

The questions are arranged roughly in the order of the key areas highlighted by the notes. But it is difficult, and undesirable, to keep topics completely separate: there's a great deal of overlapping.

The general principle has been for questions *on each topic* to get progressively harder. The result of this is that within a single chapter the level of difficulty will rise, and then fall back to begin rising again. So if you have trouble with two or three questions, don't assume that you have to give up on the whole chapter: there may be easier questions ahead!

If you can, try to work through a whole chapter before turning to the solutions. If you refer to the marking schedule after each question you will find it almost impossible to avoid seeing the answer to the next question, and the value of the book will be lessened.

Finally, don't rush your answers. Distractors are exactly what their name suggests: they are meant to look plausible and distract you from the correct option. Unless you are absolutely certain you know the answer, look carefully at each option in turn before making your choice. You will need a calculator and a pen, and paper for rough workings would be helpful, although you could use the blank space on each page for any rough workings that you need to do.

The marking schedules

The marking schedules indicate the correct answer to each question and the number of marks available. You should add up the marks on all the questions you got right and compare your total with the maximum marks available.

At the foot of each marking schedule there is a rating, which is intended to be helpful in indicating the amount of work you still need to do on each topic. You'll need to use your discretion in interpreting your rating, though. The book may be used by a very wide range of readers, from college students and students of professional, business and accountancy courses, to qualified managers with years of practical experience. A mark of 8 out of 25 might be worryingly low for an experienced person, while representing a very creditable achievement for someone at an earlier stage of his or her studies.

The comments

The answers to purely factual questions generally need no explanation, but for most questions there is a commentary or a numerical solution, usually set out in some detail.

These comments will usually describe why a particular option is correct and (more commonly) set out the calculations leading to the correct answer. Distractors are usually chosen to illustrate common misconceptions, or plausible, but incorrect, lines of calculation. The comments will often highlight what is wrong about particular distractors and this should help in clarifying your ideas about topics that you may have misunderstood.

Tables

Mathematical tables are included at the end of the book. You may of course use your own tables if you prefer, but you could get slightly different answers if your tables give values to different numbers of significant figures.

Calculators

Although you could do an advanced business mathematics course with a four-function (+, -, ×, ÷) calculator, you will find a more sophisticated calculator a great time-saver. Particularly useful are buttons for x^y and $x^{1/y}$, for finding powers and roots. Also handy are buttons for $1/x$, $x!$, $\log x$, 10^x and e^x. If you are studying for an examination, you should of course check what types of calculator are allowed in the examination.

Conclusion

Password Advanced Business Mathematics is designed as an aid both to learning and to revision. It is not primarily aimed at those who are already expert in the subject. So don't expect to score 100%. And don't despair if your marks seem relatively low. Choosing the wrong answer to a question is not a failure, if by studying the solution and comments you learn something you did not know before. This is particularly relevant if you are using the book at an early stage in your studies, rather than in the final stages of revision.

And if you *do* score 100%? There are 14 other Password titles to get through...

SECTION 1
NOTES AND QUESTIONS

CHAPTER 1

ELEMENTARY PROBABILITY THEORY

This chapter covers the following topics:

- The importance of probability
- Basic probability computations
- Combining outcomes of several events
- Introduction to expected value

1. The importance of probability

1.1 This book covers a wide range of mathematical techniques, all intended to help people in business make effective decisions. The main problem in decision making is that the future is always uncertain, and many of the techniques we will look at try to take account of this uncertainty in a precise way. *Probability theory* is the main mathematical technique for dealing with uncertainty, so you will find it applied repeatedly in this book.

2. Basic probability computations

2.1 **Events and outcomes**

Very often, doing the computations is far easier than working out which computations to do. It is always a good first step to distinguish clearly between the following:

- Events - an *event* (also called a *trial*) is an occasion on which something happens, and there may be various results (outcomes)

- Outcomes - an *outcome* is a possible result of an event.

For example, you might invest in the shares of a particular company (an event) and the shares might do well or badly (two possible outcomes).

2.2 **Finding probabilities by counting**

If there are a number of *equally likely* possible outcomes of an event, we can find probabilities of different sets of outcomes by counting.

2.3 For example, consider the event of rolling two dice, a red die and a blue die. There are 36 equally likely possible outcomes (red = 1, blue = 1; red = 1, blue = 2; ... red = 6, blue = 6). We might be interested in the probability of scoring 10. There are three outcomes in which the total score is 10 (red = 4, blue = 6; red = 5, blue = 5; red = 6, blue = 4), so the probability of scoring 10 is 3/36.

2.4 **Permutations and combinations**

It is because we can often find probabilities by counting that permutations and combinations are important in probability theory. They give us the number of possible ways of choosing x items from n. Any one particular random choice is as likely as any other, so the probability of getting any one choice is 1/(number of possible choices).

2.5

- Number of permutations of x items from n = $_nP_x$ = $\dfrac{n!}{(n-x)!}$

- Number of combinations of x items from n = $_nC_x$ = $\dfrac{n!}{(n-x)!x!}$

2.6 We use the permutations formula when the order of choice matters, eg choosing two people to be senior manager and junior manager respectively. We use the combinations formula when the order of choice is irrelevant, eg choosing three people to be junior managers.

3. Combining outcomes of several events

3.1 We may be interested in the probability of a particular set of outcomes, for example doubling turnover *and* increasing profit by 50%.

3.2 If A and B are particular outcomes, the rules we need are these:

- *Addition rule:* P(A or B) = P(A) + P(B) - P(A and B)

- *Multiplication rule:* P (A and B)   = P(A) × P(B|A) = P(B) × P(A|B)

- *Conditional probabilities rule:* P(A|B) = $\dfrac{P(A)\ P(B|A)}{P(B)}$

In the addition rule, A *or* B means A or B or both. Use this rule if we are interested in at least one of the outcomes occurring, and use the multiplication rule if we are interested in both outcomes occurring.

P(A|B) means the probability of outcome A occurring, given that outcome B occurs. This is sometimes written $P_B(A)$.

3.3 Mutual exclusivity and independence

Two outcomes, A and B, are *mutually exclusive* if they cannot both happen. In that case, P(A and B) = 0 and the addition rule becomes P(A or B) = P(A) + P(B).

Two events are *independent* if the outcome of either event is unaffected by the outcome of the other. So for any outcome A of one event and any outcome B of the other, $P(A|B) = P(A)$ and $P(B|A) = P(B)$. The multiplication rule then becomes P(A and B) = P(A) × P(B).

3.4 If we want to know the probability of one outcome occurring, given that another outcome occurs, we can use the conditional probabilities rule or we can draw up a table. For example, if P(A) = 0.5, $P(B|A)$ = 0.3, and P(B) = 0.6, we could imagine the event happening a large number of times, say 100 (any number will do, but round numbers usually make the arithmetic easier), and draw up a table:

	A	Not A	Total	Workings
B	15	45	60	0.5 × 100 = 50 (bottom left)
Not B	35	5	40	0.3 × 50 = 15 (top left)
Total	50	50	100	0.6 × 100 = 60 (top right)
				All other figures: balancing figures

$P(A|B)$ = (Number with B and A)/(Number with B) = 15/60 = 0.25.

4. Introduction to expected value

4.1 Decision making under uncertainty is covered in the next chapter. Expected value is an important aspect of decision making under uncertainty, and it is introduced in this chapter because it applies probability theory very directly.

4.2 An expected value can be worked out when the possible outcomes are given in numerical terms (for example, units sold or pounds of profit). The expected value is found by multiplying each outcome figure by the probability of that outcome's occurring, and adding the results.

> Expected value = EV = Σpx
>
> where x = an outcome's figure
>   p = probability of that outcome.

QUESTIONS

1 Three coins are tossed. What is the probability of getting precisely two heads?

A 0.125
B 0.25
C 0.375
D 0.5

Circle your answer

A   B   C   D

2 In how many different ways can a committee of three men and two women be formed from a council of eight men and nine women?

A 92
B 2,016
C 2,352
D 6,188

Circle your answer

A   B   C   D

3 There are six winners of a business competition. There are eleven prizes, eight new cars and three books on management. If each winner is allocated a prize at random, what is the probability that every winner gets a new car?

A 0.061
B 0.364
C 0.727
D 0.75

Circle your answer

A   B   C   D

4 Nine internal auditors, A, B, C, D, E, F, G, H and I, are to be divided into three teams of three. Each team must include one of A, B and C, as they are the three most experienced. In how many different ways can the teams be made up?

A 21
B 90
C 270
D 360

Circle your answer

A   B   C   D

5 Five cards are dealt from an ordinary 52-card pack. What is the probability that they are all of the same suit?

A 0.000495
B 0.000977
C 0.001981
D 0.003906

Circle your answer

A   B   C   D

6 A card game uses the jacks, queens, kings and aces from an ordinary pack. Each of four players is dealt four cards. In what proportion of games will every player be dealt four cards of the same suit?

A 1 game in 7,280
B 1 game in 2,627,625
C 1 game in 63,063,000
D 1 game in 42,859,350,625

Circle your answer

A   B   C   D

7 If, for two outcomes R and S, P (R and S) = P(R) × P(S), the two outcomes must be

A mutually exclusive
B outcomes of independent events
C both mutually exclusive and outcomes of independent events
D neither mutually exclusive nor outcomes of independent events

Circle your answer

A   B   C   D

8 If two outcomes, R and S, are both mutually exclusive and outcomes of independent events, it follows that

A at least one of them is impossible
B at least one of them must happen
C they are both impossible
D their probabilities add up to 1

Circle your answer

A   B   C   D

9 The probability that it will rain on Sunday is 0.3. The probability that it will rain on Monday is 0.2 if it is dry on Sunday, but 0.4 if it rains on Sunday. What is the probability that it will rain on at least one of the two days?

A 0.12
B 0.38
C 0.44
D 0.88

Circle your answer

A   B   C   D

10 In a large business school, 52% of the students are women and 8% of the students are mathematicians. There is no correlation between gender and subject. If two students are chosen at random, what is the probability that each of them is a woman or a mathematician or both?

A 0.08
B 0.31
C 0.36
D 0.56

Circle your answer

A   B   C   D

7

11

Three outcomes, J, K and L, may occur. The probability of J occurring is 0.4. The probability of K occurring is 0.6 if J occurs, but 0.3 if J does not occur. The probability of L occurring is 0.2 if K occurs, but 0.7 if K does not occur. What is the probability of precisely one of the outcomes occurring?

A   0.048
B   0.476
C   0.486
D   0.874

Circle your answer

A   B   C   D

12

A bank manager classifies each clerk as good or bad at counting cash, at writing reports and at telephoning customers. The probability of a clerk being good at counting cash is 0.4. The probability of a clerk being good at writing reports is 0.6. The probability of a clerk being good at telephoning customers is 0.2 if he is good at neither of the other skills, 0.4 if he is good at only one of the other skills, and 0.7 if he is good at both of the other skills. What is the probability that a clerk is good at precisely two skills?

A   0.280
B   0.352
C   0.472
D   0.640

Circle your answer

A   B   C   D

13

Plates produced in a pottery are inspected for size and colour. 4% of plates are the wrong size and 3% are the wrong colour. There is no correlation between the incidence of these defects. There is an 0.06 probability that a plate of the wrong size will pass the size inspection, and an 0.03 probability that a plate of the wrong colour will pass the colour inspection. What percentage of defective plates will pass both inspections?

A   0.33%
B   4.64%
C   8.82%
D   9.00%

Circle your answer

A   B   C   D

14

A company has three departments, each with a profit target. Department S will exceed its target (probability 0.4) or meet it. Department T will meet its target (probability 0.7) or fall short. Department U will meet its target (probability 0.8) or fall short. The results of the three departments are independent of one another. The company will meet its overall target only if (i) all three departments at least meet their targets, or (ii) S exceeds its target and only one of T and U falls short of its target. What is the probability that the company meets its overall target?

A   0.488
B   0.560
C   0.712
D   0.940

Circle your answer

A   B   C   D

15 A shopkeeper has found the following probability distribution for daily demand for a product:

Demand (units)	Probability
100	0.1
200	0.3
300	0.4
400	0.2
	1.0

What is the probability that, over a 3-day period, demand will be 1,000 units or more?

A 0.068
B 0.152
C 0.188
D 0.204

Circle your answer

A   B   C   D

16 A company produces mirrors. 82% of mirrors are perfect, 15% are fit to be sold as seconds, and 3% should not be sold at all. All mirrors which are sent out to shops are categorised by the company and inspected by the shopkeepers (who never make mistakes) and the company incurs financial penalties for wrongly categorising mirrors. The company's inspection process passes all perfect mirrors as perfect, passes 2% of seconds as perfect, rejects 6% of seconds as unsaleable, passes 4% of unsaleable mirrors as seconds, and rejects 96% of unsaleable mirrors. What is the probability that a mirror sent out to a shop will be wrongly categorised?

A 0.0036
B 0.0042
C 0.0044
D 0.0132

Circle your answer

A   B   C   D

17 If the finance director is ill, the probability of a particular board meeting being cancelled is 0.8. If he is not ill the probability of cancellation is 0.1. The probability of his being ill is 0.4. If the board meeting is cancelled, what is the probability that he is ill?

A 0.38
B 0.61
C 0.80
D 0.84

Circle your answer

A   B   C   D

18 A company makes black ball point pens and red ball point pens, making twice as many black pens as red pens. Both colours are made in both of the company's factories. In factory X, 2% of black pens and 3% of red pens are defective. In factory Y, 1% of black pens and 4% of red pens are defective. Factory X produces three times as many pens of each colour as factory Y. If a pen is selected at random from the combined output of the two factories and is found to be defective, what is the probability that it came from factory Y?

A   0.22
B   0.25
C   0.29
D   0.46

Circle your answer

A   B   C   D

19 If, for two outcomes R and S, P(R|S) > P(R), we may conclude that:

A   R tends to cause S
B   S tends to cause R
C   the events of which R and S are possible outcomes are dependent events
D   the occurrence of R makes the occurrence of S less likely

Circle your answer

A   B   C   D

20 The profitability of a new product depends on the cost of a raw material. If the cost is high, the probability of the product making a profit is 0.1. The probability of a high cost is 0.3. The overall probability of a low cost and the product being profitable is 0.6. What is the overall probability of the product not being profitable?

A   0.36
B   0.37
C   0.63
D   0.67

Circle your answer

A   B   C   D

21 Which of the following is *not* a limitation of the use of the expected value method in decision making?

A   The method requires knowledge of probabilities

B   Sensitivity of expected value to errors in predictions cannot be measured

C   The method is of limited use for one-off decisions

D   The consequences of extreme outcomes may not be adequately taken into account

Circle your answer

A   B   C   D

22 Joe has an opportunity to play a game of chance, in two stages. It costs £1 to enter. In stage 1, he has an 0.2 probability of having his £1 refunded, and an 0.5 probability of going on to stage 2. In stage 2, he has an 0.3 probability of receiving £4. What is the expected value to Joe of playing the game?

   A   -40p
   B   -20p
   C   40p
   D   80p

Circle your answer

A	B	C	D

23 A company is going to sell a new type of pen. The pens will be sold for £2 each. Variable costs per pen may be 60p (probability 0.4) or 80p. Fixed costs per week will be £900. Demand per week may be 2,000 pens (probability 0.4) or 3,000 pens. What is the expected weekly profit, if production is always adjusted to demand?

   A   £2,380
   B   £2,428
   C   £3,280
   D   £3,328

Circle your answer

A	B	C	D

24 A gambler plays a game which uses five cards, bearing the numbers 1 to 5. The cards are face down on a table. He pays £8 to enter, and then selects two cards. He is then paid the same number of pounds as the sum of the numbers on the two cards. What is the expected value to him of playing the game?

   A   -£5
   B   -£2
   C   £3
   D   £6

Circle your answer

A	B	C	D

25 Mary bets Ken that she can predict tomorrow whether or not the stock market will go up the day after. The actual probability of the stock market going up on any day is 0.4. If it will in fact go up on any day, Mary has an 0.6 probability of correctly predicting this the day before. If it will in fact not go up on any day, she has an 0.8 probability of correctly predicting this the day before. If Mary is right, Ken will pay her £10. How much will Mary pay Ken if she is wrong, given that the bet has an expected value to her of £2?

   A   £5.20
   B   £14.29
   C   £18.57
   D   £20.57

Circle your answer

A	B	C	D

CHAPTER 2

DECISION MAKING UNDER UNCERTAINTY

This chapter covers the following topics:

- Choosing between actions
- Maximising expected value
- The value of information
- Utility
- Criteria which ignore probabilities
- The assessment of risk

1. Choosing between actions

1.1 In business we often have to choose between possible actions, not knowing what the outcome will be.

1.2 The criteria for making such decisions which we will look at differ in the way in which they attach relative importance to different possible outcomes. The choice of criterion depends on circumstances and on our attitudes. For repetitive decisions, expected value may be best; but where certain outcomes would be exceptionally favourable or disastrous, such outcomes alone should perhaps determine the choice of action.

2. Maximising expected value

2.1 Expected value was introduced in the last chapter.

> The *expected value criterion* is to choose the action with the highest expected value.

2.2 Sometimes a sequence of choices has to be made, and the outcome of one choice restricts the options at a later stage. Thus if you choose to build a small factory rather than a large one, you may be unable to choose a high volume of production to take advantage of high demand.

To find the expected value of an early option, first work out the expected values of later options. Then work out the values of outcomes of the earlier options, assuming that at any later point of choice you reach you will choose the option with the highest expected value.

3. The value of information

3.1 Sometimes, uncertainty may be reduced or eliminated by obtaining information.

- *Perfect information* is information about the future which will certainly be right.

- *Imperfect information* is information about the future which may be wrong.

3.2 Information costs money to obtain, so it is useful to be able to work out how much it is worth paying for information. Information is usually valued by the difference it would make to the expected value obtainable.

> The expected value of information = Expected value of the decision with the information - Expected value of the decision without the information.

3.3 The expected value of the decision without the information is the expected value of the option with the highest expected value (because that is the option you would choose).

3.4 The expected value of the decision with the information is:

Σ (expected value of each option you might select) $\times$ (probability you will select that option)

3.5 Where information is perfect, you would always make the right decision (eg build only a small factory if you know that demand will be low). Where information is imperfect, you must allow for the possibility that you will make the wrong decision in computing the expected value of each option.

4. Utility

4.1 The values of outcomes need not be measured only in money terms. A business may have goals other than profit, such as environmental responsibility. However, mathematical decision making techniques do require that the values of outcomes be quantified.

4.2 *Utility* is a general concept of worth of outcomes to an individual or a company. It is measured in *utiles*. One could convert all sorts of rewards into utiles. For example, each £1,000 of profit could equal 1 utile, and each 1% reduction in toxic waste could equal 3 utiles. One could then aim to maximise expected utiles, rather than expected profit.

4.3 The disadvantage of using utility rather than cash amounts is that it is hard to justify any particular conversion rates. Why, for example, should £1,000 of profit equal 1 utile instead of 2?

5. Criteria which ignore probabilities

5.1 Sometimes, it may be appropriate to ignore the relative likelihood of different possible outcomes, and to concentrate solely on particular outcomes. For example, a pessimist might well select the option for which the worst possible outcome is better than the worst possible outcomes of the other options.

5.2

- *Minimax* criterion - select the option which will *minimise* the *maximum* costs or losses.

- *Maximin* criterion - select the option which will *maximise* the *minimum* profits.

- *Minimin* criterion - select the option which will *minimise* the *minimum* costs or losses.

- *Maximax* criterion - *select the option which will maximise the maximum* profits.

5.3 The first two criteria both look at the worst that can happen (high costs, low profits), and the last two both look at the best that can happen. Options are ranked according to their worst outcomes (minimax, maximin) or their best outcomes (minimin, maximax).

5.4 If both profits and losses could arise, treat losses as negative profits and use maximin or maximax.

5.5 **Minimax regret**

We can select an option (for example, build a large factory) and then later (for example, when we find demand is low) wish we had selected a different option. We can work out the *regret* for any particular option and circumstances, as follows:

- Regret   =   Profit for what would have been the best decision in the circumstances - Profit for the actual decision in the circumstances

Where costs or losses are involved, just treat them as negative profits.

5.6 For each decision, we can then identify the highest possible level of regret, and choose the decision with the lowest of these highest regret levels.

- Minimax regret criterion - select the option which will *minimise* the *maximum* regret.

5.7 Applying this criterion, we thus limit the extent to which we might find we have missed out on the opportunity to improve our profits.

6. The assessment of risk

6.1 None of the criteria we have looked at so far take account of the spread of possible outcomes.

6.2 One possible measure of risk is the standard deviation of the values of outcomes, computed as:

$$\sigma = \sqrt{\Sigma p\ (x - \bar{x})^2}$$

where   x = the value of a particular outcome
         p = the probability of that outcome
         $\bar{x}$ = the expected value, $\Sigma p\,x$

In order to take account of the size of the amounts involved, so that the relative risk of different options may be compared, one may work out the coefficient of variation, $\sigma/\bar{x}$.

6.3 Attitudes to risk

Risk is often assumed to be a bad thing, but you should be aware that there are other possible attitudes to risk. One may be:

- *Risk averse*   -   other things being equal, risk should be reduced

- *Risk neutral* -   risk is seen as neither good nor bad

- *Risk seeking* -   other things being equal, risk should be increased (on the basis that the risk of a disastrous outcome is counterbalanced by the chance of an excellent outcome).

QUESTIONS

1 A printer can produce 1,000 or 2,000 copies of a book. Each copy costs £1.50 to produce, and if sold will yield gross revenue of £4. Unsold copies will be pulped, yielding gross revenue of 10p each. The demand for the book may be 1,000 copies (probability 0.3), or 2,000 copies. What is the best achievable expected profit?

A	£2,500
B	£3,830
C	£4,250
D	£5,000

Circle your answer

A   B   C   D

2 A hotelier must decide how many rooms to set aside for delegates at a conference to take place in his town. Any rooms not set aside can be let to tourists for £100, but any rooms set aside but not taken up by conference delegates cannot be let to tourists, because by the time he releases them for tourists they will all have made other arrangements. A room can be let to a conference delegate for £160. He could set aside 40, 45, 50 or 55 rooms. The probabilities of different numbers of delegates applying for rooms are:

Number	Probability
40	0.2
45	0.3
50	0.4
55	0.1

How many rooms should the hotelier set aside to maximise expected revenue?

A	40
B	45
C	50
D	55

Circle your answer

A   B   C   D

3 A concert promoter can hire either of two halls for a concert, as follows:

Hall	Capacity (seats)	Cost
		£
Y	400	590
Z	500	670

Tickets will cost £5 each, and the promoter will be able to sell precisely 300, 400 or 500 of them. The probability of 300 tickets being demanded is 0.2. There are no costs apart from the cost of the hall. If the expected profit from hiring hall Y is the same as that from hiring hall Z, what is the probability of 400 tickets being demanded?

A	0.16
B	0.36
C	0.62
D	0.64

Circle your answer

A   B   C   D

4 In decision-making, perfect information is information which

    A certainly states future conditions or events with perfect accuracy

    B covers every aspect of the business in detail

    C certainly states past conditions or events with perfect accuracy

    D has been obtained from the best available sources

Circle your answer

A	B	C	D

5 In which of the following situations would perfect information have no expected value?

    A One option would be the most profitable in all circumstances

    B The expected values of the two best options, assuming perfect information, are £1,000,000 and £1,000,001

    C The costs of obtaining perfect information exceed its most likely value

    D All options (including doing nothing) would result in losses in all circumstances

Circle your answer

A	B	C	D

6 A professional punter can pick the winning horse in 40% of races. If he is right, he wins on average £50 (plus the return of his stake). If he is wrong, he loses his standard stake of £10. A stable lad can pick the winner every time, and has offered to sell his expertise to the punter. What is the most the punter should pay per race?

    A £26
    B £36
    C £40
    D £50

Circle your answer

A	B	C	D

7 A company considering a new product has already spent £500 on preliminary research. It can now abandon the product, go ahead, or have a market survey done. If the market is good, sales less production costs will be £30,000. If the market is poor, sales less production costs will be -£10,000. It is thought that the probability of a poor market is 0.3. A survey, at a cost of £4,000, could determine with certainty the state of the market. The expected value of the best decision (by reference to the expected value criterion) is

A	£5,000
B	£14,000
C	£17,000
D	£18,000

Circle your answer

A   B   C   D

8 An advertising campaign will begin on radio, and may then move on to television. The advertiser can choose high or low radio exposure, but there is only one level on television. Possible outcomes are as follows:

Option	Cost £	Profit £	Probability	Profit £	Probability
				Possible extra gross profit	
Radio-high	4,000	8,000	0.6	3,000	0.4
Radio-low	1,500	2,000	0.7	500	0.3
Television	50,000				
- if radio high		49,500	1.0		
- if radio low and					
extra profit £2,000		60,000	0.5	46,000	0.5
- if radio low and					
extra profit £500		48,000	1.0		

The results of radio advertising will be known when a decision is taken about television. What is the expected extra gross profit less advertising costs?

A	£1,500
B	£1,550
C	£2,000
D	£2,150

Circle your answer

A   B   C   D

9 A company can make either of two new products, X and Y, but not both. The profitability of each product depends on the state of the market, as follows:

Market state	Profit from product X £	Y £	Probability of market state
Good	20,000	17,000	0.2
Fair	15,000	16,000	0.5
Poor	6,000	7,000	0.3

What is the expected value of perfect information as to the state of the market?

A	£0
B	£600
C	£800
D	£1,000

Circle your answer

A   B   C   D

10 An investor has to choose whether to invest in business P or in business Q. If the business she invests in does not do well, she will make neither a profit nor a loss. If she invests in business P and it does well (probability 0.6), she will make a profit of £18,000. If she invests in business Q and it does well, she will make a profit of £10,000. If the expected value to the investor of perfect information about the future performance of both businesses is £1,500, what is the probability (before obtaining the perfect information) of business Q doing well?

A   0.15
B   0.375
C   0.4
D   0.85

Circle your answer

A   B   C   D

11 A civil engineering company has been offered a contract abroad, payment to be made in a foreign currency which the company would convert into sterling on receipt. Unfortunately the company cannot protect itself against fluctuations in the value of this currency. The sterling eventually received will be £25,000 (probability 0.55) or £19,000 (probability 0.45). Costs (all paid in sterling) will be £18,000 (probability 0.2) or £22,000 (probability 0.8). The company can obtain perfect information on future exchange rates for £1,500, and on costs for £50. The company should obtain perfect information on

A   exchange rates only
B   costs only
C   both exchange rates and costs
D   neither exchange rates nor costs

Circle your answer

A   B   C   D

12 Imperfect information is information which

A   costs more to collect than its value to the business

B   is available only after preliminary decisions on a business venture have been taken

C   does not take into account all factors affecting a business

D   may contain inaccurate predictions

Circle your answer

A   B   C   D

13 An umbrella maker wants to know whether next winter's rainfall will be heavy or light. He believes there is an 0.35 probability of heavy rain. A forecast can be bought. If rainfall will in fact be heavy, the probability of the forecast predicting this is 0.6. If rainfall will in fact be light, the probability of the forecast predicting this is 0.7. What is the probability that the forecast will, if it predicts heavy rainfall, be correct?

A   0.21
B   0.316
C   0.519
D   0.6

Circle your answer

A   B   C   D

14 The pound will either rise or fall next Monday. A currency speculator believes there is an 0.55 probability of its rising. He could buy a computer forecast. If the pound will in fact rise, there is an 0.7 probability that the computer forecast will predict this. If the pound will in fact fall, there is an 0.9 probability that the computer forecast will predict this. What is the overall probability of the computer forecast making a correct prediction?

A   0.21
B   0.63
C   0.79
D   0.8

Circle your answer

A   B   C   D

15 A dealer in grain futures would like to know whether next year's harvest will be good or poor. He believes the probability of a good harvest is 0.5, and on that basis he will buy futures, because the profits he could make are as follows.

		Harvest	
		Good	Poor
Action	Buy	£2,000	£20,000
	Sell	£12,000	£0

He could buy a forecast, from someone who has in the past made correct predictions in 90% of all years, both good and poor. What is the expected value to him of this information?

A   £0
B   £3,500
C   £5,000
D   £6,000

Circle your answer

A   B   C   D

16 A camera maker may choose to increase production for the summer. Profit levels are as follows:

		Demand	
		High	Low
Production increase?	Yes	£25,000	£ 8,000
	No	£16,000	£15,000

He thinks there is an 0.63 probability of high demand. He could buy a survey, which if demand were really to be high would have an 0.8 probability of predicting that, while if demand were really to be low would have an 0.9 probability of predicting that. What is the most he should pay for the survey (to the nearest £100)?

A	£0
B	£1,200
C	£2,300
D	£3,100

Circle your answer

A   B   C   D

17 A manufacturer could buy a new machine. There is an 0.35 probability that its purchase will increase profits by £20,000 over the life of the machine, and an 0.65 probability that its purchase will decrease profits by £5,000. A management consultant could investigate the likely outcome. If profits would in fact be increased, he will certainly predict this. If profits would in fact be cut, there is an 0.8 probability that he will predict this. At the moment, the cost of his services is under negotiation. The manufacturer would like to pay £2,000. The consultant wants £4,000. The final price will definitely be one of these two figures. The manufacturer should

A   abandon the purchase of the machine

B   buy the machine without an investigation

C   buy the investigation but only if he can get it for £2,000

D   buy the investigation even if he has to pay £4,000.

Circle your answer

A   B   C   D

18 Which of the following statements about the use of expected utility in decision-making is/are correct?

Statement
1. The attitude of the decision-maker to risk can be taken into account.
2. The recommendation will always coincide with that of expected monetary value.
3. Computation of utilities is generally straightforward.

A   Statement 1 only
B   Statement 2 only
C   Statements 1 and 2 only
D   Statements 1 and 3 only

Circle your answer

A   B   C   D

19 A businessman is considering four mutually exclusive projects, A, B, C and D. Possible profits in thousands of pounds are as follows:

		Economic climate		
		Boom	Stable	Recession
	A	32	31	28
Project	B	34	26	14
	C	42	30	20
	D	59	35	27
Probability of economic climate		0.3	0.5	0.2

Applying the maximin criterion, which project should he choose?

A Project A
B Project B
C Project C
D Project D

Circle your answer

| A | B | C | D |

20 An investor can invest £20,000 in business P and/or business Q. If he makes neither investment, he may put his money into a deposit (R). R will certainly make him a profit of £2,000. The possible profits and losses per £10,000 invested from investment in P and Q are:

	State of market	
	Good	*Bad*
Invest in P	+ £20,000	- £ 500
Invest in Q	+ £12,000	+ £3,000
Probability of market state	0.6	0.4

On the basis of the maximin criterion, the investor should

A Invest all his money in P only
B Invest all his money in Q only
C Invest half his money in each of P and Q
D Put all his money in deposit R

Circle your answer

| A | B | C | D |

21 Which of the following statements is/are true of the maximin criterion for decision-making?

Statement
1. Once the possible profits or losses are known, there is virtually no calculation to do.
2. Treating losses as negative profits, it is the same as the minimax criterion.
3. The probabilities of possible outcomes can be taken into account.

A Statement 1 only
B Statement 2 only
C Statements 1 and 2 only
D Statements 2 and 3 only

Circle your answer

| A | B | C | D |

22 A businessman is considering which one of four computerised accounts systems to buy. The annual running costs will depend on the pattern of trade, both its volume and its seasonality, and three possible patterns have been identified. Annual running costs are as follows:

		Pattern of trade		
		I	*II*	*III*
		£	£	£
	A	185	185	185
System	B	190	160	170
	C	250	140	100
	D	50	110	200

On the basis of the minimin criterion, which system should be chosen?

A System A	
B System B	
C System C	
D System D	

Circle your answer

A	B	C	D

23 An investor is considering four possible investments. The possible profits and losses are as follows:

		State of market		
		Good	Moderate	Bad
		£	£	£
	A	1,500	900	300
Investment	B	1,400	1,000	200
	C	1,300	1,300	1,300
	D	1,600	500	-200

On the basis of the maximax criterion, which investment should be chosen?

A Investment A	
B Investment B	
C Investment C	
D Investment D	

Circle your answer

A	B	C	D

24 X Ltd is about to select one of four new products, A, B, C or D, for production. Y Ltd is about to select one of three new products, I, II or III. Each company will choose their new product at the same time, independently of one another, but Y Ltd's choice will affect the profits X Ltd can make. X Ltd's possible profits are as follows:

		Y Ltd's choice		
		I	II	III
		£'000	£'000	£'000
	A	15	25	20
X Ltd's choice	B	18	18	20
	C	20	17	23
	D	10	22	16

On the basis of the minimax regret criterion, which product should X Ltd choose?

A Product A	
B Product B	
C Product C	
D Product D	

Circle your answer

A	B	C	D

25 An investor scores companies on a points basis. He considers investing £1,000 in a company. He awards 1 point for each £1 of expected return, and deducts 0.5 points for each £1 standard deviation of expected return. In what order would he rank the following companies (company with most points first)?

Company J: Return may be £80 (probability 0.6) or £40 (probability 0.4).
Company K: Return will definitely be £62.
Company L: Return may be £90 (probability 0.5) or £30 (probability 0.5)

A J, K, L
B L, K, J
C J, L, K
D K, J, L

Circle your answer

A B C D

26 Risk averse decision makers will

A never take any risks

B prefer investments with lower variability of return, if the alternatives have
the same expected returns

C always prefer investments with lower
variability of return

D never make investments which could lead
to losses

Circle your answer

A B C D

27 An investment may yield the following returns

Return £'000	Probability
50	0.1
68	0.75
94	0.15

What is the coefficient of variation of the return?

A 0.026
B 0.16
C 1.85
D 11.38

Circle your answer

A B C D

28 Which of the following statements is/are true about the coefficient of variation, as used to assess the riskiness of an investment?

Statement
1. It is unaffected by extreme returns so long as they are unlikely.
2. It relates the size of variation in returns to the size of the expected return.
3. Where returns on investments are in pounds sterling, the coefficient of variation is also in pounds sterling.
4. It is computed from the variation of possible returns about the most likely return.

A Statements, 1, 2 and 3 only
B Statements 2 and 4 only
C Statement 2 only
D Statements 3 and 4 only

Circle your answer

A B C D

CHAPTER 3

PROBABILITY DISTRIBUTIONS

> ## This chapter covers the following topics:
>
> - Probability distributions
> - The binomial distribution
> - The Poisson distribution
> - The normal distribution

1. Probability distributions

1.1 An event may have a number of mutually exclusive possible outcomes, each with a particular probability of occurring. The total of all these probabilities must add up to 1, and so this total of 1 must be distributed among the outcomes. A probability distribution is simply a way in which the total is distributed.

1.2 A probability distribution may be given by a list (eg P(A) = 0.3, P(B) = 0.5, P(C) = 0.2), or by a mathematical formula from which the probability of any given outcome can be found. In this chapter, we will be concerned with three important distributions which are given by mathematical formulae.

1.3 The three distributions are:

(i)   the binomial distribution;
(ii)   the Poisson distribution;
(iii) the normal distribution.

1.4 Guidelines for selecting the right distribution for a problem

- If we want the probability of a continuous variable taking a value in a certain range (eg height 140-150cm, or time >3 mins), use the normal distribution

- If we want the probability of a discrete variable taking a particular value (eg number of errors = 2) or set of values (eg number of cars seen = 0, 1, 2 or 3), use the Poisson distribution

- If we want the probability of x outcomes of a given type ("successes") in n trials (eg 4 invoices out of 6 paid on time), use the binomial distribution

- If n is large, approximations to the binomial distribution can be used:

    (i)   probability of a success on one trial small: use the Poisson distribution;

    (ii)   probability of a success on one trial near 0.5: use the normal distribution.

1.5   The above are guidelines only: sometimes, other probability distributions are better. However, these guidelines will apply to most business mathematics problems.

2.   The binomial distribution

2.1

Probability of x successes in n trials

$$= \frac{n!}{(n-x)!x!} \; p^x q^{n-x} = {_n}C_x \, p^x q^{n-x}$$

where   p = probability of a success on any one trial
          q = probability of a failure on any one trial = 1 - p.

2.2   For a given n and p, we could list the probabilities for all the values of x from 0 to n. We could then work out a mean and standard deviation of the distribution, using the same formulae as for expected values and standard deviations of expected values:

    Mean = Σ x (probability of x successes)

    Standard deviation   = $\sqrt{\Sigma(\text{probability of x successes}) (x - \text{mean})^2}$

However, for the binomial distribution there are formulae which will get us to exactly the same answers much more quickly. They are:

Mean = np

Standard deviation = $\sqrt{npq}$

These are the formulae to use to find the mean and standard deviation when approximating the binomial distribution by the normal distribution or the Poisson distribution.

2.3   The mean gives us an expected number of successes. This may not be a possible number of successes in any actual event (for example, if n = 30 and p = 0.47, np = 14.1), but it is an indication of the average number of successes (per event of n trials) in the long run.

2.4   The standard deviation gives an indication of how much the actual number of successes is likely to fluctuate around the expected number in successive events. For any given n, the standard deviation will be highest when p = q = 0.5. It will be low when p is very low or very high, because it would then be very unlikely that one would get more than a few successes (low p) or more than a few failures (high p).

3. The Poisson distribution

3.1 The Poisson distribution gives the probability of something happening a certain number of times within a given span, when the occurrences are random. We could apply it, for example, to find the probability of three errors being made in an hour by a library cataloguer, or the probability of five pieces of litter being found along 1 km of a country road.

3.2

> The probability of x occurrences in a given span is
>
> $$P(x) \quad = \quad \frac{m^x \, e^{-m}}{x!}$$
>
> where m = the mean number of occurrences in the span
>   e = a special mathematical constant, which is approximately 2.71828

3.3 Tables have been published giving P(x) for various values of x and m. A set of tables is given at the end of this book.

3.4 Sometimes the mean number of occurrences for one span is known, but we want P(x) for a different span. In such cases we can simply scale m up or down.

For example, if the mean number of occurrences in one hour is 3, and we are interested in the probability of 2 occurrences in half an hour, we can apply the formula (or tables) with x = 2, m = 3 × $\frac{1}{2}$ = 1.5, to get P(2 in half an hour) =

$$\frac{1.5^2 \, e^{-1.5}}{2!} \quad = \quad 0.251$$

3.5 The mean of a Poisson distribution is m, and its standard deviation is $\sqrt{m}$.

3.6 The Poisson distribution as an approximation to the binomial distribution

> For large n (say, over 10) and small p (say, under 0.1), the binomial probability of x successes in n trials is approximately the Poisson probability P(x), with m = np.

The larger n is, and the smaller p is, the better is the approximation.

4. The normal distribution

4.1 The normal distribution gives the probability of the value of a variable being in any particular range, where the range is measured in standard deviations from the mean. The mean is normally denoted by μ, and the standard deviation by σ.

4.2 Normal distribution tables

The formula for the normal distribution is too complicated to be of use in business applications, but luckily a single page table will suffice for all such purposes. The table is given at the end of this book. The table in this book gives the probability of the variable taking a value between the mean and a given number of standard deviations away from the mean.

4.3 For example:
(i)   P(between μ and $\mu + 2\sigma$) = 0.4772
(ii)   P(between μ and $\mu - 1.5\sigma$) = 0.4332
(iii) P(between $\mu - 1.5\sigma$ and $\mu + 2\sigma$) = 0.4332 + 0.4772 = 0.9104
(iv)   P(between μ and $\mu + 0.75\sigma$) = 0.2734
(v)   P(between $\mu + 0.75\sigma$ and $\mu + 2\sigma$) = 0.4772 - 0.2734 = 0.2038
(vi)   P(over $\mu + 2\sigma$) = 0.5 - 0.4772 = 0.0228

In (v), we deduct P(between μ and $\mu + 0.75\sigma$) from P(between μ and $\mu + 2\sigma$), to leave the range of values ($\mu + 0.75\sigma$ to $\mu + 2\sigma$) we want.

In (vi), we use the fact that P(over μ) = 0.5, and deduct P(between μ and $\mu + 2\sigma$) to leave the range of values (over $\mu + 2\sigma$) we want.

4.4 Some normal distribution tables give the probability of the variable being more than the given number of standard deviations above the mean. Thus they would have 0.0228 against 2.0 standard deviations instead of 0.4772.

4.5 The normal distribution and discrete variables

The normal distribution is appropriate for continuous variables, such as time. However, it can be used for discrete variables, such as number of employees, with very little loss of accuracy so long as the range of values of interest is fairly large (eg 450 - 520 employees, rather 450-452 employees).

4.6 When small ranges of values of a discrete variable are involved, the *continuity correction* should be used. This involves going an extra half a step beyond the range involved. Thus '450 - 452 employees inclusive' would become '449.5 - 452.5 employees', and the end points of this range would be converted into standard deviations above or below the mean. Similarly, 'precisely 440 employees' would become '439.5 - 440.5 employees'.

4.7 The normal distribution as an approximation to the binomial distribution

> For large n with p close to 0.5 (np and n(1-p) should both be over 5), the binomial probability of between x and y successes (inclusive) in n trials is approximately the probability of a normally distributed variable having a value between x and y.
>
> Use μ = np and $\sigma = \sqrt{npq}$.

4.8 When x and y are close together, the continuity correction should be applied giving x - 0.5 and y + 0.5.

QUESTIONS

1 Which of the following are necessary conditions for the use of the binomial distribution?

Condition
1. The outcomes are specified as two alternatives only
2. The trials are independent
3. The probability of one outcome is approximately 0.5
4. There are a small number of trials.

A   Conditions 1 and 2 only
B   Conditions 2 and 4 only
C   Conditions 1 and 3 only
D   Conditions 3 and 4 only

Circle your answer

A   B   C   D

2 The binomial distribution formula incorporates the formula for $_nC_x$ because

A   it combines the probabilities of success and failure

B   the binomial distribution can be approximated by the normal distribution

C   the number of ways of selecting x trials from n to be successes is required

D   the number of possible orders of different trials is required.

Circle your answer

A   B   C   D

3 What is the term containing $p^3 q^{12}$ in the expansion of $(p + q)^{15}$?

A $15 \, p^3 q^{12}$
B $36 \, p^3 q^{12}$
C $455 \, p^3 q^{12}$
D $2{,}730 \, p^3 q^{12}$

Circle your answer

A   B   C   D

4 The probability that a shop will take more than £2,000 in a day is 0.3. What is the probability that it will take more than £2,000 a day on precisely four days in a six-day week?

A   0.0040
B   0.0595
C   0.0705
D   0.1215

Circle your answer

A   B   C   D

29

5   The probability of the mail arriving after 9.30am on any one day is 0.4. What is the probability of the mail arriving after 9.30am on more than one day in a five-day week?

A   0.64
B   0.66304
C   0.7408
D   0.8704

Circle your answer

A   B   C   D

6   Either or both of two computer faults, type A and type B, may occur on any day. There are never two or more faults *of the same type* on the same day. On any one day, the probability of a type A fault is 0.4, and the probability of a type B fault is 0.35. Each type A fault costs the company £50, and each type B fault costs the company £40. Over a 3-day period, what is the probability that total costs due to faults will be £220 or more?

A   0.011956
B   0.018032
C   0.027636
D   0.030380

Circle your answer

A   B   C   D

7   The probability of any one employee being off sick on a Monday is 0.35. Out of a group of six employees, what is the probability of between two and five (inclusive) being off sick on a Monday?

A   0.67908
B   0.68092
C   0.75450
D   0.88213

Circle your answer

A   B   C   D

8   In a calculator factory, there is a constant probability of any one calculator being defective. In batches of 2,000 calculators, the mean number of defective calculators per batch is 50. What is the standard deviation of the number of defective calculators per batch?

A   6.98
B   7.07
C   40.00
D   48.75

Circle your answer

A   B   C   D

9   On average, a typist makes 3.5 errors an hour. What is the probability of fewer than 3 errors in any one hour?

A   0.2907
B   0.3209
C   0.5065
D   0.5367

Circle your answer

A   B   C   D

10 On average, 1.2 police cars pass a particular point each day. What is the probability of exactly three police cars passing that point over a period of three days?

A 0.0867
B 0.2125
C 0.3614
D 0.8333

Circle your answer

A   B   C   D

11 What is the probability of seven occurrences of an event where a Poisson distribution with a mean of five applies?

A 0.1044
B 0.1277
C 0.1737
D 0.3452

Circle your answer

A   B   C   D

12 In a Poisson distribution, the probability of five occurrences is 0.0735. For this distribution, the standard deviation is

A 1.05
B 1.10
C 1.61
D 2.60

Circle your answer

A   B   C   D

13 The Poisson distribution is a good approximation to the binomial distribution when

A there are many trials and a low probability of success

B there are many trials and the probability of success is near 0.5

C there are very few trials

D there are few trials and a high probability of success

Circle your answer

A   B   C   D

14 In a binomial distribution, the probability of a success in any one trial is 0.03. What is the approximate probability of four or more successes in sixty trials?

A 0.0364
B 0.1087
C 0.4500
D 0.8913

Circle your answer

A   B   C   D

31

15 In a binomial distribution, $p = 0.1$ and $n = 12$. If the Poisson distribution were used to compute the probability of two successes, what would the error be as a percentage of the true probability?

    A 1.32%
    B 5.74%
    C 6.09%
    D 7.06%

Circle your answer

A   B   C   D

16 A builder buys bricks in batches of 50,000. A batch with 200 or fewer defective bricks is acceptable. He checks a sample of 600 bricks from each batch, and rejects the batch if the sample contains more than three defective bricks. What is the approximate probability of his rejecting a batch which in fact contains exactly 200 defective bricks?

    A 0.2090
    B 0.2213
    C 0.3120
    D 0.4303

Circle your answer

A   B   C   D

17 What is the probability of the value of a normally distributed variable being more than 1.52 standard deviations away from the mean?

    A 0.0643
    B 0.1286
    C 0.3421
    D 0.6842

Circle your answer

A   B   C   D

18 The weights of elephants are normally distributed. The mean weight is 5,200 kg, and the probability of an elephant weighing over 6,000 kg is 0.0314. What is the standard deviation of the weights of elephants?

    A 186 kg
    B 215 kg
    C 372 kg
    D 430 kg

Circle your answer

A   B   C   D

19 The lives of light bulbs are normally distributed with a mean of 8,000 hours and a standard deviation of 330 hours. What is the probability that a bulb will last for between 7,900 hours and 8,200 hours?

    A 0.3186
    B 0.347
    C 0.653
    D 0.6814

Circle your answer

A   B   C   D

20 The durations of telephone calls made from an office are normally distributed. The probability of a call lasting more than 12 minutes is 0.1, and the probability of a call lasting less than 4 minutes is 0.33.

The mean of the distribution is

    A   3.96 minutes
    B   4.98 minutes
    C   6.05 minutes
    D   9.53 minutes

Circle your answer

A   B   C   D

21 The lengths of politicians' speeches are normally distributed. The probability of a speech being less than 1,480 words long is 0.2. The probability of a speech being between 1,480 and 1,560 words long is 0.4. What is the probability of a speech being over 1,600 words long?

    A   0.200
    B   0.215
    C   0.250
    D   0.295

Circle your answer

A   B   C   D

22 The normal distribution is a good approximation to the binomial distribution with n trials and a probability of success p when

    A   n is large and p is small
    B   n is large and p is nearly equal to 1-p
    C   np is much greater than n(1-p)
    D   the mean and standard deviation of the binomial distribution are nearly equal

Circle your answer

A   B   C   D

23 A gambler plays a game, in which the probability of his winning any one bet is 0.45. What is the approximate probability of his winning more than 470 out of 1,000 bets? (Ignore the continuity correction.)

    A   0.0778
    B   0.102
    C   0.398
    D   0.4222

Circle your answer

A   B   C   D

24 A normal distribution is used to approximate a binomial distribution. If the normal distribution's mean is 79.9 and its standard deviation is 6.507, then for the binomial distribution n is

    A   87
    B   121
    C   151
    D   170

Circle your answer

A   B   C   D

25 A coin is tossed 250 times. Applying the continuity correction, what is the approximate probability of getting 122, 123, 124 or 125 heads?

A   0.1480
B   0.1700
C   0.1939
D   0.2467

Circle your answer

A   B   C   D

26 In a binomial distribution, n = 50 and the probability of a failure on any one trial is 0.38. What is the approximate probability of 39 successes?

A   0.0055
B   0.0077
C   0.0108
D   0.0163

Circle your answer

A   B   C   D

CHAPTER 4

SAMPLING THEORY

> ## This chapter covers the following topics:
>
> - Taking samples
> - Inferences from samples
> - The standard error of the mean
> - The standard error of the proportion

1. Taking samples

1.1 There are two main aspects of sampling theory:

(i)   reasons for, and the different ways of, taking samples;
(ii) the mathematics of drawing inferences from samples.

1.2 When studying a population, we generally take samples, because surveying every member of the population would be too expensive. We should expend enough resources to achieve the results we require, and no more.

1.3 Two points to consider in seeking to obtain cost-effective data are these:

- Should we obtain *primary data* (data collected specifically for the current purpose) or could we make do with *secondary data* (data already collected for some other purpose or for general use, such as published Government statistics)?

- If primary data are to be collected, should we try out our collection methods with a *pilot enquiry* to make sure they work?

1.4 Methods of sampling

The main methods of sampling are these:

- Random sampling - every member of the population has an equal chance of being selected.

- Systematic sampling - members of the population at regular intervals (the *sampling interval*), eg every 50th, are selected.

- Stratified sampling - the population is broken down into layers (strata), for example bands of income, and samples taken within each layer.

- Quota sampling - interviewers are given a quota of people, possibly broken down into sub-quotas (eg 100 males and 100 females), and they just interview the first people to come along until their quotas are fulfilled.

The choice of method depends on available resources, and the degree to which the sample must be representative of the population. However, most mathematical inferences from samples can only be drawn if the sample is random, so we will look at random sampling in more detail.

1.5 Random sampling

To take a random sample, we need

(i)   a *sampling frame* - a numbered list of all the members of the population;

(ii)   a list of random numbers, so we can select members of the population with the corresponding numbers in the sampling frame. The list of random numbers may be generated by a computer program, or it may be obtained from random number tables. These tables will generate random numbers so long as you work systematically (up, down, left or right) through the table.

Often, it is impossible or too costly to get a complete list of a population, so we then use some other sampling method.

2.   Inferences from samples

2.1 We can take a sample, and find from it the sample mean or proportion. We can then estimate:

(i)   the value of the population mean or proportion - a *point estimate*;

(ii)   a *confidence interval* within which we can have a certain level of confidence that the population mean or proportion lies - an *interval estimate*.

2.2 It is common to use Roman letters for sample means etc, and Greek letters for population means etc, as follows:

	Sample	*Population*
Mean	$\bar{x}$	μ
Proportion	p	π
Standard deviation	s	σ

n is used for the sample size.

2.3 We will be concerned with interval estimates, but the point estimates to use are $\bar{x}$ (for μ) and p (for π).

2.4 If we take a measurement of $\bar{x}$ or p from a sample, it may be equal to or very close to the corresponding population value (μ or π), or it may be far away from that value. However, most samples are likely to produce results fairly close to the population values.

2.5 The sampling distribution and the standard error

The *sampling distribution* (of the mean or proportion) is the distribution of all possible sample values ($\bar{x}$ or p) for a given sample size. Its standard deviation is called the *standard error* (of the mean or proportion). For n $\geqslant$ 30, it is approximately a normal distribution, so because 95% of a normal distribution lies within mean $\pm$ 1.96 standard deviations, we can say with 95% confidence that population value = sample measurement $\pm$ 1.96 standard errors.

For 99% confidence, substitute 2.58 for 1.96. Figures for other levels of confidence can be found using normal distribution tables.

2.6 For small samples (n < 30), we use a t distribution with n - 1 degrees of freedom (unless σ is known - see below). If you look at the t distribution tables at the end of this book, you will see that as the degrees of freedom increase, the table values (in columns $t_{0.025}$ for 95% (= 100% - 2 $\times$ 2.5%) confidence and $t_{0.005}$ for 99% (= 100% - 2 $\times$ 0.5%) confidence) get closer to the normal distribution figures of 1.96 and 2.58. Apart from using these t figures, the formula in the preceding paragraph is unchanged.

2.7 Whenever n < 30, the formula for a confidence interval only applies if the population is approximately normally distributed.

3. The standard error of the mean

3.1 The standard error of the mean is $\dfrac{\sigma}{\sqrt{n}}$

This indicates how widely spread possible sample means are about μ. The larger the sample size (n), the smaller the standard error, as large samples are more likely than small ones to give a good idea of the population mean, μ.

3.2 We will usually not know σ, and have to estimate it as $s \times \sqrt{\dfrac{n}{n-1}}$. The factor $\sqrt{\dfrac{n}{n-1}}$ is Bessel's correction. It is often ignored if n $\geqslant$ 30. s (with or without Bessel's correction) is also the estimate to use for σ when we want an estimate of σ for its own sake, rather than to find the standard error of the mean.

3.3 If we do know σ (as opposed to estimating it from s), we use the normal distribution figures (1.96, etc) even if n < 30.

3.4 Sometimes we will have the results of two samples to combine into one larger sample. If we call them samples 1 and 2, so $\bar{x}_1$ is sample 1's mean and so on, then:

Pooled mean $= \dfrac{n_1\overline{x}_1 + n_2\overline{x}_2}{n_1 + n_2}$

Pooled estimate of $\sigma = \sqrt{\dfrac{n_1 s_1^2 + n_2 s_2^2}{n_1 + n_2 - 2}}$

4. The standard error of the proportion

4.1 The standard error of the proportion is $\sqrt{\dfrac{\pi(1-\pi)}{n}}$

4.2 As we will not know π (it is what we are trying to find out), we use p as an estimate for π.

4.3 If we start with an idea of the maximum acceptable size of confidence interval, we need to be able to find the sample size to give a confidence interval which is narrow enough. The closer π is to 0.5, the larger is the standard error and hence the wider is the confidence interval; so considering $\pi = 0.5$ gives us a 'worst case' to use in finding n.

QUESTIONS

1 A sampling frame is

    A   a list of every member of a population

    B   a framework of mathematical theory used to compute sample sizes

    C   a table of random numbers suitable for selecting a sample

    D   a list of the members of a sample

Circle your answer

A	B	C	D

2 Secondary data are

    A   data collected from a non-random sample

    B   data collected for purposes other than the research they are now being used for

    C   data collected over 12 months ago

    D   data collected in a follow-up survey after the main one

Circle your answer

A	B	C	D

3 Which of the following are advantages of postal questionnaires over interviews?

1.   The questions are presented to all respondents in the same way.
2.   The respondents can put their own interpretations on questions, without help from interviewers.
3.   Respondents can omit questions.
4.   Larger samples can generally be obtained for the same expenditure.

    A   1 and 2 only
    B   2 and 4 only
    C   2 and 3 only
    D   1 and 4 only

Circle your answer

A	B	C	D

4 A population comprises 100 members, numbered from 00 to 99. Which of the following methods of using random number tables will produce a random sample of ten members?

   A   Taking the last two digits from each row of the table as a two-digit number, discarding numbers which equal a number already obtained, until ten two-digit numbers have been selected

   B   As in A, but also discarding two digit numbers which only differ from those already selected by one (eg 87, if 88 has already been selected)

   C   As in A, but also discarding any even (or odd) numbers once five even (or odd) numbers have been selected, so that the final list includes five even numbers and five odd numbers

   D   Listing digits from the start of the table, discarding duplicates, until a list of the digits 0-9 has been obtained, in a random order, then prefixing the first digit on the list with 0, the second with 1, and so on, so that the final list contains one number in the range 00-09, one in the range 10-19 and so on.

Circle your answer

A   B   C   D

5 A random sample of five two-digit numbers is to be obtained, using the following extract from random number tables: 88768 24194 90126 13108.

Which of the following samples has been properly selected?

   A   88 68 41 49 12
   B   24 41 19 94 49
   C   88 24 90 13 08
   D   80 13 16 21 10

Circle your answer

A   B   C   D

6 The adult population is divided by age into the groups 18-27 years, 28-37 years and so on, and then 0.1% of the members of each age group are selected for a survey. This is an example of

   A   Random sampling
   B   Stratified sampling
   C   Cluster sampling
   D   Quota sampling

Circle your answer

A   B   C   D

7   A survey is to be carried out to obtain views on a proposed sports centre. 52% of the population are male. 32% of the population play sports at least once a week, and 12% play sports less often. 40% of men play no sports, and 23.3% of women play sports at least once a week. If a sample of 1,000 people is to be selected using quota sampling, how many men who play sports, but less than once a week, should be interviewed?

     A   104
     B   112
     C   120
     D   208

Circle your answer

A   B   C   D

8   In surveys of a population, a pilot enquiry is used

     A   instead of a full survey when resources are limited

     B   to see whether potential customers will pay enough for the results of the survey

     C   to study members of the sample who will be unavailable at the time of the main survey

     D   to test the questions or other data collection methods

Circle your answer

A   B   C   D

9   The standard error of the mean is

     A   the difference between the population mean and the mean of the sample actually taken

     B   the standard deviation of the distribution of means of all samples of a given size

     C   the difference between the mean of all sample means and the population mean

     D   the standard deviation of a representative sample

Circle your answer

A   B   C   D

10 A sample of 70 items is taken from a population. The sample mean is 85 units and the sample standard deviation is 25 units. The standard error of the mean is

    A   0.29 units
    B   0.33 units
    C   0.36 units
    D   2.99 units

Circle your answer

A   B   C   D

11 A sample is taken from a population. The sample standard deviation is 2,770 units, and the standard error of the mean is 30.22 units. How large is the sample?

    A   92 items
    B   504 items
    C   2,800 items
    D   8,402 items

Circle your answer

A   B   C   D

12 A sample of 100 items is taken from a population. The standard error is 839 units. If a sample of 500 items had been taken instead, the standard error would have been

    A   34 units
    B   168 units
    C   375 units
    D   839 units

Circle your answer

A   B   C   D

13 In a study of the annual profits of plumbers, a random sample of 75 plumbers was taken. The sample mean was £18,000 and the sample standard deviation was £1,500. What is the 95% confidence interval for the mean annual profits of all plumbers?

    A   £17,714 to £18,286
    B   £17,661 to £18,339
    C   £17,596 to £18,404
    D   £17,553 to £18,447

Circle your answer

A   B   C   D

14 To establish the mean amount of a quarterly telephone bill, a random sample of 150 bills was taken. The sample mean was £42.57 and the sample standard deviation was £8.92. How wide is the 99% confidence interval for the mean amount of a telephone bill?

    A   £1.88
    B   £2.85
    C   £3.39
    D   £3.76

Circle your answer

A   B   C   D

15 All possible samples of 100 items are taken from a very large population. Which of the following is true of the interval

$$\text{population mean} \pm 1.65 \times \text{population standard deviation} / \sqrt{100} \text{ ?}$$

 A   90% of all the sample means lie within
     the interval

 B   The mean of a specified sample is within
     the interval 90% of the time

 C   5% of all the sample means lie outside
     the interval

 Circle your answer

 D   There is a 90% probability that all the
     sample means lie within the interval

 A   B   C   D

16 A random sample of bottles of typist's correction fluid was taken to establish the average life of a bottle. A 95% confidence interval 5.835 days wide was obtained, with a sample standard deviation of 12 days. What was the size of the sample?

 A   46 bottles
 B   65 bottles
 C   92 bottles
 D   113 bottles

 Circle your answer

 A   B   C   D

17 A baker wishes to find the mean weight of a large loaf of bread, to within 10g, with 99% confidence. If the standard deviation of weights is 46g, how large a sample should he take?

 A   81 loaves
 B   115 loaves
 C   141 loaves
 D   563 loaves

 Circle your answer

 A   B   C   D

18 On the basis of a sample of 65 packets, the 95% confidence interval for the true weight of the contents of a 1kg packet of sugar has been found to be 1.05 kg ± 0.04 kg. If the sample size had been 195 packets, and the sample mean and standard deviation had been the same, what would the 95% confidence interval have been?

 A   1.05kg ± 0.0133kg
 B   1.05kg ± 0.0231kg
 C   1.05kg ± 0.0693kg
 D   1.05kg ± 0.12kg

 Circle your answer

 A   B   C   D

19 To determine the mean life of a central heating boiler, a sample of 20 was taken. The sample mean was 137 months and the sample standard deviation was 42 months. What is the 99% confidence interval for the population mean?

  A   112.14 months to 161.86 months
  B   112.77 months to 161.23 months
  C   110.14 months to 163.86 months
  D   109.44 months to 164.56 months

Circle your answer

A   B   C   D

20 If, in a sample of 320 people, 64 were found to buy products mainly because of their packaging, what is the 95% confidence interval for the proportion of people in the whole population who buy products mainly because of their packaging?

  A   0.2 ± 0.001
  B   0.2 ± 0.037
  C   0.2 ± 0.044
  D   0.2 ± 0.055

Circle your answer

A   B   C   D

21 40% of a sample of 25 people are found to be interested in buying football souvenirs. How wide, in terms of a percentage of the population, is the 99% confidence interval for the percentage of the whole population which is interested in buying football souvenirs?

  A   38%
  B   40%
  C   51%
  D   55%

Circle your answer

A   B   C   D

22 A sample of consumers was taken, and it was found that 45% of them liked product X. The 99% confidence interval for the proportion of the whole population liking product X was 45% ± 5.034%. How large was the sample?

  A   161 consumers
  B   375 consumers
  C   530 consumers
  D   650 consumers

Circle your answer

A   B   C   D

23 A population proportion is to be determined to within ± 0.02, with 95% confidence. The proportion is not less than 0.7. How many members of the population should be included in the sample?

  A   1,430
  B   1,702
  C   2,017
  D   2,401

Circle your answer

A   B   C   D

24 A population proportion is to be determined to within ± 0.016, with 99% confidence. Nothing is known about the population proportion. What size of sample will guarantee that a confidence interval no wider than that required is obtained?

A   1,626
B   3,752
C   5,302
D   6,501

Circle your answer

A   B   C   D

25 In a survey to find how much cash people carry with them, the standard deviation of amounts in a sample of 25 people was £4.32. What is the best estimate of the population standard deviation, applying Bessel's correction?

A   £4.15
B   £4.23
C   £4.41
D   £4.50

Circle your answer

A   B   C   D

26 At what sample size does Bessel's correction give an estimate for the population standard deviation differing from the sample standard deviation by only 1% of the latter figure?

A   49
B   51
C   99
D   101

Circle your answer

A   B   C   D

27 Two samples (with no members in common) are taken from a large population. The first sample comprises 12 items, and the sample standard deviation is 14 units. The second sample comprises 16 items, and the sample standard deviation is 11 units. What is the estimated population standard deviation?

A   12.29 units
B   12.38 units
C   12.50 units
D   12.84 units

Circle your answer

A   B   C   D

28 Three samples are taken from a large population. The first sample comprises 26 items and has a mean of 47 units; the second sample comprises 18 items and has a mean of 44 units; and the third sample comprises 37 items and has a mean of 46 units. No item is included in more than one sample. What is the estimated population mean?

A   45.317 units
B   45.877 units
C   45.885 units
D   45.921 units

Circle your answer

A   B   C   D

CHAPTER 5

HYPOTHESIS TESTS

This chapter covers the following topics:

- General scheme of hypothesis tests
- Table of tests of means and proportions
- Standard deviations and goodness of fit
- Contingency tests and analysis of variance

1. General scheme of hypothesis tests

1.1 When finding confidence intervals (see the previous chapter), we obtain the data first, and then make deductions. In hypothesis testing, we take a more active role. We start with a specific hypothesis, and then see whether the data support or refute that hypothesis.

1.2 In hypothesis testing, we start by deciding what hypothesis we want to test (the *null hypothesis*, denoted by H_0), and what alternative we are concerned with (the *alternative hypothesis*, H_1).

1.3 H_0 will be an equality, for example that a population mean μ equals some specified value, μ_0.

1.4 H_1 will contradict H_0, in one of three ways.

H_1 Form	H_1 Example	Corresponding H_0
... ≠ ...	Mean cost of a telephone call in the UK does not equal mean cost in Denmark	The two mean costs are equal
... > ...	Mean height of a human being exceeds 170cm	Mean height equals 170cm
... < ...	Proportion of left handed people is below 0.2	Proportion equals 0.2

1.5 It is important to choose the right alternative hypothesis, as it will affect our test. If, for example, only a population mean in excess of a particular value would lead to our taking action, the appropriate H_1 will be ... > ...

1.6 We can now undertake our test, by performing the following steps.

(i) Decide on a significance level. As we are only taking samples, there is always the risk of error. There are two types of error we can make:

● Type I error: rejecting H_0 when it is true
● Type II error: accepting H_0 when it is false.

The significance level is the risk of making a type I error. A common level is 5%. This means that on 5% of the occasions when we test H_0 and H_0 is in fact true, we will reject H_0. Unfortunately, we cannot just set a very low level, such as 0.01%, because that increases the probability of a type II error.

(ii) Take our sample, and compute the *test statistic* we need. This will depend on what H_0 is about (eg one mean, two proportions) and a table is given later in these notes.

(iii) See whether the probability of getting the test statistic value we did would be less than the significance level, assuming H_0 to be true. If that probability would be less than the significance level, reject H_0; otherwise accept H_0.

For example, if you tested the hypothesis that the mean UK income is £13,000 by sampling 100 people, then if this is true you might well get a sample mean of £13,100, and you would then accept H_0. If the sample mean turned out to be £20,000, you would reject H_0, because your chances of getting a sample mean of £20,000 if the population mean was £13,000 are tiny.

1.7 There is a close connection between confidence intervals and hypothesis testing. Confidence intervals set limits to the likely gap between a sample mean or proportion and the corresponding population figure. In hypothesis testing, we see what the gap is between the sample result and the population figure based on H_0, and ask how likely such a gap is.

1.8 Thus, for example, if H_0 is that $\mu = 38$ and H_1 is that $\mu \neq 38$, and we are using a 5% significance level and taking a sample of 30 or over, we expect the test statistic

$$\frac{\text{sample mean} - 38}{\text{standard error}}$$

to fall within the range ± 1.96. The end points of this range are called the *critical values*, and if the test statistic falls outside this range we reject H_0.

1.9 We need to look at H_1 before working out our critical values. Hypothesis tests are of two types:

● Two-tailed: H_1 has the form ... ≠ ...
● One-tailed: H_1 has the form ... > ... or ... < ...

In the latter case, we are only interested in the population value (mean etc) differing from that under H_0 in one direction.

Our value of 1.96 in the preceding paragraph was based on the fact that 95% (= 100% - 5%) of a normal distribution lies in the range mean ± 1.96 standard deviations. If we are only interested in straying outside the acceptable range on one side, we would need, for example, to set a single critical value at + 1.65. This is because 5% of a normal distribution lies above the point 1.65 standard deviations above the mean.

2. Table of tests of means and proportions

2.1

H_0	H_1	Test statistic	Critical values (see 2.2 below)	Notes (see 2.3 below)
$\mu = \mu_0$	$\mu \neq \mu_0$		(a)	
	$\mu > \mu_0$ or $\mu < \mu_0$	$\dfrac{\bar{x} - \mu_0}{\sigma/\sqrt{n}}$	(b)	(i), (ii)
$\pi = \pi_0$	$\pi \neq \pi_0$		(a)	
	$\pi > \pi_0$ or $\pi < \pi_0$	$\dfrac{p - \pi_0}{\sqrt{\pi_0(1 - \pi_0)/n}}$	(b)	(iii)
$\mu_1 = \mu_2$	$\mu_1 \neq \mu_2$		(a)	
	$\mu_1 > \mu_2$ or $\mu_1 < \mu_2$	$\dfrac{\bar{x} - \bar{x}_2}{\sqrt{\dfrac{s_1^2}{n_1} + \dfrac{s_2^2}{n_2}}}$	(b)	(iii) (iv)
$\mu_1 = \mu_2$	$\mu_1 \neq \mu_2$		(a)	
	$\mu_1 > \mu_2$ or $\mu_1 < \mu_2$	$\dfrac{\Sigma(x_1 - x_2)}{\sigma/\sqrt{n}}$	(b)	(v)
$\pi_1 = \pi_2$	$\pi_1 \neq \pi_2$		(a)	
	$\pi_1 > \pi_2$ or $\pi_1 < \pi_2$	$\dfrac{p_1 - p_2}{\sqrt{p(1-p)\left(\dfrac{1}{n_1} + \dfrac{1}{n_2}\right)}}$	(b)	(iii) (vi)

2.2   Critical values

(a)   Derive from normal distribution tables, or t distribution tables (n - 1 degrees of freedom) if n <30.

For example: 1% significance, n ⩾ 30: ± 2.58

5% significance, n = 25: ± 2.06

If σ is known (rather than estimated from s), use normal distribution tables even if n <30.

(b)   As for (a), but the significance level equals the probability on *one side only* of the distribution.

For example: 1% significance, n ⩾ 30: 2.33
5% significance, n = 25: 1.71

Critical value will be positive for H_1 of form ... >..., negative for H_1 of form ... <....

2.3   Notes

(i)   Estimate σ with s, or s $\sqrt{\dfrac{n}{n-1}}$ for small n.

(ii)   If n <30, the population must be approximately normally distributed.

(iii)   n must be at least 30.

(iv)   This test is for data which are not paired (see note (v)).

(v)   This test is for paired data. For example, each of 20 consumers might give ratings of two products on a scale of 1 to 10. We would then have 20 pairs of values of x_1 and x_2.

σ is the standard deviation of the values $x_1 - x_2$, multiplied by $\sqrt{\dfrac{n}{n-1}}$ for small n

(vi) $p = \dfrac{p_1 n_1 + p_2 n_2}{n_1 + n_2}$

3.   Standard deviations and goodness of fit

3.1   As well as tests concerned with particular values (means or proportions), we can make tests concerned with the shapes of distributions.

● An F test shows whether two populations have the same standard deviation
● A goodness of fit test shows whether a population fits a given distribution

3.2 Test of two standard deviations

Null hypothesis: $\sigma_1 = \sigma_2$

Alternative hypothesis: $\sigma_1 \neq \sigma_2$

Test statistic: F, = the larger of $\dfrac{s_1^2}{s_2^2}$ and $\dfrac{s_2^2}{s_1^2}$

Critical value: F, from tables (at the end of this book)
Degrees of freedom for numerator and denominator =
n for corresponding sample - 1

Significance level is double the subscript on F: eg 10% for $F_{0.05}$

We must assume that the populations are approximately normally distributed.

3.3 Test of goodness of fit

Null hypothesis: a distribution with n classes has a certain shape

Test statistic: χ^2 (chi-squared) $= \dfrac{\Sigma(O\text{-}E)^2}{E}$

O = observed frequency in a class

E = expected frequency in that class

Critical value: χ^2 from tables (at end of this book) with n - 1 degrees of freedom (but see below)

For example: 5% significance, n = 8, critical value = 14.1

Degrees of freedom for specific distributions:

normal: n - 3
binomial: n - 2
Poisson: n - 2

4. Contingency tables and analysis of variance

4.1 Business decisions often depend on the influence of one variable on another. For example, before deciding whether to spend more on advertising, we need to know whether the level of sales is really influenced by the level of advertising.

4.2 There are two main tests of the null hypothesis that one variable has no effect on another. We use the *contingency table test* when our data are in the form of a contingency table, and the *analysis of variance test* when that is not so.

4.3 Contingency table test

A contingency table has a row for each value of one variable (for example, advertising high, medium or low) and a column for each value of the other (for example, sales high or low).

4.4 For each cell in the table, we will have a number of observations to go in that cell (for example, there might be 32 months in which high advertising was combined with high sales). These are the observed values, O.

For each cell, there will also be an expected figure E. This is the number of observations we would expect if one variable had no effect on the other.

For any one cell

$$E = \frac{\Sigma O \text{ for row} \times \Sigma O \text{ for column}}{\Sigma O \text{ for whole table}}$$

4.5 The test is then as follows.

Null hypothesis: One variable has no effect on another

Alternative hypothesis: One variable does have an effect on the other

Test statistic: $\chi^2 = \frac{\Sigma(O\text{-}E)^2}{E}$

For a 2 × 2 table add or subtract 0.5 to each O-E (to bring it nearer zero) before squaring; this adjustment is *Yates' correction* .

Critical value: χ^2 from tables. For a m × n table, degrees of freedom = (m-1)(n-1).

4.6 Analysis of variance test

Sometimes, we have as data some values of one variable observed under each of several conditions (called treatments). For example, a typist might experiment with two different keyboards, flat and sloping, and might record the number of words typed per minute with each keyboard on several occasions during a day.

4.7 To perform the test, we compare the variation in values of the variable due to the choice of treatment (the mean sum of treatment squares, MSTr) with the variation due to other causes (the mean sum of error squares, MSE). Only if the ratio of MSTr to MSE is high enough do we conclude that the choice of treatment affects the value of the variable.

4.8 The test is as follows

Null hypothesis: One variable has no effect on the other

Alternative hypothesis: One variable does have an effect on the other

x = data values
n = number of data values for each treatment
k = number of different treatments
T = Σx for each treatment

SST (total sum of squares) = $\Sigma x^2 - (\Sigma T)^2 / \Sigma n$

SSTr (treatment sum of squares) = $\Sigma(T^2/n) - (\Sigma T)^2 / \Sigma n$

SSE (error sum of squares) = SST - SSTr

MSTr = SSTr/(k-1)

MSE = SSE/(Σn-k)

Test statistic: $\dfrac{MSTr}{MSE}$

Critical values: F (from tables at the end of this book), with k - 1 degrees of freedom for the numerator and Σn - k for the denominator.

Significance level is the subscript on F (5% for $F_{0.05}$).

QUESTIONS

1 In a hypothesis test, for which a sample of 100 items is taken, the null hypothesis is that μ = 2,000 units and the alternative hypothesis is that $\mu \neq$ 2,000 units. If the test is at 1% significance, within what range must the sample mean fall for the null hypothesis to be accepted?

    A   2,000 units ± 1.65 standard errors
    B   2,000 units ± 1.96 standard errors
    C   2,000 units ± 2.33 standard errors
    D   2,000 units ± 2.58 standard errors

Circle your answer

A   B   C   D

2 X maintains that the mean income, μ, in the UK is £13,000. Y says that it is more than this. A sample of 200 people is taken. The sample mean income is £13,250 and the sample standard deviation of incomes is £2,000. A hypothesis test at 5% significance is used. Which of the following is true?

    A   The null hypothesis is that μ = £13,000, and this hypothesis should be accepted

    B   The null hypothesis is that μ = £13,000, and this hypothesis should be rejected

    C   The null hypothesis is that μ > £13,000, and this hypothesis should be accepted

    D   The null hypothesis is that μ > £13,000, and this hypothesis should be rejected

Circle your answer

A   B   C   D

3 It is thought that the mean number of letters written by any one person in a year does not differ from 180. To test this hypothesis, a sample of 55 people is taken. The sample mean is 192 letters and the sample standard deviation is 50 letters. The null hypothesis should be

    A   accepted at 5% significance but rejected at 1% significance

    B   accepted at 1% significance but rejected at 5% significance

    C   accepted at both 5% significance and 1% significance

    D   rejected at both 5% significance and 1% significance

Circle your answer

A   B   C   D

4 A test is made of the hypothesis that the mean weight of all books in a library is 700g against the hypothesis that the mean weight is greater than 700g. A sample of 80 books is taken. The sample mean is 730g, and the sample standard deviation is 141g. The null hypothesis is only just accepted. What is the significance level?

A 5.74%
B 5.00%
C 2.87%
D 1.00%

Circle your answer

A   B   C   D

5 It is thought that blue is the favourite colour of one quarter of the population, neither more nor less. If a sample of 80 people is taken, within what range would the number of people saying that blue was their favourite colour have to lie for the null hypothesis to be accepted at 1% significance?

A 16 to 24
B 14 to 26
C 13 to 27
D 11 to 29

Circle your answer

A   B   C   D

6 It is thought that 3% of batteries produced in a factory, and not more, are defective. If a sample of 200 batteries is chosen, what is the smallest number of defective batteries which would lead you to reject the null hypothesis at 5% significance?

A 6
B 10
C 12
D 14

Circle your answer

A   B   C   D

7 Mary thinks that the proportion of the population who have a video recorder is at least 0.4. Of 300 people questioned, 99 said they had a video recorder. Mary's view should be

A accepted at 5% significance but rejected at 1% significance

B accepted at 1% significance but rejected at 5% significance

C accepted at both 5% significance and 1% significance

D rejected at both 5% significance and 1% significance

Circle your answer

A   B   C   D

8 In a two-tailed test of the hypothesis that 50% of the British population can speak French, 44% of a sample of 150 people could speak French, and the null hypothesis was just rejected. What was the significance level?

A   14%
B   7%
C   5%
D   1%

Circle your answer

A   B   C   D

9 It is claimed that the mean annual salary in Britain is no higher than that in France. A test of this claim at the 5% significance level is carried out. The mean salary of 150 Britons is £13,200 (sample standard deviation £700) and the mean salary of 120 French people is £13,020 (sample standard deviation £900). Which of the following is true?

A   The null hypothesis is that the population means are equal, and this hypothesis should be accepted

B   The null hypothesis is that the British population mean exceeds the French, and this hypothesis should be accepted

C   The null hypothesis is that the population means are equal, and this hypothesis should be rejected

D   The null hypothesis is that the British population mean exceeds the French, and this hypothesis should be rejected

Circle your answer

A   B   C   D

10 In a two-tailed test at 1% significance of the hypothesis that two population means are equal, a sample of 80 items from the first population has a standard deviation of 47 units and a sample of 130 items from the second population has a standard deviation of 32 units. If the null hypothesis is only just accepted, what is the difference between the means of the two populations?

A   10 units
B   12 units
C   14 units
D   15 units

Circle your answer

A   B   C   D

11 Samples are taken from two populations. A sample of 50 items from the first population has a standard deviation of 75 units, and a sample of 60 items from the second population has a standard deviation of 45 units. It will be accepted that the two population means differ if the sample means differ by more than 26.6 units. What level of significance is being used?

A 5.00%
B 2.78%
C 1.39%
D 1.00%

Circle your answer

A   B   C   D

12 The hypothesis that the mean lives of jackets made by two different manufacturers are equal is to be tested against the hypothesis that they are unequal. Eight people, who have different lifestyles, were chosen to test the jackets. The results were as follows:

Wearer	Life (days) Manufacturer X	Manufacturer Y
P	300	310
Q	350	370
R	280	260
S	320	310
T	400	410
U	420	420
V	450	470
W	230	240

The null hypothesis should be

A accepted at 5% significance but rejected at 1% significance

B accepted at 1% significance but rejected at 5% significance

C accepted both at 5% significance and at 1% significance

D rejected both at 5% significance and at 1% significance

Circle your answer

A   B   C   D

13 A two-tailed test of the hypothesis that a population mean equals 148 is performed at 5% significance, with a sample size of 45. If the population standard deviation is known to be 24 and the true population mean is 162, what is the probability of a type II error?

A 0.0128
B 0.025
C 0.0256
D 0.05

Circle your answer

A   B   C   D

14 In a test of the hypothesis that the proportion of homes with central heating equals the proportion of homes with two or more televisions, 60% of a sample of 90 homes were found to have central heating and 55% of a sample of 80 homes were found to have two or more televisions. The null hypothesis should be

A   accepted at both 5% significance and 1% significance

B   accepted at 5% significance but rejected at 1% significance

C   accepted at 1% significance but rejected at 5% significance

D   rejected at both 5% significance and 1% significance

Circle your answer

A   B   C   D

15 In a two-tailed test at 1% significance of a hypothesis that two proportions were equal, the first sample proportion was 0.4 and the second sample proportion was 0.5. Both samples were of the same size, and the null hypothesis was only just rejected. How large was each sample?

A   134
B   190
C   269
D   329

Circle your answer

A   B   C   D

16 It is thought that the mean life of a pre-recorded videotape is not more than 1,000 playings. A sample of 14 tapes was tested. They had a mean life of 1,150 playings and a standard deviation of lives of 235 playings. It is accepted that the lives of tapes are normally distributed. The null hypothesis should be

A   accepted at 5% significance but rejected at 1% significance

B   accepted at 1% significance but rejected at 5% significance

C   accepted both at 5% significance and at 1% significance

D   rejected both at 5% significance and at 1% significance

Circle your answer

A   B   C   D

17 In a test of the hypothesis that a bottle of ink will last for 56,000 words of handwriting, neither more nor less, a sample of six bottles was used. The sample mean was 62,000 words and the sample standard deviation was 6,000 words. It is accepted that the lives of bottles of ink are normally distributed. The null hypothesis should be

A   accepted at 5% significance but rejected
     at 1% significance

B   accepted at 1% significance but rejected
     at 5% significance

C   accepted both at 5% significance and at
     1% significance

D   rejected both at 5% significance and at
     1% significance

Circle your answer

| A | B | C | D |

18 A test of whether two populations have the same standard deviation is to be made, using these sample results:

	Population 1	*Population 2*
Number in sample	40	45
Sample standard deviation	12	27

What is the value of F to be used in the test?

A   0.1975
B   2.2500
C   5.0625
D   5.6953

Circle your answer

| A | B | C | D |

19 To test the hypothesis that two populations have the same standard deviation, against the alternative hypothesis that their standard deviations differ, two samples were taken as follows:

	Population 1	*Population 2*
Number in sample	10	7
Sample standard deviation	35	80

The null hypothesis should be

A   accepted at 10% significance but rejected
     at 2% significance

B   accepted at 2% significance but rejected
     at 10% significance

C   accepted both at 10% significance and at
     2% significance

D   rejected both at 10% significance and at
     2% significance

Circle your answer

| A | B | C | D |

20 In a goodness of fit test, the observed and expected frequencies were as follows:

Observed	Expected
12	10
9	10
8	8
2	5
7	5

What was the value of χ^2 ?

A   0.57
B   3.1
C   5.5
D   8

Circle your answer

A   B   C   D

21 A distribution of car colours was hypothesised, and 300 cars were then observed, as follows.

Colour	Hypothesised %	Observed
Red	17	47
Green	15	50
Blue	20	70
Yellow	10	37
Other	38	96

The hypothesis should be

A   accepted at 5% significance but rejected at 1% significance

B   accepted at 1% significance but rejected at 5% significance

C   accepted both at 5% significance and at 1% significance

D   rejected both at 5% significance and at 1% significance

Circle your answer

A   B   C   D

22 A variable is thought to have a Poisson distribution. What value of χ^2 would be computed in a goodness of fit test based on the following data? (Use the mean of observed values as the Poisson distribution mean.)

Value	Number of observations
0	32
1	40
2	14
3	14
> 4	0

A   3.25
B   3.88
C   3.96
D   8.25

Circle your answer

A   B   C   D

23 It is thought that a certain variable fits a normal distribution, with a given mean (μ) and standard deviation (σ). Results from 1,000 observations were as follows:

(Value - μ)/σ	Proportion of cases
< - 2	0.04
$\geqslant$ - 2, < - 1	0.15
$\geqslant$ - 1, < 0	0.30
$\geqslant$ 0, < + 1	0.35
$\geqslant$ + 1, < + 2	0.10
$\geqslant$ + 2	0.06

The null hypothesis should be

A   accepted at 10% significance but rejected at 1% significance

B   accepted at 1% significance but rejected at 10% significance

C   accepted both at 10% significance and at 1% significance

D   rejected both at 10% significance and at 1% significance

Circle your answer

A   B   C   D

24 A farmer tests the hypothesis that the choice of fertiliser has no effect on the yield of arable land. He experiments on 100 different plots, with the following results:

| | | Fertiliser | | | |
		X	Y	Z	Total
	High	5	8	25	38
Yield	Medium	10	6	10	26
	Low	15	16	5	36
	Total	30	30	40	100

The hypothesis should be

A   accepted at 10% significance but rejected
    at 5% significance

B   accepted at 5% significance but rejected
    at 10% significance

C   accepted both at 10% significance and
    at 5% significance

D   rejected both at 10% significance and
    at 5% significance

Circle your answer

A	B	C	D

25 What is the value of χ^2 for the following contingency table of observed results, assuming a null hypothesis of no connection between actions and outcomes and applying any appropriate correction?

		Action		
		P	Q	Total
Outcome	R	25	46	71
	S	15	14	29
Total		40	60	100

A   0.3393
B   1.7018
C   2.3393
D   3.0779

Circle your answer

A	B	C	D

26 A restaurateur is experimenting with the effects of different typefaces in his menus. He takes one dish, and prints three different types of menu: one with the dish in normal type, one with the dish in bold type and one with the dish in italic type. Numbers of the dish sold on 10 different days are as follows:

Normal type: 30, 27, 28, 42
Bold type: 45, 37, 32
Italic type: 38, 29, 35

The sum of the squares of these ten sales figures is 12,105.

The null hypothesis that the choice of typeface makes no difference to sales is tested using an analysis of variance test. The null hypothesis should be

A   accepted at 5% significance but rejected at 1% significance

B   accepted at 1% significance but rejected at 5% significance

C   accepted both at 5% significance and at 1% significance

D   rejected both at 5% significance and at 1% significance

Circle your answer

A   B   C   D

CHAPTER 6

CORRELATION AND REGRESSION

This chapter covers the following topics:

- Correlation
- Regression
- Regression - confidence limits and hypothesis tests
- Regression - special cases

1. Correlation

1.1 We may be given pairs of values of two variables (for example, sales of two products each month for a year), and wonder whether there is a link between the two variables. Such a link is called *correlation*.

1.2 Correlation may be *positive* (high values of one variable associated with high values of the other) or *negative* (high values of one variable associated with low values of the other). But however strong correlation is, it does not prove a causal link between the two variables. Both may be affected by a third variable, or the correlation may be due to chance: in either case, we speak of *spurious correlation*.

1.3 The larger the number of pairs of values collected, the more significant is any given level of correlation. This is because there is more chance of any lack of connection between the variables showing up if more data are collected.

1.4 The main measure of correlation is the *Pearsonian correlation coefficient*, r.

For n pairs of data for two variables, x and y,

$$r = \frac{n\Sigma xy - \Sigma x \, \Sigma y}{\sqrt{[n\Sigma x^2 - (\Sigma x)^2] \, [n \, \Sigma y^2 - (\Sigma y)^2]}}$$

$$= \frac{\Sigma xy - n\bar{x}\,\bar{y}}{n \, \sigma_x \, \sigma_y} = \frac{\Sigma(x - \bar{x}) \, (y - \bar{y})}{\sqrt{\Sigma(x - \bar{x})^2 \, \Sigma(y - \bar{y})^2}}$$

r can take values between +1 (perfect positive correlation) and -1 (perfect negative correlation).

1.5 The *coefficient of determination*, r^2, is the proportion of variation in one variable explained by variation in the other.

1.6 If, instead of the actual values of variables, we are only given pairs of ranks or positions (such as first (1) in Latin and fourth (4) in Greek), we cannot work out r, but we can work out *Spearman's rank correlation coefficient*, r_s.

For each of n pairs of ranks, compute the difference in ranks, d, ignoring minus signs (first - fourth = 1-4 = 3)

$$r_s = 1 - \frac{6\Sigma d^2}{n(n^2 - 1)}$$

---

r_s can also take values between +1 and -1.

2. Regression

2.1 A correlation coefficient can show us whether there is a relationship between two variables, but not exactly what the relationship is. The methods of *regression* are used to establish the relationship. Once it is established, we can use it to predict values of one variable for given values of the other.

2.2 Before computing the relationship between two variables, we must first identify the independent variable (usually denoted by x) and the dependent variable (usually denoted by y). The independent variable is the one which affects the other. If x is the independent variable, we can compute the *regression line of y on x*, and use it to predict values of y for given values of x (but not vice versa).

2.3 The usual regression line to compute is the least-squares regression line, so called because it minimises the sum $\Sigma(y - y_e)^2$, where y is each observed value of the dependent variable and y_e is the value which the line would have predicted for the corresponding observed value of the independent variable.

For n data pairs, the least-squares linear regression line is y = a + bx, where

$$b = \frac{n\Sigma xy - \Sigma x \Sigma y}{n\Sigma x^2 - (\Sigma x)^2}$$

$$a = \overline{y} - b\overline{x} = \frac{\Sigma y}{n} - \frac{b\Sigma x}{n}$$

2.4 There are some links between regression and correlation which can be handy in solving problems.

> In the regression line $y = a + bx$,
>
> $$b = \frac{\text{Covariance of } x \text{ and } y}{\text{Variance of } x}$$

The covariance of x and y is $\dfrac{\Sigma(x - \bar{x})(y - \bar{y})}{n}$

> If we have a regression line of y on x, $y = a + bx$ and one of x on y, $x = c + dy$, then we can find the Pearsonian correlation coefficient between x and y:
>
> $$r = \sqrt{bd}$$
>
> Take the positive square root if b and d are positive, and the negative square root if they are negative.

3. Regression - confidence limits and hypothesis tests

3.1 We compute a regression line from a sample of data pairs, and rely on the line to make predictions. We must therefore allow for the possibility of error. As with means, proportions and standard deviations, we can compute confidence limits and perform hypothesis tests.

3.2 Before doing either of these things, we need to work out the standard error of the estimated regression line, SE.

> For a line $y = a + bx$
>
> $$SE = \sqrt{\frac{\Sigma(y - y_e)^2}{n - 2}} = \sqrt{\frac{\Sigma y^2 - a\Sigma y - b\Sigma xy}{n - 2}}$$
>
> where $y_e = a + bx$ for each observed value of x

3.3 Confidence limits are then as follows.

For a specific predicted value of y from a specific value x_0:

$$a + bx_0 \pm t\, SE \sqrt{1 + \frac{1}{n} + \frac{n(x_0 - \bar{x})^2}{n\Sigma x^2 - (\Sigma x)^2}}$$

Thus if x = advertising expenditure and y = sales, we might use this formula to reach a conclusion such as: for x = £20,000, y = £500,000 ± £15,000 with 95% confidence.

For a:

$$a \pm t\, SE \sqrt{\frac{1}{n} + \frac{n\bar{x}^2}{n\Sigma x^2 - (\Sigma x)^2}}$$

For b:

$$b \pm \frac{t\, SE}{\sqrt{\dfrac{n\Sigma x^2 - (\Sigma x)^2}{n}}}$$

In each case, t is the value from t distribution tables (for n - 2 degrees of freedom) for the appropriate confidence level, eg $t_{0.025}$ for 95% confidence. If n is over 30, normal distribution tables can be used (eg t = 1.96 for 95% confidence).

3.4 Significance tests can be performed on both a and b, as follows.

3.5 Null hypothesis: a = some particular value, α

Test statistic:

$$\frac{a - \alpha}{SE \sqrt{\dfrac{1}{n} + \dfrac{n\bar{x}^2}{n\Sigma x^2 - (\Sigma x)^2}}}$$

Critical values: $\pm$ t. Values are found from t distribution tables with n - 2 degrees of freedom, or from normal distribution tables, as for a test for one sample mean. Thus for n = 20 and 5% significance, the critical value for a two-tailed test (H_1 is a $\neq \alpha$) would be 2.10, and for a one-tailed test (H_1 is a $> \alpha$, or H_1 is a $< \alpha$) it would be 1.73.

3.6 Null hypothesis: b = some particular value, β

Test statistic: $\dfrac{b - \beta}{SE} \sqrt{\dfrac{n\Sigma x^2 - (\Sigma x)^2}{n}}$

Where the null hypothesis is that b = 0, this equals $\sqrt{\dfrac{r^2(n - 2)}{1 - r^2}}$, where r is the Pearsonian correlation coefficient.

Critical values: as for hypothesis test for a.

3.7 We could, for example, test the hypothesis that a = 0 (so that y is simply a multiple of x), or that b = 0 (so that the value of y is uninfluenced by the value of x).

4. Regression - special cases

4.1 Multiple regression

It may be that the value of y depends on the values of several variables, $x_1, x_2, \ldots x_n$. In that case, a *multiple regression* equation may be computed, of the form

$$y = a + b_1 x_1 + b_2 x_2 + \ldots + b_n x_n$$

4.2 Non-linear relationships

The relationship between two variables may not be linear. In some cases, the least-squares regression formulae can still be used, because logarithms can be used to convert the non-linear relationship to a linear one.

4.3 A geometric relationship, $y = ax^b$, can be converted to $\log y = \log a + b \log x$. A regression line of log y on log x can be found, giving values for log a (from which a can be found) and for b.

4.4 An exponential relationship, $y = ab^x$, can be converted to $\log y = \log a + x \log b$. A regression line of log y on x can be found, giving values for log a and log b, and hence for a and b.

QUESTIONS

1

The Pearsonian correlation coefficient (r) between two variables, our sales (x) and a competitor's sales (y), is -1. We may conclude that

A increases in the value of x cause decreases in the value of y

B increases in the value of y cause decreases in the value of x

C if the value of x doubles, the value of y will halve

D all the variation in the value of y is explained by variation in the value of x

Circle your answer

A   B   C   D

2

Which of the following statements about the Pearsonian correlation coefficient is/are true?

Statement
1. In exceptional circumstances its value may exceed 1
2. High positive correlation in past data shows that future changes in one variable will certainly be accompanied by changes in the other
3. Strong correlation is more significant if it has been found from a larger sample of data pairs
4. It is important to identify the independent variable when computing r.

A Statements 1 and 3 only
B Statements 2 and 4 only
C Statement 3 only
D Statements 3 and 4 only

Circle your answer

A   B   C   D

3

Between sales of cold drinks and sales of suntan cream, one would expect (assuming spending money to be unlimited)

A positive, but spurious correlation

B negative, but spurious, correlation

C positive correlation indicating direct causation

D negative correlation indicating direct causation

Circle your answer

A   B   C   D

4 What is the Pearsonian correlation coefficient, r, for the following data:

x	y
1	6
2	5
3	3
4	8

A   -0.25
B   -0.06
C   +0.06
D   +0.25

Circle your answer

A   B   C   D

5 For a set of six data pairs for the variables x (net office furniture expenditure) and y (sales) the following values have been found:

Σx = 1
Σy = 15
Σx^2 = 15
Σy^2 = 65
Σxy = 7

What is the Pearsonian correlation coefficient?

A   0.05
B   0.07
C   0.22
D   0.47

Circle your answer

A   B   C   D

6 For a set of four data pairs for the variables x (average salary) and y (staff turnover), the following values have been found:

Σx = 10
Σy = 9
Σxy = 17
σ_x = 1.118
σ_y = 1.299

What is the Pearsonian correlation coefficient?

A   -0.90
B   -0.92
C   -0.95
D   -0.97

Circle your answer

A   B   C   D

7 Which of the following statements is/are true of the coefficient of determination?

Statement
1. It is the square of the Pearsonian correlation coefficient
2. It is the square root of the Pearsonian correlation coefficient
3. It can never quite equal 1
4. If it is high, this proves that variations in one variable cause variations in the other

A Statement 1 only
B Statements 1 and 4 only
C Statements 2 and 3 only
D Statements 2 and 4 only

Circle your answer

| A | B | C | D |

8 For a set of five data pairs of the variables x and y, the following values have been found

$$\Sigma (x - \bar{x})(y - \bar{y}) = -6$$
$$\Sigma (x - \bar{x})^2 = 10$$
$$\Sigma (y - \bar{y})^2 = 4$$

What is the coefficient of determination between these two variables?

A 0.85
B 0.90
C 0.95
D 0.97

Circle your answer

| A | B | C | D |

9 The following data give five skaters' marks for technical merit and artistic impression.

Skater	Technical merit	Artistic impression
P	6.0	5.5
Q	5.2	5.6
R	5.4	5.4
S	5.7	5.8
T	5.9	5.9

What is the value of Spearman's rank correlation coefficient between the two sets of positions?

A -0.8
B -0.2
C + 0.2
D + 0.8

Circle your answer

| A | B | C | D |

10 Six competitors in two competitions achieved the following scores:

Competitor	Competition 1	Competition 2
U	38	50
V	36	54
W	36	56
X	32	50
Y	30	50
Z	27	45

What is the value of Spearman's rank correlation coefficient between the two sets of positions?

A -0.64
B -0.36
C +0.36
D +0.64

Circle your answer

A   B   C   D

11 When data pairs are plotted on a scatter diagram, with the independent variable along the horizontal axis, the least-squares regression line minimises

A the sum of the squares of the horizontal distances from the points to the line

B the sum of the squares of the perpendicular distances from the points to the line

C the sum of the squares of the vertical distances from the line of points above the line less the sum of the squares of the horizontal distances from the line of points below the line

D the sum of the squares of the vertical distances from the points to the line

Circle your answer

A   B   C   D

12 What is the equation of the least-squares regression line of y (sales in £m) on x (number of sales staff) for the following four data pairs?

x	y
1	2
2	3
3	5
4	5

A $y = 1 + 1.1x$
B $y = 1.1 + x$
C $y = 1.75 + 0.8x$
D $y = 0.8 + 1.75x$

Circle your answer

A   B   C   D

13 What is the equation of the least-squares regression line of x on y for the following five data pairs?

x	y
4	1
7	2
9	3
8	3
9	3

A   x = 6.4 + 0.42y
B   x = 0.42 + 6.4y
C   x = 2.25 + 2y
D   x = 2 + 2.25y

Circle your answer

A   B   C   D

14 The following values have been obtained from data for two variables, x (number of employees ill, the independent variable) and y (thousands of units of production lost).

$\bar{x}$ = 2
$\bar{y}$ = 6
covariance (x,y) = 10
variance (x) = 4

If a regression line were computed, what value of y would be predicted for a value of x of 5?

A   3
B   5.4
C   7.5
D   13.5

Circle your answer

A   B   C   D

15 For two variables, x and y, the least-squares regression line of y on x is y = 2 - 1.8x, and the regression line of x on y is x = 1.18 - 0.53y. What is the Pearsonian correlation coefficient between x and y?

A   -0.910
B   -0.954
C   -0.977
D   -0.988

Circle your answer

A   B   C   D

16 A multiple regression computation has yielded the equation y = 475 + 0.7x + 3.2w + 1.9z. What value of y would be predicted for w = 42, x = 7, z = -0.9?

A   525.09
B   528.51
C   612.59
D   616.01

Circle your answer

A   B   C   D

17 Six data pairs have been used to find a regression line. The actual values of the dependent variable, and the values which would have been predicted from the regression line, are as follows.

y (actual)	y_e (predicted)
1	1.3
4	3.8
7	6.5
2	2.0
6	6.4
9	9.0

What is the standard error of the estimated regression line?

A 0.09
B 0.135
C 0.3
D 0.367

Circle your answer

A   B   C   D

18 40 pairs of observed values of x (the independent variable) and y have been collected, with the following results:

Σx = 820
Σy = 1,320
Σx^2 = 22,140
Σy^2 = 58,640
Σxy = 35,890

The regression line is y = -1.03 + 1.66x. What is the 95% confidence interval for the predicted value of y when x = 14.5?

A 17.46 to 28.62
B 16.41 to 29.67
C 15.16 to 30.92
D 14.31 to 31.77

Circle your answer

A   B   C   D

19 A regression line of cost (y) on output (x) was found using 15 data pairs. The equation was y = 12 + 12x, and the standard error of the line was 6. Σx^2 = 1,240, and Σx = 120. It is hypothesised that in fact y is a purely variable cost, with no fixed component (so the value of a, 12, arose by chance because of the sample taken). This hypothesis should be

A accepted at 5% significance but rejected at 1% significance

B accepted at 1% significance but rejected at 5% significance

C accepted both at 5% significance and at 1% significance

Circle your answer

D rejected both at 5% significance and at 1% significance

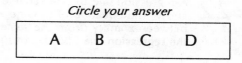

A   B   C   D

20 A regression line has been established using twelve data pairs. The line is $y = a + bx$. The standard error of the line is 27. $\Sigma x = 78$ and $\Sigma x^2 = 650$.

What is the 95% confidence interval for the slope of the regression line?

A $b \pm 0.87$
B $b \pm 0.99$
C $b \pm 4.42$
D $b \pm 5.03$

Circle your answer

A   B   C   D

21 It is hypothesised that daily sales, y, are uninfluenced by number of newspaper advertisements on the same day, x. 20 readings of x and y were taken, and the regression line computed was $y = 324 + 0.25x$. The standard error of the regression line is 2.5, $\Sigma x^2 = 2,870$, and $\Sigma x = 210$. The hypothesis should be

A   accepted at 5% significance but rejected at 1% significance

B   accepted at 1% significance but rejected at 5% significance

C   accepted both at 5% significance and at 1% significance

D   rejected both at 5% significance and at 1% significance

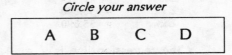

Circle your answer

A   B   C   D

22 A regression line of one variable, y, on another, x, was computed from seven readings of x and y. The equation of the line was $y = 42 - 0.4x$. The Pearsonian correlation coefficient, r, between x and y (from the same seven readings) was -0.6. The hypothesis that the slope of the regression line (-0.4) is not significantly different from zero should be

A   accepted at 5% significance but rejected at 1% significance

B   accepted at 1% significance but rejected at 5% significance

C   accepted both at 5% significance and at 1% significance

D   rejected both at 5% significance and at 1% significance

Circle your answer

A   B   C   D

23 Two variables, x and y, are related by an expression of the form $y = ax^b$. The following readings have been obtained.

x	y
2	32
3	108

What is the value of a?

A 2
B 3
C 4
D 5

Circle your answer

A   B   C   D

24 It is thought that one variable, y, depends on another, x, and that the relationship is of the form $y = ax^b$. The following readings have been obtained.

x	y
1	2
2	5
3	15
4	22

Using logarithms and applying least-squares linear regression, what is the value of b?

A   0.26
B   1.46
C   1.79
D   7.00

Circle your answer

A   B   C   D

25 It is thought that two variables, x and y, are related by an expression of the form $y = ab^x$. The following readings have been obtained:

x	y
1	2
2	2
3	2.7
4	3.3

Using logarithms and least-squares linear regression, what value for y would be predicted for a value of x of 6?

A   3.5
B   4.1
C   4.6
D   5.2

Circle your answer

A   B   C   D

CHAPTER 7

TIME SERIES ANALYSIS

This chapter covers the following topics:

- The components of a time series
- Finding the trend
- Seasonal variations and residuals
- Predictions

1. The components of a time series

1.1 A *time series* is any series of data over time, for example production costs each month for a year. The usual reason for collecting such a series is to be able to make predictions for the future. To do this, we need to analyse the time series into its components, so we can work out the likely influence of each component on future values.

1.2 The four components into which time series are normally analysed are:

(i)   *Trend* - the general long-term movement
(ii)   *Cyclical variations* - cycles over a long period, for example 10 years
(iii) *Seasonal variations* - cycles over a shorter period, often a year but sometimes a month or some other period
(iv)   *Random variations* - these do not recur predictably.

2. Finding the trend

2.1 The trend is the long-term movement. In common with most computational examination questions, we will concentrate on separating the trend from seasonal variations, ignoring for the moment cyclical and random variations.

2.2 If we consider a company whose sales are high each spring and summer and low each autumn and winter, we would expect the time series of their sales to show a marked up and down pattern from one season to another within each year, which might hide any long-term rise or fall. On the other hand, looking at a series of *averages* of four consecutive quarters' sales (spring year 1 - winter year 1; summer year 1 - spring year 2; etc) might well reveal such a trend, because each average would include results from one spring, one summer, one autumn and one winter. This is the method of *moving averages*, and is a common way of finding a trend.

76

2.3 There is one refinement, appropriate when a time period is divided into an even number of seasons (eg four quarters in a year, but not seven days in a week). An average for spring year 1 - winter year 1 hovers between summer and autumn, rather than belonging to one particular quarter. So as to line up the averages with seasons, a moving total of two four-season totals is taken, and this is divided by $2 \times 4 = 8$.

2.4 Here is an example with a small amount of data.

Season	Data	Four-quarter total	Eight-quarter total	Moving average
Spring	4			
Summer	5			
		22		
Autumn	7		47	5.875
		25		
Winter	6		54	6.75
		29		
Spring	7			
Summer	9			

3. Seasonal variations and residuals

3.1 If T = trend, S = seasonal variations, C = cyclical variations and R = random variations, we may analyse a time series using either of two models:

- *Additive model:* Actual = T + S + C + R

- *Multiplicative model:* Actual = T × S × C × R

In the additive model, all of T, S, C and R will be in the same units (eg pounds). In the multiplicative model (also called the proportional model), S, C and R will be percentage adjustments.

The multiplicative model makes the arithmetic a bit harder, but is generally better when the trend is rising or falling rapidly, as variations are more likely to be stable percentages of the trend than stable amounts.

In the following analysis, we will continue to ignore C and R.

3.2 The additive model

If actual = trend + seasonal variation, then for each period for which we have a trend value we can find a seasonal variation:

Seasonal variation = actual - trend

In seasons of high values, the actual figure will exceed the trend and the seasonal variations will be positive. In seasons of low values, the seasonal variations will be negative.

3.3 If we are to make reliable predictions, we need to take account of as much data as possible. We should therefore work out average variations for each season, taking an arithmetic mean of (for example) all the seasonal variations for the summers for which we have them.

There is one last refinement. The net effect of seasonal variations over a year should be nil. If the average seasonal variations do not add up to 0, the same amount should be added to or subtracted from each one so that they do so add up. In practice, a bit of rounding is acceptable.

3.4 **The multiplicative model**

If actual = trend × seasonal variation, then seasonal variation = $\dfrac{\text{actual}}{\text{trend}} \times 100\%$

In seasons of high values, the seasonal variations will exceed 100%, while in the seasons of low values they will be below 100%.

3.5 The seasonal variations thus found can be averaged just as for additive model seasonal variations. However, they should not add up to 0, but to n × 100% where there are n seasons in each time period (eg to 400% for four quarters in a year). The same amount should be added to or subtracted from each average variation to achieve this.

3.6 **Residuals**

Average seasonal variations are unlikely to equal the actual seasonal variations for individual seasons, so if we combine a season's trend figure with its appropriate average seasonal variation we will not in general get back to the actual figure. The gap is the *residual*, measured as follows:

(i) Additive model: residual = actual - (trend + average seasonal variation)

(ii) Multiplicative model: residual = $\dfrac{\text{actual}}{\text{trend} \times \text{average seasonal variation}} \times 100\%$

3.7 The size of the residual indicates the extent to which factors other than the trend and seasonal variations are needed to explain the actual figures. If the residuals are large (additive model) or very different from 100% (multiplicative model), this suggests that the analysis into trend and seasonal variations is inadequate, so that predictions based on this analysis are likely to be unreliable.

3.8 **Seasonally adjusted figures**

Seasonally adjusted figures (for example, for unemployment) are frequently quoted in the media. They are meant to reflect the trend, without the effect of seasonal variations, and are also called *deseasonalised data*.

3.9   Seasonally adjusted figures are computed as follows:

(i)   Additive model: actual - average seasonal variation

(ii)   Multiplicative model: actual/average seasonal variation

Normally, such figures are produced as the data become available, so the average seasonal variations used will be based on data for a number of previous periods.

4.   Predictions

4.1   To make a prediction using either the additive model or the multiplicative model, we first extrapolate the trend then apply the appropriate average seasonal adjustment. The trend is normally extrapolated by taking its average rise per season over the longest interval for which we have trend values (unless either end point of that interval is known to be unrepresentative in some way, or the rate of change of trend values has changed markedly within that interval, in which case a different interval may be preferable).

4.2   Predictions made in this way must be treated with caution. The trend could change direction at any time, the pattern of seasonal variations could change, and random factors could influence individual seasons' results. The further into the future predictions are made, the riskier they become.

4.3   Exponential smoothing

A quite different method of making predictions is *exponential smoothing*. Each predicted figure is a weighted average of (1) the previous period's predicted figure and (2) that period's actual figure, as follows.

$$\text{Forecast}_{t+1} = (1 - \alpha)\,\text{Forecast}_t + \alpha(\text{Actual}_t)$$

$$= \text{Forecast}_t + \alpha\,(\text{Actual}_t - \text{Forecast}_t)$$

α is the *smoothing constant*, and $0 \leqslant \alpha \leqslant 1$

4.4   The effect, seen particularly clearly in the second version of the formula, is to take as each period's forecast the previous period's forecast plus an adjustment for the extent to which that previous period's forecast was in error.

At one extreme, $\alpha = 0$, and the forecast will never change, whatever actual results are. At the other extreme, $\alpha = 1$, and the forecast for any period will always equal the previous period's actual results. In between these extremes, a balance is struck between previous forecasting and actual results.

4.5   Exponential smoothing can be a useful technique when analysis of data into a trend and seasonal variations is inappropriate. However, the smoothing constant needs to be chosen carefully.

QUESTIONS

1 Which of the following is *not* one of the four components of a time series?

    A   The historical data
    B   The trend
    C   Cyclical variations
    D   Random variations

Circle your answer

A   B   C   D

2 A time series has been compiled of the number of cars passing a given point each day. The series has been analysed into the following four components. Which one would be designated the seasonal variation?

    A   A basic level which was 1,000 cars a day thirty years ago and has increased by 25 to 30 cars a day each year since then

    B   Variations of up to 50 cars a day which occur at unpredictable times, but on average four times each year

    C   An extra 65-85 cars a day in the first six months each year

    D   An extra 50-60 cars a day in the first half of each decade

Circle your answer

A   B   C   D

3 Which of the following is true of cyclical variations?

    A   They always repeat every 5 to 10 years

    B   They always reflect the trade cycle

    C   Their magnitude is constant from one cycle to the next

    D   Their period is longer than that of seasonal variations

Circle your answer

A   B   C   D

4 Using the following data, what is the three-month moving average for April?

Month	Number of new houses finished
January	500
February	450
March	700
April	900
May	1,250
June	1,000

A 683 houses
B 800 houses
C 860 houses
D 950 houses

Circle your answer

A B C D

5 What is the eight-quarter moving total centred on year 1, quarter 4 for the following data?

Year	Quarter	Data
1	1	52
	2	54
	3	56
	4	55
2	1	57
	2	60
	3	59
	4	62

A 439
B 448
C 450
D 459

Circle your answer

A B C D

6 Assuming that seasonal variations show a four-quarter cycle, and that the moving averages method is used, what would be the trend value for year 2, quarter 1 for the following data?

Year	Quarter	Data
1	1	47
	2	38
	3	45
	4	35
2	1	36
	2	30
	3	33
	4	29

A 32.75
B 35.00
C 36.50
D 37.25

Circle your answer

A B C D

7 Assuming that seasonal variations show a weekly cycle, and that the moving averages method is used, what would be the trend value for Saturday of week 1 for the following data?

Week	Day	Data
1	Monday	15
	Tuesday	17
	Wednesday	19
	Thursday	22
	Friday	18
	Saturday	16
	Sunday	15
2	Monday	17
	Tuesday	20
	Wednesday	21
	Thursday	25
	Friday	23
	Saturday	21
	Sunday	20

A   17.6
B   17.7
C   18.1
D   18.4

Circle your answer

A   B   C   D

8 A time series for weeks 1-12 has been analysed into a trend and seasonal variations, using the additive model. The trend value is 84 + 0.7w, where w is the week number. The actual value for week 9 is 88.7. What is the seasonal variation for week 9?

A   -1.6
B   -0.9
C   + 0.9
D   + 1.6

Circle your answer

A   B   C   D

9 The following data are to be analysed into a trend and seasonal variations, using the additive model and assuming that the seasonal variations have a period of three months (ie follow a pattern of rises and falls which lasts three months). What is the seasonal variation for April?

Month	Data
March	8
April	13
May	16
June	11

A   -0.67
B   -0.17
C   + 0.17
D   + 0.67

Circle your answer

A   B   C   D

10 The following data are to be analysed into a trend and seasonal variations, using the additive model and assuming that the seasonal variations have a period of four days. What is the seasonal variation for day 6?

Day	Data
1	5
2	6
3	7
4	2
5	6
6	8
7	9
8	6

A -1.75
B -1.25
C +1.25
D +1.75

Circle your answer

A   B   C   D

11 The following seasonal variations have been found in a time series analysis using the additive model. What is the average seasonal variation for summer?

		Spring	Summer	Autumn	Winter
Year	1			+5	+6
	2	-6	-4	+4	+7
	3	-5	-5		

A -4.25
B -4.50
C -4.75
D -5.00

Circle your answer

A   B   C   D

12 The following data are to be analysed into a trend and seasonal variations, using the additive model and assuming that the seasonal variations have a four-quarter period. What is the average seasonal variation for quarter 2?

		Quarter 1	2	3	4
Year	1	32	36	40	28
	2	36	39	42	32
	3	45	48	50	39

A +1.7920
B +2.6875
C +2.8125
D +5.3750

Circle your answer

A   B   C   D

13 The following data are to be analysed into a trend and seasonal variations, using the multiplicative model and assuming a four-quarter period for seasonal variations. What is the seasonal variation for quarter 4?

		Quarter 1	2	3	4
Year	1	157	140	100	120
	2	170	155	110	130

A 88.1%
B 89.3%
C 90.6%
D 92.3%

Circle your answer

A   B   C   D

14 A time series has been analysed into trend and seasonal variations, using the multiplicative model and assuming a five-day period for seasonal variations. The following are the actual and the trend figures. What is the average seasonal variation for day 4?

Week	Day	Actual	Trend
1	3	35	37.6
	4	40	36.0
	5	50	34.6
2	1	22	33.6
	2	26	32.8
	3	30	30.8
	4	36	30.0
	5	40	29.6
3	1	18	28.6
	2	24	26.6
	3	25	24.2

A 111.1%
B 115.2%
C 115.6%
D 120.0%

Circle your answer

A   B   C   D

15 A time series analysis has been performed on data for weeks 1-20. The trend line is given by 3,150 + 72x, where x is the week number. The average seasonal variation (using the additive model) for weeks whose numbers are divisible by 4 (ie weeks 4, 8, 12 etc) is -47. The actual figure for week 12 was 4,000. What was the residual for that week?

A   -61
B   -14
C   + 19
D   + 33

Circle your answer

A   B   C   D

16 A time series analysis using the additive model has been performed on monthly employment figures, and the following average seasonal adjustments to the trend have been arrived at:

July	- 20,000
August	+ 40,000

The actual numbers of unemployed for July and August in a particular year are 2,030,500 and 2,027,000 respectively. What are the seasonally adjusted numbers for these two months?

A July: 2,050,500; August: 2,067,000
B July: 2,050,500; August: 1,987,000
C July: 2,010,500; August: 2,067,000
D July: 2,010,500; August: 1,987,000

Circle your answer

A   B   C   D

17 A company analyses the time series of its quarterly sales figures using a multiplicative model. The seasonal adjustments for spring and summer (based on data up to 19X8) are 92% and 115% respectively. Seasonally adjusted figures for 19X9 (based on these adjustments) were £32,567 for spring and £44,098 for summer. What were the actual sales for these two quarters?

A Spring: £35,399; Summer: £38,346
B Spring: £29,962; Summer: £38,346
C Spring: £35,399; Summer: £50,713
D Spring: £29,962; Summer: £50,713

Circle your answer

A   B   C   D

18 A company collects data on the number of orders received each day for a new product in the first fourteen days after launch, and analyses them using the additive model and assuming that the seasonal variations have a period of seven days, so as to predict orders for the next fourteen days. Days are numbered sequentially from 1 onwards. The trend is found to be $37 + 3x$, where x is the day number, and the seasonal variation for days whose numbers are divisible by 7 (ie days 7, 14 etc) is +5. What number of orders would be predicted for day 21?

A 53
B 63
C 95
D 105

Circle your answer

A   B   C   D

19 A time series has been analysed into trend and seasonal variations, using the additive model and assuming a period of four quarters for the seasonal variations. The trend values for year 1, quarter 3 and year 3, quarter 2 are 189 and 231 respectively, and the average seasonal variation for quarter 3 is -8. What is the predicted actual figure for year 4, quarter 3?

A 248
B 253
C 264
D 269

Circle your answer

A   B   C   D

20 A time series has been analysed into trend and seasonal variations, using the multiplicative model and assuming a twelve month period for the seasonal variations. The trend value for January 19X9 was 452, and the trend is increasing by 16 each month. The average seasonal variation for May is 103%. What is the predicted actual figure for May 19X9?

A 501
B 517
C 531
D 548

Circle your answer

A   B   C   D

21 A time series has been analysed into trend and seasonal variations, using the multiplicative model and assuming a period of four quarters for seasonal variations. The trend value for year 1, quarter 3 was 1,475, and for year 5, quarter 2 it was 1,190. The average seasonal variation for quarter 1 was 95%. What is the predicted actual value for year 6, quarter 1?

A 1,076
B 1,080
C 1,193
D 1,197

Circle your answer

A   B   C   D

22 A company forecasts the number of employees absent each day by exponential smoothing, using a smoothing constant of 0.3. The forecast number of absentees for Wednesday was 470, and the actual number was 520. What is the forecast number of absentees for Thursday?

A 485
B 505
C 520
D 535

Circle your answer

A   B   C   D

23 A restaurant uses exponential smoothing to forecast the number of plates broken each day. The forecast for Tuesday was 4 plates, and the actual number for Tuesday was 8 plates. If the forecast for Wednesday was 5 plates, what was the smoothing constant?

A 0.25
B 0.33
C 0.50
D 0.75

Circle your answer

A   B   C   D

CHAPTER 8

LINEAR PROGRAMMING

This chapter covers the following topics:

- Formulation of problems and graphical solution
- Dual prices
- Sensitivity analysis
- The dual problem
- The simplex method

1. Formulation of problems and graphical solution

1.1 Linear programming is a technique for solving problems with the following components:

(i)   a set of *decision variables*, such as quantities of different products to make;

(ii)   an *objective*, such as the maximisation of profit or the minimisation of costs;

(iii)   a set of *constraints* on possible values of the decision variables, such as that total units produced cannot exceed 6,000. These constraints often reflect limited *resources*, such as labour hours available.

Both the objective and the constraints must be formulated as linear functions of the decision variables. Thus if those variables are x and y, $3x + 2y \leqslant 10,000$ would be a possible constraint, but $x^2 + y \leqslant 1,000$ would not be. This requirement explains the name of the technique, *linear programming*, and also highlights an important limitation. In the real world, objectives and constraints are often not linear.

1.2 If there are only two decision variables, linear programming problems can be solved graphically. Typical graphs are as follows.

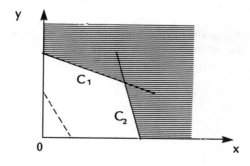
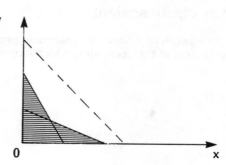

1.3 Consider the left hand graph first. The decision variables are x and y. The constraints are represented by lines C_1 and C_2, and both constraints are satisfied in the unshaded area, the *feasible region*.

The dotted line is a *trial objective*, ie a line obtained by giving a specific value to the objective function. Any value will do; for example, if the objective is to maximise x + 2y, we could plot the line x + 2y = 1,000.

The optimum is found by moving the edge of a ruler parallel to the trial objective as far up and to the right as possible while still touching the feasible region. The last point when the edge touches the feasible region is the optimum.

1.4 The right hand graph corresponds to a linear programming problem where the value of the objective function has to be minimised. In this case a line parallel to the trial objective is moved as far down and to the left as possible.

2. Dual prices

2.1 We can extract more information from a solution to a linear programming problem than simply the values we should choose for the decision variables. In particular, we can find out how much it would be worth paying for extra resources.

2.2 Say we are limited by a constraint, that x + 2y ≤ 3,000, where this represents the fact that we are limited to 3,000 units of gas a week. If we could buy one extra unit of gas a week, this constraint would change to x + 2y ≤ 3,001, and the position of our optimum would change slightly, leading (we hope) to increased profits.

However, profits per unit of x and y are worked out taking account of the normal cost of gas, so the increase in profit is the maximum *extra* we should be prepared to offer, above the normal rate, for the one extra unit. This increase in profit is the *dual price* per unit of gas (also called the *shadow price*).

2.3 Note that if we had spare gas anyway, perhaps because we ran out of labour first, it would not be worth buying any more gas. We would then say that the gas constraint was *non-critical,* and the dual price of gas would then be zero.

3. Sensitivity analysis

3.1 On a graph of a linear programming problem, the gradient of the objective will be between the gradients of the constraints which intersect at the optimum. For example:

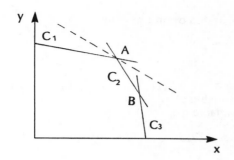

The solid lines represent constraints, and the dotted line the objective. The optimum is at point A, because the objective line is steeper than C_1 but not as steep as C_2.

3.2 The optimum would change to B if the objective line became steeper than C_2. This could happen if the coefficients of x and/or y in the objective function changed enough. If, for example, the gradient of C_2 is -2 and the initial objective is to maximise $3x + 4y$, a change of objective function to $8x + 4y$ (gradient = $-8/4 = -2$) or to $3x + 1.5y$ (gradient = $-3/1.5 = -2$) would be almost enough to tip the balance in favour of B. A change to $8.001x + 4y$ or to $3x + 1.4999y$ would mean that B would be a better choice than A.

4. The dual problem

4.1 Given a linear programming problem (the *primal problem*), we can formulate another problem, the *dual problem*, which is related to the primal problem in several useful ways. The relationship is symmetrical: each problem is the other's dual.

4.2 Two problems, say A and B, which are each other's duals, are related as follows:

(i)   each constraint in A corresponds to a decision variable in B;

(ii)   the values of the variables at the optimum in A are the dual prices of the corresponding constraints in B;

(iii) if a constraint is non-critical at the optimum in A, the value of the corresponding variable at the optimum in B is zero.

4.3 A consequence of (ii) is that we can solve the dual problem as a way of finding dual prices of constraints in the primal problem, rather than recomputing the value of the objective following a slight change in a constraint.

4.4 A consequence of (iii) is that if we have a problem with three decision variables and two constraints, which cannot be solved graphically because of the number of decision variables, we can solve the dual problem (which will have two decision variables and three constraints), note which constraint is non-critical, set the value of the corresponding variable in the primal problem to zero, and then solve the remaining two-variable primal problem.

4.5 The method of finding the dual problem is best illustrated by an example:

Primal problem

Maximise 5x + 8y

Subject to: 2x + y ≤ 10,000 (dual problem variable p)
4x + 3y ≤ 3,000 (dual problem variable q)
x, y ≥ 0

Dual problem

Minimise 10,000p + 3,000q

Subject to: 2p + 4q ≥ 5 (primal problem variable x)
p + 3q ≥ 8 (primal problem variable y)
p, q ≥ 0

5. The simplex method

5.1 The simplex method is an alternative to the graphical method of solving linear programming problems. It is not restricted to two decision variables, but the computations can get quite complicated so a computer program is often used, rather than manual calculations.

5.2 The first step in using the method is to turn all constraints into equations, by the insertion of slack or surplus variables. For example:

3x + 2y ≤ 1,000 becomes 3x + 2y + slack = 1,000
4x + y ≥ 50 becomes 4x + y - surplus = 50

The slack and surplus variables indicate how far one is from coming up against the limits the constraints impose.

5.3 A tableau is then formulated. This has

(i) a column for each decision variable, plus one for each slack variable and each surplus variable, and a solution column;

(ii) a row for each constraint;

(iii) a solution row, the figures in which show the results achieved and any scope for improvement.

5.4 Successive tableaux are then produced, until there is no more scope for improvement. The final tableau shows the values of variables and of the objective function at the optimum, which constraints are critical, the dual prices of the constraints and how the optimum would change were constraints to change slightly.

5.5 The method is illustrated in questions at the end of this chapter.

QUESTIONS

1   A company is using linear programming to decide how many units of each of its two products to make each week. Weekly production will be x units of product X and y units of product Y. At least 50 units of X must be produced each week, and at least twice as many units of Y as of X must be produced each week. Each unit of X requires 30 minutes of labour, and each unit of Y requires 2 hours of labour. There are 5,000 hours of labour available each week. Which of the following is the correct set of constraints?

A $0.5x + 2y \leqslant 5,000$
           $x \geqslant 50$
           $y \geqslant 2x$

B $x + 4y \leqslant 5,000$
           $x \geqslant 50$
           $y \geqslant 2x$

C $0.5x + 2y \leqslant 5,000$
           $x \geqslant 50$
           $y \geqslant 100$

D $0.5x + 2y \leqslant 10,000$
           $x \geqslant 0.5y$
           $y \geqslant 100$

Circle your answer

A   B   C   D

2   A businessman is trying to visit a large number of banks and building societies in London in five days. He wants to know what numbers of each he could visit, given that he has six hours available each day. Each bank will take two hours, and each building society will take one hour. For every two banks he visits, he wants to visit at least three building societies. He wants to visit at least two banks. If x is the number of banks visited, and y is the number of building societies visited, which of the following is the correct set of constraints on the visits to be made?

A $2x + y \leqslant 30$
           $3x \geqslant 2y$
           $x \geqslant 2$

B $2x + y \leqslant 30$
           $2y \geqslant 3x$
           $x \geqslant 2$

C $2x + y \geqslant 30$
           $3x \geqslant 2y$
           $x \geqslant 2$

D $2x + y \leqslant 30$
           $2y \geqslant 3x$
           $x \geqslant 0$

Circle your answer

A   B   C   D

3

A farmer wants to find the possible amounts of two different chemicals, P and Q, to use on arable land, and is using linear programming. He must use at least 50 kg of P per hectare. The weight of Q per hectare may be between two and five times the weight of P per hectare. The total weight of chemicals per hectare must not exceed 500 kg. If p = kg per hectare of chemical P, and q = kg per hectare of chemical Q, which of the following is the correct set of constraints?

A $\quad p \geqslant 50$
$\quad\quad q \geqslant 2p$
$\quad\quad q \leqslant 5p$
$\quad\quad p + q \leqslant 1,000$

B $\quad p \geqslant 50$
$\quad\quad p \geqslant 2q$
$\quad\quad p \leqslant 5q$
$\quad\quad p + q \leqslant 500$

C $\quad p \geqslant 50$
$\quad\quad q \geqslant 100$
$\quad\quad q \leqslant 250$
$\quad\quad p + q \leqslant 500$

D $\quad p \geqslant 50$
$\quad\quad q \geqslant 2p$
$\quad\quad q \leqslant 5p$
$\quad\quad p + q \leqslant 500$

Circle your answer

A	B	C	D

4

A company wishes to maximise its annual profit. It has two products, F and G. F sells for £20 a unit, and costs are 60% of selling price. G costs £15 a unit to make, and is sold at a profit of 40% of cost. There are no other costs. The company is using linear programming to determine the best sales mix. If f is the number of units of F sold each year, and g is the number of units of G sold each year, which of the following is the correct objective?

A Maximise 6f + 8g
B Maximise 8f + 9g
C Maximise 6f + 9g
D Maximise 8f + 6g

Circle your answer

A	B	C	D

5

A travelling salesman wishes to maximise the total value of orders he gets each week. He can visit small or large companies, and is using linear programming to decide how many visits to make. Each small company visit has a 60% probability of yielding an order of £500. Each large company visit has a 70% chance of yielding no order, but if an order is obtained it will amount to £3,000. If s is the number of visits to small companies made each week, and l is the number of visits to large companies made each week, what is the salesman's objective?

A   Maximise 500s + 3,000l
B   Maximise 500s + 900l
C   Maximise 300s + 900l
D   Maximise 300s + 2,100l

Circle your answer

A   B   C   D

6   An office manager wishes to minimise the cost of telephone calls made. 40% of calls in peak hours cost £1 each and the remainder of such calls cost £1.50 each. 30% of calls at other times cost 80p each, 50% of them cost 90p each, and 20% of them cost £1 each. These proportions cannot be varied, though the total numbers of calls made in peak hours and of calls made at other times can be. If x = the number of calls made each day in peak hours, and y = the number of calls made each day at other times, which of the following is the office manager's objective?

A   Minimise 120x + 89y
B   Minimise 120x + 90y
C   Minimise 130x + 89y
D   Minimise 130x + 90y

Circle your answer

A   B   C   D

7   In a linear programming problem, the constraints are as follows:
     $x \geqslant 0$
     $y \geqslant 150$
     $x + y \leqslant 450$
     $4x + y \leqslant 600$
What is the maximum possible value of the objective function, 3x + y, given these constraints?

A   450.0
B   487.5
C   537.5
D   550.0

Circle your answer

A   B   C   D

8   A company wishes to maximise its contribution from making records and compact discs (CDs). Relevant data are as follows:

	Per record	Per CD	Total available each day
Labour (minutes)	1	2	4,000
Machine time (minutes)	2	0.4	5,000
Administration time (minutes)	1	1	3,000
Contribution (£)	2	6	

What is the maximum contribution the company can make each day from these two products together?

A   £5,000
B   £8,500
C   £10,000
D   £12,000

Circle your answer

A   B   C   D

9 A marketing manager may use large posters and/or small posters to advertise a new product. There must be at least half as many large posters as small posters and at least 50 large posters. There must be at least 100 posters in total, and not more than 150 small posters. Each large poster costs £4 and each small poster costs £2. What is the minimum total cost?

A   £300
B   £400
C   £500
D   £600

Circle your answer

A   B   C   D

10 In a linear programming problem, a company's objective was to minimise its total spending per week on two materials, G and H. Each unit of G cost £3 and each unit of H cost £8. The optimum was found to be at the intersection of two constraints. The first was a contractual obligation to buy at least 50 units of H each week, and the second was a requirement to buy at least twice as many units of G as units of H each week. What is the maximum the company should be prepared to pay for a reduction in its contractual obligation by one unit of H per week?

A   £8.00
B   £9.50
C   £11.00
D   £14.00

Circle your answer

A   B   C   D

11 In a linear programming problem involving two variables, x and y, the objective was to maximise contribution in pounds, $2x + 4.5y$. The optimum was found to be at the intersection of a constraint on the electricity supply, $2x + 5y \leqslant 10,000$ units of electricity, and a constraint on machine time, $x + 2y \leqslant 4,300$ hours. What was the dual price per unit of electricity?

A   £0.40
B   £0.50
C   £2.25
D   £2.50

Circle your answer

A   B   C   D

12 Linear programming has been used to maximise contribution earned by a factory from two products, J and K. Among the variable costs is direct labour. Each unit of J needs 2 hours of direct labour. If the direct labour constraint is plotted on a graph with units of K on the vertical axis, it has a gradient of -2/3. The direct labour per unit of K costs £10.50. The dual price of labour is £5.30 an hour. What is the maximum hourly rate that should be paid for additional direct labour, assuming there is no change in the rate paid for the currently available direct labour time?

A   £5.30
B   £7.40
C   £8.80
D   £13.18

Circle your answer

A   B   C   D

13 A linear programming problem involves finding the production mix of two products, X and Y, which will maximise contribution. x units of product X and y units of product Y are to be made each week.

The constraints are:

$$x + 2y \leqslant 10,000$$
$$3x + y \leqslant 18,000$$
$$x \geqslant 0$$
$$y \geqslant 0$$

The contribution per unit of X is £5, and that per unit of Y is £3. By what amount would the contribution per unit of X have to rise for the optimum production mix to change?

A £4
B £7
C £9
D £10

Circle your answer

A   B   C   D

14 In a linear programming problem, the objective is to minimise the total expenditure on two products, V and W. v units of V are to be bought at £17 each, and w units of W at £25 each. The optimum lies at the intersection of two constraint lines, which (with v on the horizontal axis) have gradients of -0.6 and -1.2 respectively. Which of the following changes in the unit price of W would both cause changes in the optimum purchase mix?

A A rise of 43.3% and a fall of 13.3%
B A rise of 13.3% and a fall of 43.3%
C A rise of 76.5% and a fall of 11.8%
D A rise of 11.8% and a fall of 76.5%

Circle your answer

A   B   C   D

15 A linear programming problem is as follows:

Maximise $14x + 9y$,
Subject to $2x + 3y \leqslant 10,000$
                    $5x + y \leqslant 12,000$
                    $x,y \geqslant 0$

Which of the following is the dual problem?

A   Minimise $10,000p + 12,000q$
      Subject to $2p + q \geqslant 14$
                              $3p + 5q \geqslant 9$
                              $p,q \geqslant 0$

B   Minimise $12,000p + 10,000q$
      Subject to $2p + q \geqslant 14$
                              $3p + 5q \geqslant 9$
                              $p,q \geqslant 0$

C   Minimise   10,000p + 12,000q
                        2p + 5q   ⩾ 14
                        3p + q   ⩾ 9
                        p, q   ⩾ 0

D   Minimise   12,000p + 10,000q
                        2p + 5q   ⩾ 14
                        3p + q   ⩾ 9
                        p, q   ⩾ 0

Circle your answer

A   B   C   D

16 A linear programming problem involved finding the optimum production mix to maximise contribution. There were two products. The only two constraints, litres of oil and hours of machine time, intersected at the optimum. The variables in the dual problem corresponding to these constraints were p and q respectively. The dual problem was as follows:

Minimise   200p + 250q
Subject to   p + 2q ⩾ 10
                  3p + q ⩾ 8
                  p, q   ⩾ 0

What was the dual price per litre of oil in the original problem?

A   £1.20
B   £2.67
C   £4.40
D   £5.00

Circle your answer

A   B   C   D

17 A nutritionist wishes to minimise the total weight of a pre-packed food bar for mountaineers, subject to two nutritional constraints. The bar is made of three ingredients, S, T and U. The bar must contain at least 50g of protein and 70g of carbohydrate. The problem has been formulated as follows:

Let   s   =   grams of S per bar
       t   =   grams of T per bar
       u   =   grams of U per bar

Minimise s + t + u

Subject to   0.2s + 0.3t + 0.1u ⩾ 50 (protein)
                0.4s + 0.2t + 0.5u ⩾ 70 (carbohydrate)

What is the dual price (in terms of grams of total weight) per gram of protein required?

A   0g
B   1.00g
C   1.25g
D   2.50g

Circle your answer

A   B   C   D

18 A linear programming problem is as follows:

Maximise $3x + 4y + z$
Subject to $2x + 2y + 3z \leqslant 1{,}200$
$x + 4y + z \leqslant 800$
$x, y, z, \geqslant 0$

Which variable or variables would have a value of zero at the optimum?

A x only
B x and z only
C y and z only
D z only

Circle your answer

A   B   C   D

19 Which of the following statements is/are true of the simplex method?

Statement

1. It requires that there be at least as many variables (excluding slack variables) as constraints

2. Slack variables will always all be zero in the final solution

3. There are as many slack or surplus variables as there are constraints

A Statements 1 and 2 only
B Statements 2 and 3 only
C Statement 1 only
D Statement 3 only

Circle your answer

A   B   C   D

20 Which of the following is the correct initial simplex method tableau for the following linear programming problem?

Maximise $3x + 2y + z$
Subject to $2x + 2y + 3z \leqslant 2{,}000$
$x + 2y \leqslant 1{,}000$
$x, y, z \geqslant 0$

A		x	y	z	a	b	Solution
	a	2	2	3	1	0	2,000
	b	1	2	0	0	1	1,000
	Solution	-3	-2	-1	0	0	0

97

B		x	y	z	a	b	Solution
	a	2	2	3	1	0	1,000
	b	1	2	0	0	1	2,000
	Solution	-3	-2	-1	0	0	0

C		x	y	z	a	b	Solution
	a	-2	-2	-3	1	0	-2,000
	b	-1	-2	0	0	1	-1,000
	Solution	3	2	1	0	0	0

D		x	y	z	a	b	Solution
	a	2	2	3	0	1	2,000
	b	1	2	0	1	0	1,000
		-3	-2	-1	0	0	0

Circle your answer

A   B   C   D

21 In the simplex method, the following steps must be performed to move from one tableau to the next:

Step

1. Divide the values in the solution column by the corresponding values in the column of the variable being introduced, and select the row with the lowest positive resulting value as the one in which to introduce that variable.

2. In the column of the variable being introduced, get 1 in the row in which it is being introduced and 0 elsewhere by multiplying the row in which 1 is required by an appropriate figure, and adding multiples of that row to other rows.

3. Identify the column with the largest negative value in the solution row as the column of the variable to be introduced.

In what order should these steps be performed?

A 1, 2, 3
B 2, 3, 1
C 3, 2, 1
D 3, 1, 2

Circle your answer

A   B   C   D

Data for questions 22 - 25

The following final simplex tableau was obtained in a linear programming problem involving three variables (x, y and z) and three constraints (corresponding to slack variables a, b and c).

	x	y	z	a	b	c	Solution
x	1	0.75	0	1	0	-0.25	62.5
b	0	2.25	0	-1	1	0.25	17.5
z	0	0.25	1	0	0	0.25	37.5
Solution	0	1.25	0	3	0	0.25	337.5

The values of x, y and z are quantities of output (in kg) per week of three different products.

22 Naming the constraints by their slack variables, which constraint(s) is/are not critical at the optimum?

A   Constraint a only
B   Constraint b only
C   Constraints a and c only
D   None of the constraints

Circle your answer

A   B   C   D

23 How many kg in total would be produced each week at the optimum?

A   100
B   117.5
C   337.5
D   338.75

Circle your answer

A   B   C   D

24 If one more unit of the resource which is the subject of constraint c were to become available, which of the following would happen?

A   Output of x would fall by 0.25 kg a week and outputs of y and z would each rise by 0.25 kg a week.

B   Output of x would rise by 0.25 kg a week and outputs of y and z would each fall by 0.25 kg a week.

C   Output of x would fall by 0.25 kg a week,
    output of z would rise by 0.25 kg a week
    and an extra 0.25 units a week of the
    resource which is the subject of constraint
    b would go unused.

D   Output of x would fall by 0.25 kg a week,
    output of z would rise by 0.25 kg a week
    and an extra 0.25 units a week of the
    resource which is the subject of constraint
    b would be used

Circle your answer

| A | B | C | D |

25 How many extra units of the resource which is the subject of constraint c could become available before the changes per extra unit described in the correct answer to question 24 cease to apply?

A   35 units
B   70 units
C   84 units
D   250 units

Circle your answer

| A | B | C | D |

CHAPTER 9

TRANSPORTATION AND ASSIGNMENT

This chapter covers the following topics:

- Transportation problems
- The north west corner and least cost methods
- The Vogel approximation method
- Assignment problems

1. Transportation problems

1.1 Transportation problems have the following elements:

(i)   a set of producers of an item, generally called *factories,* each with a certain production capacity;

(ii)   a set of recipients of the item, generally called *depots,* each with a certain total requirement;

(iii)   a cost per unit for each possible route from a factory to a depot;

(iv)   an objective, the minimisation of total costs.

The problem is to allocate units to routes from factories to depots, so that all depots' requirements are satisfied (unless the factories cannot produce enough to do so), and so that the objective is achieved.

1.2 Where total production exceeds total requirements, we introduce a *dummy depot*. Spare production is notionally allocated to this depot. Where total requirements exceed total production, we introduce a *dummy factory*, which notionally produces the shortfall. If a depot is allocated units from the dummy factory, its requirement is to that extent not met. Any route to a dummy depot or from a dummy factory has a cost of 0.

1.3 Where a business has *warehouses* between its factories and depots, then so long as the warehouses can handle any quantity of goods they might be called on to, they can be ignored. The cost per unit of a route from a factory to a depot is then the total cost of the cheapest factory-warehouse-depot route.

1.4 Many business problems unconnected with the allocation of goods from real factories to real depots can be formulated as transportation problems. For example, a workshop might assemble and check radios. Each assembler (factory) could assemble a certain number of radios each day, and each checker (depot) could check a certain number of radios each day. Certain assemblers might work better with some checkers than with others, giving rise to measurable costs per radio passed from particular assemblers to particular checkers (routes).

1.5 If a problem is to maximise some amount, for example profit, it can be converted to a transportation problem by subtracting the amount per unit (eg profit) for each route from the highest amount per unit. We can then treat the problem as an ordinary cost minimisation transportation problem, with the cost for each route being the difference between its profit and the maximum profit.

2. The north west corner and least cost methods

2.1 In these two methods for solving transportation problems, we first set up a table with rows for factories and columns for depots, and then make an initial allocation of units.

(i) In the *north west corner method*, the table is filled from the top left, working from left to right across each row and starting as far to the left as possible in each new row.

(ii) In the *least cost method*, the first route to be used is the cheapest one, and other routes are used in ascending order of cost, ties being settled by arbitrary choice.

This chapter concentrates on the least cost method, because it is sensible to start with a low-cost allocation. However, some examples are given of initial allocations found using the north west corner method.

2.2 Once an initial allocation of units to routes has been made, both methods proceed in exactly the same way.

(i) Work out shadow despatch and receipt costs for the factories and depots respectively. The shadow despatch cost for the factory on the first row is 0. Other costs are worked out as balancing figures, on the basis that for each route in use, shadow despatch cost of factory + shadow receipt cost of depot = cost of route.

(ii) Work out the cost of not using each unused route. This is the sum of the shadow despatch cost for its factory and the shadow receipt cost for its depot.

(iii) Work out the shadow cost of each unused route. This is the cost of using it minus the cost found in (ii).

(iv) If no unused routes have negative shadow costs, an optimum has been found. Otherwise, allocate units to the unused route with the highest negative shadow cost, reallocating units from other routes as necessary, and then return to step (i). Reallocation of units is done by the stepping stone method, illustrated in the questions, so as to keep the totals for each row (factory outputs) and column (depot requirements) unchanged.

2.3 One possible problem is *degeneracy*. This occurs when there are m factories and n depots, but fewer than m + n - 1 routes are in use. It is then not possible to work out all shadow despatch and receipt costs (stage (i)). The remedy is to select an unused route and treat it as used for transporting 0 units.

3. The Vogel approximation method

3.1 This is an alternative to the north west corner and least cost methods. It is more complicated to use, but it has the advantage that an optimum solution is often reached at the first attempt.

3.2 The steps are as follows.

(i) For each row and column, compute the penalty, equal to the difference between the lowest and second lowest costs (ignoring any routes in dummy rows or columns and any routes no longer available because the whole requirement for the corresponding row or column has already been allocated).

(ii) Allocate as many units as possible to the cheapest route in the row or column with the highest penalty. If there is a tie for highest penalty, select a row or column arbitrarily.

(iii) Return to step (i), unless all rows and columns have already been selected. In that case, complete the allocation of units in any way.

(iv) Check the solution for optimality by looking for unused routes with negative shadow costs (as in the least cost method). If the solution is not optimal, improve it in the same way as in the least cost method.

4. Assignment problems

4.1 *Assignment problems* involve the pairing off of workers and tasks, so as to minimise total costs. Each combination of a worker and a task has a certain cost, for example minutes for that worker to do that task.

4.2 Although such problems could be formulated as transportation problems, this would be unnecessarily complex, and degeneracy would frequently occur. We therefore use the *assignment algorithm* to solve such problems instead.

4.3 The first step is to equalise the numbers of workers and tasks, introducing dummies if necessary. For example, if there are 4 workers and 5 tasks, a dummy worker would be introduced, with zero costs for doing any task. The task allocated to the dummy will not get done.

4.4 A table is then set up, with rows for workers and columns for the tasks, or vice versa. The costs of the different pairings are then filled in.

4.5   Successive possible solutions are then found by the following procedure.

   (i)   Each cost is reduced by the lowest figure in the same row.

   (ii)   Each cost is reduced by the lowest figure in the same column. If a row (or a column) contains a zero, the application of (i) (or (ii)) to that row (or column) will of course have no effect on it.

   (iii)   If fewer than n straight lines through rows or columns can be drawn to cover all zeros (where n is the number of rows), reduce each uncrossed amount and increase each amount crossed by two lines by the smallest uncrossed amount. Then return to step (i). If n lines are needed to cover all zeros, an optimum has been found.

   (iv)   Pair off workers and tasks according to where the zeros are in the optimum table.

4.6   Assignment problems requiring the maximisation of a total can be handled by first deducting the value of each pairing of workers and tasks from the highest value of any pairing, and then setting out to minimise the total of these shortfalls.

4.7   The method is not limited to individual workers performing tasks. It could, for example, be used to assign six different encyclopaedias to six different locations in a library, where each pairing of encyclopaedia and location has a cost in terms of minutes per day that a typical reader would spend walking to the encyclopaedias he wants.

QUESTIONS

Data for questions 1 and 2

A company has one product, made in four factories, J, K, L and M, and sold in three shops, P, Q, and R. The output of the factories must be transported to the shops. The following table shows the units available from each factory, the units required at each shop, and the costs of transport per unit.

		P £	Shop Q £	R £	Units available
Factory	J	6	1	5	500
	K	3	2	4	400
	L	4	7	5	600
	M	5	3	7	500
Units required		800	300	900	2,000

1 Which of the following allocations would be the initial solution in the least cost method, using routes strictly in order of cost even if total cost is thereby increased?

A

		P	Shop Q	R
Factory	J		300	200
	K	400		
	L	400		200
	M			500

B

		P	Shop Q	R
Factory	J	200	300	
	K	400		
	L	200		400
	M			500

C

		P	Shop Q	R
Factory	J	500		
	K	300	100	
	L		200	400
	M			500

D

		P	Shop Q	R
Factory	J			500
	K	100	300	
	L	200		400
	M	500		

Circle your answer

A	B	C	D

105

2   What is the total cost of the allocation selected in the previous question?

A   £8,600
B   £8,700
C   £9,000
D   £10,000

Circle your answer

A   B   C   D

Data for questions 3 - 5

The following table relates to a transportation problem for a company aiming to minimise transport costs. Costs given are per unit transported.

		W	X	Depot Y	Z	Units available
		£	£	£	£	
Factory	F	2	3	4	5	300
	G	3	5	4	5	200
	H	4	8	3	2	200
Units required		200	150	250	100	700

An initial solution (found using the north west corner method) is as follows:

		W	X	Depot Y	Z
Factory	F	200	100		
	G		50	150	
	H			100	100

3   The shadow despatch cost for factory H is

A   £0
B   £1
C   £2
D   £3

Circle your answer

A   B   C   D

4   The shadow receipt cost for depot X is

A   £1
B   £2
C   £3
D   £4

Circle your answer

A   B   C   D

5 The shadow cost of the route from factory G to depot Z is

A   -£2
B   -£1
C   £1
D   £2

Circle your answer

A   B   C   D

6 In solving a transportation problem, an optimum solution has been found only when

A   all unused routes have negative shadow costs

B   no unused routes have negative shadow costs

C   all unused routes have zero shadow costs

D   all unused routes have positive shadow costs

Circle your answer

A   B   C   D

7 In the north west corner and least cost methods for solving transportation problems, an unused route must be selected for use at each stage before the optimal solution is reached. If the following are the four unused routes, which of them would be selected for use?

A   Route from factory A to depot 3, shadow cost + £4

B   Route from factory B to depot 1, shadow cost - £5

C   Route from factory C to depot 2, shadow cost - £2

D   Route from factory C to depot 3, shadow cost £0

Circle your answer

A   B   C   D

Data for questions 8 - 11

A transportation problem involving three factories (P, Q and R) and three depots (X, Y and Z) is given by the following table. Route costs are per unit transported.

		Depots X £	Depots Y £	Depots Z £	Units available
Factories	P	8	7	5	300
	Q	2	1	4	350
	R	7	5	3	200
Units required		400	150	300	850

The problem, to minimise transport costs, is to be solved using the stepping stone procedure.

The first feasible solution, found using the north west corner method, is as follows:

		Depots X	Depots Y	Depots Z
Factories	P	300		
	Q	100	150	100
	R			200

8 Which route should be introduced in getting to the next solution?

A   Route PY
B   Route PZ
C   Route RX
D   Route RY

9 What is the next feasible solution to be reached?

A

		Depots X	Depots Y	Depots Z
Factories	P	150	150	
	Q	250		100
	R			200

B

		Depots X	Depots Y	Depots Z
Factories	P	200		100
	Q	200	150	
	R			200

C		Depots		
		X	Y	Z
	P	300		
Factories	Q		150	200
	R	100		100

D		Depots		
		X	Y	Z
	P	300		
Factories	Q	100		250
	R		150	50

Circle your answer

A   B   C   D

10 In the optimum solution, what is the highest unit cost of any used route?

A   £3
B   £5
C   £7
D   £8

Circle your answer

A   B   C   D

11 What is the total transport cost for the optimum solution?

A   £3,100
B   £3,250
C   £3,600
D   £3,800

Circle your answer

A   B   C   D

12 When solving transportation problems, degeneracy can sometimes occur. Which of the following statements is/are true of degeneracy?

Statement

1. It occurs when the number of used routes is geater than m + n -1 (m = number of rows, n = number of columns).

2. It prevents calculation of all the shadow despatch and receipt costs.

3. It is dealt with by giving an unused route an allocation of 0 units.

4. It is dealt with by giving an unused route an allocation of 1 unit.

A   Statement 1 only
B   Statements 1 and 3 only
C   Statements 2 and 3 only
D   Statements 2 and 4 only

Circle your answer

A   B   C   D

13 In transportation problems, there may be no route between a particular factory and a particular depot. Which of the following statements is/are true?

Statement

1. The term 'impossible route' is used in such cases.
2. The non-availability of a route can be dealt with in solving the problem by assigning a very high cost to transport between the factory and the depot concerned.
3. The non-availability of a route can be dealt with by removing the relevant row and column from the solution.

A Statement 1 only
B Statement 3 only
C Statements 1 and 2 only
D Statements 2 and 3 only

Circle your answer

A   B   C   D

---

14 Which of the following statements is/are true of dummy depots in transportation problems?

Statement

1. They are used when demand exceeds supply.
2. Transport costs to them are zero.
3. In any one problem, one can choose to use either a dummy factory or a dummy depot.

A Statements 1 and 2 only
B Statement 2 only
C Statements 2 and 3 only
D Statement 3 only

Circle your answer

A   B   C   D

---

15 A manufacturer can make three different products. Any product can be made on any of three different machines. Demand, capacity of the machines, and profit per unit are as follows:

		Product P £	Product Q £	Product R £	Units available
Machine	J	8	6	7	50
	K	10	9	2	25
	L	12	4	5	25
Units demanded		20	50	30	100

The manufacturer will find the optimum production plan using the least cost transportation method. In preparing the initial solution, combinations of machines and products will be chosen strictly in order of profitability.

What, in the initial solution, will be the shadow cost of making product P on machine J?

A £2
B £4
C £6
D £8

Circle your answer

A   B   C   D

16 A transportation problem is given by the following table. Costs are per unit transported.

		Depot			*Units available*
		X	Y	Z	
		£	£	£	
	P	3	4	6	250
Factory	Q	2	8	5	400
	R	1	5	3	300
Units required		400	350	200	950

The problem is to be solved using the Vogel approximation method.

In the initial solution, how many units will be allocated to the route from factory R to depot Z?

A 0
B 100
C 150
D 200

Circle your answer

A   B   C   D

17 A company has three factories (P, Q and R), two warehouses with unlimited capacity (S and T), and three shops (X, Y and Z). All output of the company's one product must go from a factory via a warehouse to a shop. The costs of transport per unit, and the units available and required, are as follows:

		Warehouse		*Units available*
		S	T	
		£	£	
	P	3	2	500
Factory	Q	4	8	700
	R	7	8	400

		Shop		
		X	Y	Z
		£	£	£
Warehouse	S	2	3	5
	T	1	4	3
Units required		500	500	600

Which of the following tables correctly states the costs for the whole problem?

A

		Shop		
		X	Y	Z
		£	£	£
	P	3	6	5
Factory	Q	6	7	9
	R	9	10	11

B

		Shop		
		X	Y	Z
		£	£	£
	P	5	6	8
Factory	Q	9	12	11
	R	9	12	12

C

		Shop		
		X	Y	Z
		£	£	£
	P	5	9	9
Factory	Q	6	12	12
	R	8	11	12

D

		Shop		
		X	Y	Z
		£	£	£
	P	3	6	9
Factory	Q	6	7	10
	R	5	9	11

Circle your answer

A   B   C   D

18 Which of the following would be a suitable problem for solution by the assignment method?

A The output of two factories is to be allocated to two shops, minimising transport costs. The costs of all routes are known

B Five tasks are to be allocated to six members of staff, one task per person (with one person not getting a task), so as to minimise the total staff time spent. The number of minutes each staff member would spend on each task is known

C Three products are to be made on three machines. Any one machine can make any one or more of the products, and the profit per unit depends on both the product and the machine used. These profit figures are known, and total profit is to be minimised

D Three cars are to be allocated to three members of staff, one car each. The people concerned have expressed preferences, though not in a quantifiable way, and the objective is to maximise total staff satisfaction

Circle your answer

A   B   C   D

19 The following four solutions were reached in solving assignment problems in which jobs were to be assigned to machines so as to minimise the total machine times. Which one is an optimum solution?

A

		Machine			
		1	2	3	4
Job	E	0	2	0	0
	F	0	1	2	3
	G	0	1	2	3
	H	2	0	1	4

B

		Machine			
		5	6	7	8
Job	J	0	0	2	2
	K	2	4	0	2
	L	0	3	2	0
	M	1	3	0	0

C

		Machine			
		9	10	11	12
Job	P	0	0	2	3
	Q	2	5	0	3
	R	2	4	2	0
	S	1	4	0	1

D

		Machine			
		13	14	15	16
Job	T	2	8	0	3
	U	4	0	7	1
	V	5	0	3	1
	W	0	7	9	0

Circle your answer

A B C D

20 Four members of staff are to be assigned to four tasks, one for each member of staff. The total time spent is to be minimised. The times in hours each staff member would spend on each task are as follows:

		Staff member			
		T	U	V	W
Task	P	3	4	5	6
	Q	8	7	6	4
	R	10	8	9	8
	S	6	7	5	4

113

What is the minimum total staff time?

A   19 hours
B   20 hours
C   21 hours
D   22 hours

Circle your answer

A   B   C   D

21 A computer company can write any three of four programs for a client. There are three programmers available, and each will write one of the programs. The company wishes to minimise the total staff time used. The following table shows the number of hours each programmer would take to write each program.

		Programmer P	Programmer Q	Programmer R
		P	Q	R
Program	A	3	4	5
	B	4	3	6
	C	4	4	5
	D	2	5	3

Which program should *not* be written for the client?

A   Program A
B   Program B
C   Program C
D   Program D

Circle your answer

A   B   C   D

CHAPTER 10

NETWORK ANALYSIS

This chapter covers the following topics:

- Network problems and diagrams
- Critical paths, starting and finishing times and floats
- Crashing
- PERT

1. Network problems and diagrams

1.1 Networks are a tool for the planning and management of projects comprising several activities, some of which must be completed before others can start. They can be used to display the order in which activities must be carried out, and to work out the total time which a project will take and the effects of delays in particular activities.

1.2 There are two types of network diagram.
- Activity on arrow diagrams
- Activity on node diagrams

This chapter concentrates on activity on arrow diagrams, as they are more commonly used, but some examples of activity on node diagrams are included.

1.3 Activity on arrow diagrams

Activities are represented by arrows, which join circles, or nodes. An activity can start when all the activities leading into the node at its start have been completed. There is one node at the start of the project and one at the end.

Dummy activities are sometimes needed, either to represent the logic of the network or to avoid having two activities running between the same two nodes (which can make the network hard to read). They are normally represented by dotted arrows, and take no time and no resources to complete.

1.4 For example, a project might involve five activities, as follows:

Activity	Must be preceded by
V	-
W	V
X	V
Y	W, X
Z	X

1.5   An activity on arrow diagram would be as follows:

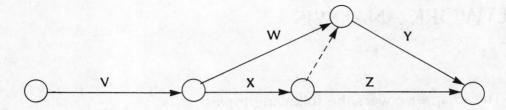

1.6   Activity on node diagrams

In these diagrams, each activity is represented by a circle, or node. There is also a node for the start of the project and one for the end. Nodes are linked by arrows, and an activity can be started only when all the activities at the start of arrows leading into its node have been completed.

2.   Critical paths, starting and finishing times and floats

2.1   A *path* through a network is any route from the beginning to the end. The *critical path* is the path with the longest total duration. Occasionally, a network will have more than one critical path. The importance of the critical path is that if any activities on it are delayed, completion of the whole project will be delayed.

2.2   For every activity, we can find:

● the *earliest starting time* (EST), the earliest time the activity could start, assuming that all preceding activities are done as early as possible

● the *latest starting time* (LST), the latest time the activity may be started, if the whole project is to be completed in minimum time

● the *earliest finishing time* (EFT), equal to EST + duration of the activity

● the *latest finishing time* (LFT), equal to LST + duration of the activity.

2.3   Activities on the critical path must be started and finished as soon as possible if the whole project is to be completed in minimum time, so for such activities EST = LST and EFT = LFT.

2.4   With other activities, there may be some latitude, or *float*. However, delaying some activities may reduce flexibility on later activities. To reflect this, three types of float are defined:

● *total float* = LFT - EST - duration: this is the amount by which an activity may be delayed, if we are prepared to disregard the possible effect on other activities' floats

● *free float* = EFT - EST - duration: this is the permissible delay, if we do not wish to reduce the float available on subsequent activities, but do not mind affecting preceding activities' floats

- *independent float* = EFT - LST - duration: this is the permissible delay, if we do not want to affect any other activities' floats.

2.5 Floats are particularly important when resources constrain work scheduling. If we need to limit the peak demand for staff, for example, it is important to know to what extent activities can be re-timed so as to avoid several activities with high staff demand running at once, while at the same time not increasing total project duration.

3. Crashing

3.1 Very often, the durations of activities can be reduced by increasing expenditure. This process is known as *crashing*.

3.2 There are two alternative goals of crashing:

(i) *minimum time* for the whole project;

(ii) *minimum cost* for the whole project.

3.3 In both cases, the best arrangement can be found by first reducing all activities to their minimum times (their *crash times*).

3.4 Where the goal is minimum time, the durations of activities not on the critical path should then be increased *(uncrashed)* to save money, seeking the largest possible savings at each stage and stopping as paths become critical or when activities reach their maximum durations.

3.5 Where the goal is minimum cost, the durations of activities should be increased whenever this will produce net savings. We weigh up the savings from uncrashing activities against the increase in costs related to overall project duration (eg overheads per day).

4. PERT

4.1 Uncertainty about the future affects project planning as much as any other aspect of business decision making, and the *Project Evaluation and Review Technique* (PERT) has been developed to allow for this uncertainty in network analysis.

The aim is to get an idea of how likely any particular duration or range of possible durations for the whole project is. If an unacceptably long duration is likely, management can plan for this and perhaps amend the project.

4.2 Each activity of uncertain duration is assigned a probability distribution of durations, so that the probabilities of different durations for the whole project can be found. The individual activities' probability distributions may be discrete or continuous.

4.3 Where continuous distributions are used, it is usually assumed that they are normal distributions, and that the durations of activities are independent of one another.

The assumption of independence allows variances to be added: in a chain of activities A - B - C, the variance of the duration of the whole chain is the sum of the variances of the durations of the three activities.

4.4 If normal distributions are to be used, the mean and standard deviation of the duration of each activity must be estimated. It is usual to estimate three durations for each activity, optimistic, most likely and pessimistic, and then to use the following conventional formulae.

o = optimistic duration
m = most likely duration
p = pessimistic duration

$$\text{Estimated mean duration} = \frac{o + 4m + p}{6}$$

$$\text{Estimated standard deviation of duration} = \frac{p - o}{6}$$

4.5 Note that some people restrict the term 'PERT' to analyses of uncertainty which use these formulae.

QUESTIONS

1   A project comprises the following activities:

Activity	Preceded by
V	-
W	-
X	V, W
Y	V, W
Z	V, W

Which of the following activity-on-arrow diagrams correctly represents this project?

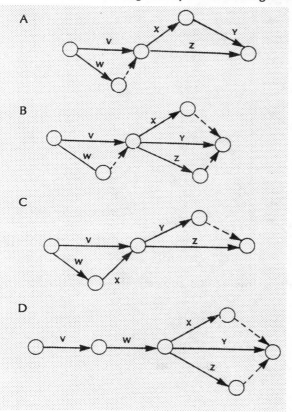

A

B

C

D

Circle your answer

A	B	C	D

2   A project comprises the following activities:

Activity	Preceded by
P	-
Q	-
R	P
S	Q, R
T	Q
U	T

Which of the following activity-on-arrow diagrams correctly represents this project?

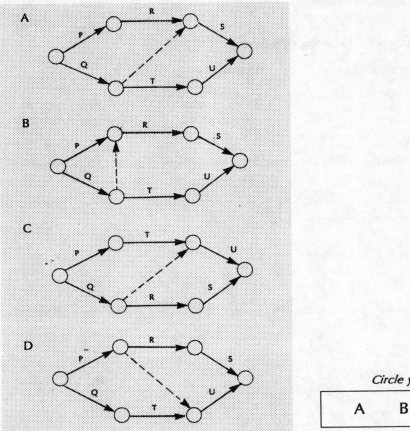

Circle your answer

A	B	C	D

3 Which of the following statements is true of the project represented by the following activity-on-arrow diagram?

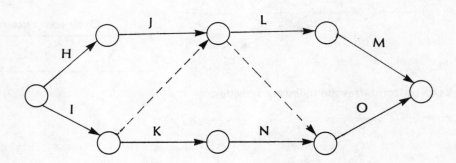

A   Activity M cannot be started unless
    activity K has been completed

B   Activity O cannot be started until
    activity H has been completed

C   The two dummy activities can both be
    treated as completed as soon as activity
    I has been completed

D   Activities M and N may not be performed
    simultaneously.

Circle your answer

| A | B | C | D |

4   Which of the following projects is correctly represented by this activity-on-arrow diagram?

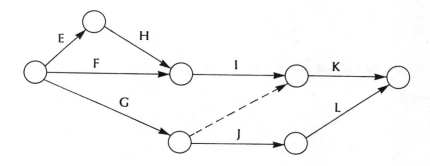

Answer	A	B	C	D
Activity		*Preceded by*		
E	-	-	-	-
F	-	-	-	-
G	-	-	-	-
H	E	E	E,F	E
I	E,F	F,H	E,F,H	F,H
J	G	G	G	G
K	G,I	I	I	G,I
L	G,J	J	G,J	J

Circle your answer

| A | B | C | D |

5   Which of the following statements about the critical path through a network is/are true?

Statement

1.   The total duration of the critical path is greater than that of any non-critical path.

2.   For a project to be completed in the minimum total time, the total duration of the critical path must not exceed that of any other path.

121

3.   The critical path always contains at least as many activities as any non-critical path.

4.   The activities on the critical path all have zero total float.

A   Statement 1 only
B   Statements 2 and 3 only
C   Statements 1 and 4 only
D   Statements 2 and 4 only

Circle your answer

| A | B | C | D |

6   A project comprises the following activities:

Activity	Preceded by	Duration (days)
J	-	5
K	-	6
L	J	12
M	K	10
N	L,M	5
O	N	4
P	N	6

What is the total duration of the critical path?

A   25 days
B   26 days
C   27 days
D   28 days

Circle your answer

| A | B | C | D |

7   A project comprises the following activities:

Activity	Preceded by	Duration (days)
T	-	4
U	T	11
V	T	12
W	T	13
X	U	3
Y	U,V,W	7
Z	X	3

What is the minimum time within which the whole project can be completed?

A   21 days
B   22 days
C   23 days
D   24 days

Circle your answer

| A | B | C | D |

Data for questions 8 - 11

A project is as follows (activity durations (in days) in brackets):

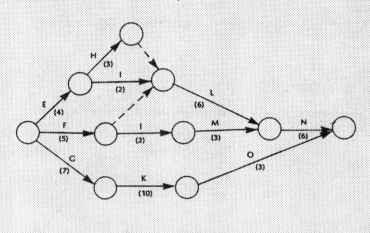

8 What is the earliest starting time for activity N?

A   Day 10
B   Day 11
C   Day 12
D   Day 13

Circle your answer

A	B	C	D

9 What is the latest starting time for activity O?

A   Day 15
B   Day 16
C   Day 17
D   Day 18

Circle your answer

A	B	C	D

10 What is the earliest finishing time for activity L?

A   Day 12
B   Day 13
C   Day 14
D   Day 15

Circle your answer

A	B	C	D

11 What is the latest finishing time for activity F?

A   Day 6
B   Day 7
C   Day 8
D   Day 9

Circle your answer

| A | B | C | D |

Data for questions 12 - 14

A project is as follows (activity durations (in days) in brackets):

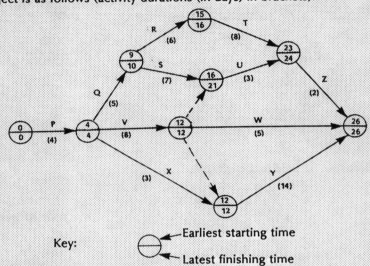

Key:

Earliest starting time
Latest finishing time

12 What is the total float of activity U?

A   3 days
B   4 days
C   5 days
D   6 days

Circle your answer

| A | B | C | D |

13 What is the free float of activity R?

A   0 days
B   1 day
C   2 days
D   3 days

Circle your answer

| A | B | C | D |

14 What is the independent float of activity W?

  A   8 days
  B   9 days
  C   10 days
  D   11 days

Circle your answer

A   B   C   D

Data for questions 15 and 16

A project comprises the following activities:

Activity	Preceded by	Normal Duration (weeks)	Normal Cost £	Crash Duration (weeks)	Crash Cost £	Extra cost of crashing per week £
H	-	4	200	3	300	100
I	-	5	100	2	220	40
J	-	4	40	3	50	10
K	H	3	150	3	150	-
L	K	4	130	1	280	50
M	H	6	30	2	230	50
N	I	7	80	5	140	30
O	L,M	4	60	2	180	60
			790		1,550	

Overheads are £300 for each day the project lasts. All activities can be crashed one week at a time at the costs shown.

15 What is the minimum time in which the project may be completed?

  A   7 weeks
  B   8 weeks
  C   9 weeks
  D   10 weeks

Circle your answer

A   B   C   D

16 What is the minimum cost at which completion in the minimum time may be achieved?

  A   £3,960
  B   £3,980
  C   £4,060
  D   £4,150

Circle your answer

A   B   C   D

Data for questions 17 and 18

A project comprises the following activities:

Activity	Preceded by	Normal Duration (weeks)	Normal Cost £	Crash Duration (weeks)	Crash Cost £	Extra cost of crashing per week £
P	-	7	300	6	320	20
Q	-	3	100	3	100	-
R	Q	2	100	2	100	-
S	P,R	7	140	5	230	45
T	P	2	130	2	130	-
U	T	7	10	6	40	30
V	T	4	20	3	40	20
W	V	2	30	1	50	20
X	U,W	2	90	1	140	50
Y	S	6	30	3	135	35
			950		1,285	

Overheads are £80 for each week the project lasts. All activities may be crashed one week at a time at the costs shown.

17 What is the minimum cost for the project?

A   £2,385
B   £2,400
C   £2,445
D   £2,485

Circle your answer

A   B   C   D

18 What is the minimum time in which this minimum cost may be achieved?

A   14 weeks
B   15 weeks
C   16 weeks
D   17 weeks

Circle your answer

A   B   C   D

19 A project comprises the following activities:

Activity	Preceded by	Duration (days)	Staff required
T	-	5	8
U	-	3	7
V	T	6	6
W	U	3	4
X	V,W	5	6
Y	X	6	8
Z	V,W	3	8

The numbers of staff stated are required throughout the activities' durations. Once an activity has been started, it cannot be interrupted. The whole project is to be completed in the minimum possible time.

What is the lowest possible figure for the maximum number of staff required simultaneously?

A 13
B 14
C 15
D 16

Circle your answer

A   B   C   D

Data for questions 20 and 21

A project comprises the following activities:

Activity	Preceded by	Optimistic	Most likely	Pessimistic
M	-	2	4	10
N	-	10	10	10
O	-	6	6	6
P	M	2	3	4
Q	M	4	5	9
R	N	12	12	12
S	O	3	4	5
T	P,Q	3	7	11
U	T	4	6	10
V	S	5	8	9
W	V	4	6	10

(Duration (days) spans Optimistic, Most likely, Pessimistic columns.)

The standard PERT formulae are to be used, with activity durations assumed to be independent and normally distributed.

20 What is the expected duration of the path MQTU?

    A   20 days
    B   21 days
    C   22.33 days
    D   23.5 days

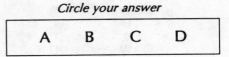

Circle your answer

A   B   C   D

21 Identifying the critical path as the one with the longest expected duration, and considering only uncertainty on that path, what is the probability that the whole project will take more than 25 days?

    A   0.2119
    B   0.2611
    C   0.2881
    D   0.3085

Circle your answer

A   B   C   D

22 A project comprises the following activities:

Activity	Preceded by
P	-
Q	-
R	P,Q
S	P
T	R

Which of the following activity-on-node diagrams correctly represents the project?

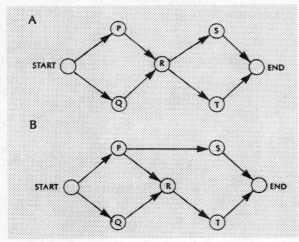

A

B

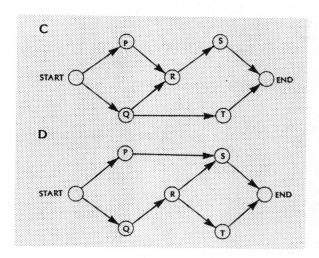

Circle your answer

| A | B | C | D |

23 The following activity-on-node diagram represents a project:

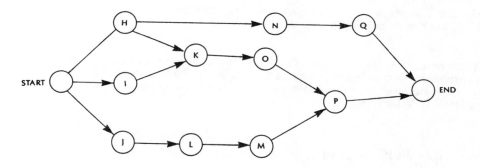

Which of the following projects does this diagram represent?

Answer	A	B	C	D
Activity		*Preceded by*		
H	-	-	-	-
I	-	-	-	-
J	-	-	-	-
K	H,I	H,I	H,I	H,I
L	I,J	J	I,J	J
M	L	L	L	L
N	H,I	H	H	H
O	H,I,K	K	H,I	K
P	O,M	K,L	H,O,M	O,M
Q	N	N	N	N

Circle your answer

| A | B | C | D |

CHAPTER 11

STOCK CONTROL

This chapter covers the following topics:

- The aim of stock control
- The simple EOQ model
- Production in batches
- Stock outs
- Uncertainty

1. The aim of stock control

1.1 The aim of stock control is to minimise the total costs associated with holding and ordering stock. These costs include storage, insurance, the cost of capital tied up in stock, and administrative costs of placing an order.

1.2 Only relevant costs, that is, costs affected by stock ordering and stockholding decisions, need be considered. Thus unless discounts are available for large orders, the cost of the stock itself is irrelevant because total purchases per year will be the same, whether a few large orders or many small orders are made.

2. The simple EOQ model

2.1 The simple economic order quantity (EOQ) model gives a formula for the size of order which should be placed to minimise total costs (the EOQ).

If Q = the economic order quantity
c = the cost of placing one order
d = demand per time period
h = the cost of holding one unit in stock for one time period

then $Q = \sqrt{\dfrac{2cd}{h}}$

2.2 The formula is derived by taking the total costs per time period as the sum of the costs of holding stock ($h \times$ average stock $= Qh/2$) and the cost of placing orders ($c \times$ number of orders $= cd/Q$), and setting the first derivative of this sum with respect to Q equal to zero.

2.3 The simple model makes several assumptions:

(i) that demand is at a constant rate;

(ii) that the *lead time* (time between placing an order and receiving the goods) is fixed;

(iii) that no *stock outs* (running out of stock and being unable to meet demand) are permitted.

Consequences of (i) and (ii) are that no *buffer stock* (safety stock to cope with unexpected demand) need be held, and that the *re-order level* (the level of stocks at which a fresh order is placed) is constant.

2.4 If bulk purchase *discounts* are available for large orders, it will be worth ordering in larger quantities than the simple model would indicate if the savings on purchases exceed the increase in the total of stock ordering and stock holding costs.

The decision should be made by starting at the order size indicated by the simple model, and then calculating the net effect of increasing the order size just enough to qualify for each level of discount.

3. Production in batches

3.1 Stock control theory can be applied to goods produced internally, as well as to goods bought externally. However, the formula needs to be modified, because when goods are bought, the whole order will normally arrive at once, while when they are made, stock will normally be replenished gradually.

3.2

If Q = the economic batch quantity (EBQ)
c = the cost of setting up for one batch
d = demand per time period
h = the cost of holding one unit in stock for one time period
r = the quantity which would be produced in one time period by continuous production

then $Q = \sqrt{\dfrac{2cd}{h(1-d/r)}}$

3.3 The change from h to h(1-d/r) reflects the fact that average stock will be Q(1-d/r)/2 rather than Q/2. The reduction is caused by the fact that some units will be taken out of stock for use even as stock is being replenished by fresh production. If production is very fast so r is very high in relation to d, periods of production will be very short, so this will have little effect, d/r will be small and (1-d/r) will be nearly equal to 1.

131

4. Stock outs

4.1 The simple economic order quantity model, and its extension to production in batches, assume that stock outs (not having enough stock to meet all demand immediately) will not be allowed. However, it may be in the business's interests to allow stock outs, if the costs of holding stock are high and the costs of stock outs (eg loss of customer goodwill) are low.

4.2 There are two cases to consider:

(i) when stocks do arrive, orders placed when there were no stocks are fulfilled;

(ii) orders placed when there are no stocks are lost permanently (ie the customer goes elsewhere).

4.3 If Q, c, d and h have the same meanings as in the simple model, and s is the cost of being out of stock by one unit per unit time (ie cost per unit of one unsatisfied order × number of times per period stock runs out (= number of orders per period)), then

(i) if orders are held and fulfilled when stocks arrive,

$$Q = \sqrt{\frac{2cd}{h}} \times \sqrt{\frac{s+h}{s}} \qquad \text{Maximum shortage} = \frac{Qh}{h+s}$$

(ii) if orders not fulfilled immediately are lost permanently,

$$Q = \sqrt{\frac{2cd}{h}} \times \sqrt{\frac{s}{s+h}} \qquad \text{Maximum shortage} = \frac{Qh}{s}$$

5 Uncertainty

5.1 In practice, neither the length of the lead time nor the daily demand is likely to be certain. The best that can normally be done is to minimise the expected annual total costs.

5.2 The usual approach is to start with a re-order level such that average demand in lead time will be catered for, and then to consider various re-order levels above that, weighing up the incremental costs and savings of each increase in re-order level.

5.3 Incremental costs will be increased stockholding costs. Note that the re-order *level* chosen will have no effect on the number of orders per time period, and so no effect on the cost of placing orders. Savings would be reduced costs of stock outs, through a reduction in the size of stock outs.

5.4 An alternative approach is to attach overriding importance to customer service, and to set a re-order level so as to reduce the probability of a stock out to some acceptably low level.

QUESTIONS

1 A company is trying to compute a re-order level to minimise the sum of its stockholding and re-ordering costs for a particular item. No quantity discounts are available. Which of the following costs would be relevant?

Cost

1. The supplier's fixed charge per order placed.
2. The company's own (incremental) administrative costs in placing an order.
3. Insurance costs, based on the average quantity of stock held.
4. The cost of the stock bought.
5. The cost of maintaining the company's existing warehouse (which is large enough for any order size).

A   Costs 1, 3 and 4 only
B   Costs 1, 2 and 3 only
C   Costs 2, 4 and 5 only
D   Costs 1 and 3 only

Circle your answer

A   B   C   D

2 Which of the following statements is/are correct?

Statement

1. *Lead time* is the time between placing an order and receiving stock.
2. A *stock out* occurs when stocks are run down to zero just when new stocks arrive.
3. *Buffer stock* is stock which is held but never actually used.
4. *Re-order level* is the size of a fresh order placed when stocks are running low.

A   Statements 1, 2 and 4 only
B   Statements 1 and 3 only
C   Statements 3 and 4 only
D   Statement 1 only

Circle your answer

A   B   C   D

Data for questions 3 and 4

A business works a 250 day year. Demand for widgets is always 200 per working day. When widgets are ordered, the goods are always received the next day. The cost of holding one widget for one year is £2 (storage) plus 10% of cost (insurance). The cost of placing an order is £30. Each widget costs £50.

3 What is the total annual holding cost if the order size is 900 widgets?

   A   £900
   B   £2,250
   C   £3,150
   D   £4,817

Circle your answer

A   B   C   D

4 What is the total annual ordering cost if the order size is 500 widgets?

   A   £3,000
   B   £3,500
   C   £4,250
   D   £4,750

Circle your answer

A   B   C   D

5 In the simple economic order quantity model, with

   Q   = order quantity
   T   = total of holding and ordering costs per time period,

which of the following is true when Q equals the economic order quantity?

(*Reminder about calculus:* dT/dQ is a derivative, not a fraction involving annual demand.)

A $\dfrac{dT}{dQ} > 0, \qquad \dfrac{d^2T}{dQ^2} = 0$

B $\dfrac{dT}{dQ} = 0, \qquad \dfrac{d^2T}{dQ^2} < 0$

C $\dfrac{dT}{dQ} < 0, \qquad \dfrac{d^2T}{dQ^2} = 0$

D $\dfrac{dT}{dQ} = 0, \qquad \dfrac{d^2T}{dQ^2} > 0$

Circle your answer

A   B   C   D

6 In the simple economic order quantity model, with:

   Q   = order quantity
   c   = cost of placing one order
   d   = demand per time period
   h   = holding cost per unit per time period,

which of the following equations holds when Q = the economic order quantity?

A $\quad Q^2 = \dfrac{cd}{h}$

B $\quad d = \dfrac{2Q^2 h}{c}$

C $\quad h = \dfrac{2cd}{Q^2}$

D $\quad c = \dfrac{2Q^2}{hd}$

Circle your answer

A   B   C   D

7 A company has found that its demand for wotsits is steady at 300 a week; the company works a 52 week year. The cost of placing an order is £45. The cost of holding a wotsit is £2 a year. The purchase price per wotsit is £47, with no bulk discounts. Orders are always fulfilled five working days after being placed. What is the economic order quantity?

A   419 wotsits
B   592 wotsits
C   838 wotsits
D   1,185 wotsits

Circle your answer

A   B   C   D

8 A wholesaler wishes to establish the economic order quantity for calculators (which it buys from the manufacturer and sells to retailers), and has obtained the following information:

demand per week = 28,000 calculators
trading weeks per year = 50
cost of storing one calculator for one year = 35p
delivery charge = £22 per order plus 10p per calculator
internal administration costs = £14 direct costs per order plus £300 per year apportioned fixed overheads

What is the economic order quantity?

A   10,583 calculators
B   13,266 calculators
C   16,971 calculators
D   22,978 calculators

Circle your answer

A   B   C   D

9 A company wishes to calculate the economic order quantity for the sofas which it buys and sells. It has a warehouse large enough to cope with any realistic order size. Each sofa occupies 2m² of warehouse floor space. Warehouse space not required can be let for a year at a time, for £1.30 per m². Once let, space cannot be used by the company at any time during the year. The company also has to pay a stores manager an annual salary of £15,000, plus an annual bonus of £1 × average number of sofas held. The company insures its stock, for an annual premium of £16 × maximum number of sofas held during the year. The direct costs of ordering are £70 per order, and all orders are fulfilled immediately. Annual demand is 12,000 sofas, with no seasonal variations. What is the economic order quantity?

A   210 sofas
B   217 sofas
C   275 sofas
D   293 sofas

Circle your answer

A   B   C   D

10 In the economic batch quantity formula, with:

Q   = batch quantity
c   = cost of setting up for one batch
d   = demand per time period
h   = holding cost per unit per time period
r   = production per time period assuming continuous production,

which of the following equations holds when Q = the economic batch quantity?

A $(1 - d/r)h = \dfrac{cd}{2Q^2}$

B $(1 - r/d)h = \dfrac{2cd}{Q^2}$

C $(1 - d/r)c = \dfrac{2d}{Q^2 h}$

D $\dfrac{Q^2 (1 - d/r)h}{2} = cd$

Circle your answer

A   B   C   D

11 A company makes a component for its output in batches. Weekly demand is for 5,000 units, and if the machine which makes the component operated throughout the company's 50-week working year it would make 1,000,000 units. The cost of storing one component for a year is £2, and the cost of setting up the machine to make a batch is £230. What is the economic batch quantity?

A   7,583 units
B   8,756 units
C   12,382 units
D   15,166 units

Circle your answer

A   B   C   D

12 A company buys in a part for use in its output. The annual requirement is for 50,000 units, with the same quantity being required each day. Annual storage costs per unit are £1.50, and the incremental administrative cost per order is £135. The normal cost of the part is £3 per unit, but discounts are available as follows:

Order size at least units	Discount on normal cost %
2,000	2
4,000	5
5,000	6

What is the economic order quantity?

136

A   2,000 units
B   3,000 units
C   4,000 units
D   5,000 units

Circle your answer

A   B   C   D

13 A company orders a particular product regularly, always ordering the economic order quantity. The company's annual requirement is 40,000 units, the incremental administrative cost per order is £100, and the cost of holding one unit for one year is £3.50. The product costs the company £8 per unit.

The supplier is considering offering a discount on the purchase price for all orders of 2,500 units or more. What is the minimum discount necessary for it to be beneficial for the company to take the discount?

A   0.11%
B   0.21%
C   0.54%
D   0.78%

Circle your answer

A   B   C   D

Data for questions 14 and 15

A company has determined the economic order quantity for a component it uses on the basis of the following data:

Annual demand = 25,000 units
Incremental administrative cost per order = £85
Holding cost per unit per year = £4

14 If in fact the incremental administrative cost per order turns out to be 10% higher than thought, but all the other data are correct, by what percentage will actual total annual costs of ordering and holding stock exceed what they would have been had the correct economic order quantity been used?

A   0.097%
B   0.12%
C   4.5%
D   4.8%

Circle your answer

A   B   C   D

15 If in fact the holding cost per unit per year turns out to be 25% lower than thought, but all the other data are correct (incremental administrative cost per order £85), by what percentage will actual total annual costs of ordering and holding stock exceed what they would have been had the correct economic order quantity been used?

A 1.00%
B 1.04%
C 14%
D 17%

Circle your answer

A B C D

16 A company buys and sells a particular product, and has established the following figures:

Annual demand = 28,000 units (no seasonal fluctuations)
Incremental cost of placing an order = £220
Cost of holding one unit for one year = £18
Stock out cost per unit per year = £7

It is the company's policy to allow stock outs if the benefits to the company exceed the costs. If an order cannot be fulfilled from stock, it is fulfilled when new stock arrives.

What is the economic order quantity?

A 702 units
B 827 units
C 1,106 units
D 1,563 units

Circle your answer

A B C D

17 A company stocks a product which it sells to the public. Fresh supplies are ordered when stocks reach a certain level, and the goods arrive three working days after the order is placed. Demand per day follows this probability distribution:

Demand (units)	Probability
6	0.5
7	0.3
8	0.2

Demand on any one day is independent of that on any other day. What is the lowest acceptable re-order level, if the probability of its not being possible to meet all demand immediately from stock is to be less than 0.1?

A 21 units
B 22 units
C 23 units
D 24 units

Circle your answer

A B C D

18 A company buys and sells a product, ordering fresh supplies when stocks reach a certain level. The lead time varies according to the following probability distribution.

Lead time (working days)	Probability
3	0.2
4	0.5
5	0.2
6	0.1

Demand is 20 units per working day. If demand cannot be fulfilled immediately from stock, the cost in lost goodwill is £15 per unit of unfulfilled demand. (This is the cost per unit per unfulfilled order, not a cost per year of being short by one unit.) The holding cost per unit per year is £25, and the company places orders 3 times a year on average. What should the re-order level be in order to minimise total costs?

A 60 units
B 80 units
C 100 units
D 120 units

Circle your answer

A   B   C   D

19 A company stocks a product, for which demand during the lead time is normally distributed with a mean of 450 units. The probability of demand in the lead time exceeding 500 units is 0.1711. What should the re-order level be, if the probability of a stock out is to be 0.05?

A 533 units
B 537 units
C 548 units
D 553 units

Circle your answer

A   B   C   D

20 A company stocks microcomputers for sale. The lead time is two days and demand in the lead time follows a Poisson distribution, with a mean of 0.5 units. The cost of holding one unit for one year is £80, and the cost in lost goodwill of not being able to satisfy a sales order from stock is £70. (This is a cost per unit per unfulfilled order, not an annual cost.) The company orders fresh supplies four times a year. What is the re-order level which will minimise total costs?

A 0 units
B 1 unit
C 2 units
D 3 units

Circle your answer

A   B   C   D

CHAPTER 12

QUEUEING THEORY. SIMULATION

This chapter covers the following topics:

- Queueing problems
- Single-channel queueing systems
- Multi-channel queueing systems
- Simulation
- Random numbers in simulations

1. Queueing problems

1.1 Queueing theory deals with situations where customers arrive at some place to obtain service. As well as shops, banks etc, queueing theory can be applied to telephone calls arriving at a switchboard, requests by factory workers for a supervisor's attention, and so on.

1.2 Possible aims of the person applying queueing theory to such situations are the reduction of queueing times to some acceptable maximum, and the minimisation of total costs. Where cost minimisation is sought, the cost of improving facilities (for example, employing extra shop staff) must be weighed against the cost of waiting time (for example, loss of customer goodwill).

1.3 A number of technical terms are used in queueing theory. Customers are drawn from the *calling population* (all possible customers). They arrive in an *arrival pattern* (eg at random, or at regular intervals), and are served according to the *service pattern* (eg first come, first served). *Queue discipline* refers to behaviour in the queue (eg whether people give up and leave the queue). There may be one server (a *single channel system*) or several servers (a *multiple channel system*). The customers waiting are the *queue*, and those waiting plus those being served are the *system*. A system is in a *transient state* when its state is a function of time (eg a bank just after opening, when there is an initial rush of customers); otherwise, it is in a *steady state*.

1.4 The time a customer spends in the system depends not only on the length of the queue when he joins it, but also on the times taken to serve him and the customers in front of him. It is normal to assume that the probabilities of *service times* (ie time spent serving individual customers) follow a particular probability distribution, called a negative exponential distribution.

140

2. Single-channel queueing systems

2.1 So long as certain assumptions (commonly referred to as the M/M/1 assumptions) are made, queueing problems can be dealt with by the use of a set of fairly simple formulae.

2.2 The assumptions are:

(i) there is one queue and one service channel, with no limit on the maximum queue size and an infinite calling population;

(ii) customer arrivals per unit time follow a Poisson distribution, customers are served on a first come, first served basis and no customers leave before being served;

(iii) service times follow a negative exponential distribution;

(iv) the system is in a steady state.

2.3 The following notation will be used:

λ = arrival rate = average number of customers arriving per unit time

μ = service rate = average number of customers who could be served per unit time (if the server worked continuously)

ρ = traffic intensity = λ/μ.

Note that the traffic intensity must not exceed 1, otherwise the queue will grow indefinitely.

2.4 On the basis of the M/M/1 assumptions:

(i) Probability of having to queue on arrival = λ/μ = ρ

(ii) Probability of being served immediately on arrival = $1 - \lambda/\mu$ = $1 - \rho$

(iii) Average number of customers in the system = $\dfrac{\rho}{1-\rho}$ = $\dfrac{\lambda}{\mu-\lambda}$

(iv) Average number of customers in the queue = $\dfrac{\lambda\rho}{\mu-\lambda}$ = $\dfrac{\lambda^2}{\mu(\mu-\lambda)}$

(v) Average time spent in the system = $\dfrac{\rho}{\mu-\lambda} + \dfrac{1}{\mu}$ = $\dfrac{1}{\mu-\lambda}$ = $\dfrac{1}{\mu(1-\rho)}$

(vi) Average time spent in the queue = $\dfrac{\rho}{\mu-\lambda}$ = $\dfrac{\lambda}{\mu(\mu-\lambda)}$ = $\dfrac{\rho}{\mu(1-\rho)}$

2.5 The formulae for average time spent in the queue and in the system could well be used in predicting levels of customer dissatisfaction or, if for example the system was one supplying stores to factory workers, lost production time.

3. Multi-channel queueing systems

3.1 We are concerned here with systems where there is a single queue but several service channels, and the customer at the head of the queue goes to the first available channel. Apart from the number of service channels, the assumptions in paragraph 2.2 will apply. The same notation as before will be used, and the number of service channels will be denoted by c.

3.2 In such a system, the traffic intensity (ρ) is given by $\lambda/\mu c$.

The other formulae make use of the probability that there are no customers in the system, P_0.

$$P_0 = \frac{c!(1-\rho)}{(\rho c)^c + c!(1-\rho)\left[\displaystyle\sum_{n=0}^{c-1}\frac{1}{n!}(\rho c)^n\right]}$$

3.3 We then have the following formulae:

(i) probability of having to queue on arrival $= 1 - P_0$

(ii) probability of being served immediately on arrival $= P_0$

(iii) average number of customers in the system $= \dfrac{\rho(\rho c)^c}{c!(1-\rho)^2}\,P_0 + \rho c$

(iv) average number of customers in the queue $= \dfrac{\rho(\rho c)^c}{c!(1-\rho)^2}\,P_0$

(v) average time spent in the system $= \dfrac{(\rho c)^c}{c!(1-\rho)^2\,c\mu}\,P_0 + \dfrac{1}{\mu}$

(vi) average time spent in the queue $= \dfrac{(\rho c)^c}{c!(1-\rho)^2\,c\mu}\,P_0$

4. Simulation

4.1 Simulation is an approach to the modelling of systems which are too complex to be represented by a set of equations which can be solved algebraically. The aim is to understand the behaviour of the system by trying out various sets of inputs into a mathematical representation of the system, and seeing what outputs are generated. For example, a complex queueing system or a company's cash flows could be simulated.

4.2 A number of technical terms are used in simulation.

(i) Models may be *continuous*, showing the state of a system at any given time, or *discrete*, showing its state only at certain times (for example, the end of each month).

(ii) A model will have a number of *input variables*. These are set by the user of the model. They may be *parameters* (set at constant values throughout the simulation), other *controllable variables* (representing factors management can control) or other *uncontrollable variables* (representing factors outside management's control). The company's selling price and market conditions would normally be input variables.

(iii) *Status variables* show the state of the model at any particular time.

(iv) *Output variables* show the results of the simulation. The company's profit for a simulated year might well be an output variable.

5. Random numbers in simulations

5.1 Rather than simply working through a systematic list of all possible inputs, a representative set of inputs is often generated using random numbers. Orders received, for example, might well vary randomly from month to month, and appropriate use of random numbers might well be the best way of representing this. Such use of random numbers is called the *Monte Carlo method*.

5.2 Different possibilities are normally allocated different ranges of random numbers according to their probabilities. Thus if two-digit random numbers are used to model an input which can either be low sales (probability 0.37) or high sales (probability 0.63), a random number in the range 00 - 36 would generate an input of low sales and one in the range 37 - 99 would generate an input of high sales.

5.3 Random numbers are not always used where probabilities are involved. Sometimes the probabilities can be applied directly to the model. This is particularly so where there is a known input (for example of new employees) to a system and different things can happen to them (for example, promotion) with known probabilities.

QUESTIONS

1 Which of the following statements about queueing theory is/are correct?

Statement
1. The *calling population* is the customers who join the queue in a given time period.
2. The *service pattern* is the number of queues which may form.
3. In a *multiple channel system* there may be either one queue or several queues.

A Statements 1 and 2 only
B Statements 1 and 3 only
C Statement 2 only
D Statement 3 only

Circle your answer

A   B   C   D

2 Which of the following statements about queueing theory are correct?

Statement
1. The *traffic intensity* is the ratio of the average arrival rate to the average service rate.
2. *Queue discipline* is the way in which customers behave in a queue.
3. The *system* includes customers in the queue, but excludes any customer being served.
4. A system is in a *steady state* when the number of customers in the queue does not fluctuate.

A Statements 1 and 2 only
B Statements 1 and 4 only
C Statements 2 and 3 only
D Statements 3 and 4 only

Circle your answer

A   B   C   D

3 In queueing theory, it is often assumed that the number of customers arriving per unit time follows a Poisson probability distribution. If this assumption is made, and the probability of 5 customers arriving in any given hour is 0.1377, what is the probability of 3 customers arriving in any given 40 minutes?

A 0.0602
B 0.1417
C 0.2090
D 0.2125

Circle your answer

A   B   C   D

4 A queueing system is in a transient state whenever

A there are no customers in the queue
B the state of the system is a function of time
C some customers have recently given up and left the queue
D the traffic intensity exceeds 0.5

Circle your answer

A   B   C   D

5 In a single-channel queueing system, the average inter-arrival time is 14 minutes and the average service rate is 7 customers per hour. What is the traffic intensity, ρ?

A 0.5
B 0.61
C 1.63
D 2

Circle your answer

A   B   C   D

6 Which of the following assumptions are made in modelling the simple (M/M/1) queue?

Assumption
1. There is no limit on the length of the queue
2. The calling population is infinite
3. The system is in a steady state for about 90% of the time
4. The number of customers arriving in a given period of time follows a normal distribution

A Assumptions 1 and 4 only
B Assumptions 2 and 3 only
C Assumptions 3 and 4 only
D Assumptions 1 and 2 only

Circle your answer

A   B   C   D

Data for questions 7 - 11

In a simple queueing system with one service channel, the average arrival rate is 20 customers an hour and the average service rate is 28.5 customers an hour

7 What is the probability of a customer having to queue on arrival?

A 0.298
B 0.425
C 0.575
D 0.702

Circle your answer

A   B   C   D

8 What is the average number of customers in the system?

A 1.65 customers
B 1.77 customers
C 2.24 customers
D 2.36 customers

Circle your answer

A   B   C   D

9 What is the average length of time a customer spends in the system?

A 3.48 minutes
B 4.96 minutes
C 7.06 minutes
D 10.06 minutes

Circle your answer

A   B   C   D

10 What is the average number of customers in the queue?

A 1.65 customers
B 1.77 customers
C 2.24 customers
D 2.36 customers

Circle your answer

A   B   C   D

11 What is the average length of time a customer spends in the queue?

A 3.48 minutes
B 4.96 minutes
C 7.06 minutes
D 10.06 minutes

Circle your answer

A   B   C   D

12 A company can use one of four types of system in its stores department for dealing with requests from the manufacturing department, as follows:

System	Direct cost of system per hour £	Average service rate per hour
1	12	20
2	14	25
3	18	32
4	20	40

There are on average 17 requests per hour. Each request requires one member of the manufacturing department staff to wait in the queue and be served. The cost per staff member per hour of waiting time or time being served is £4. Which system would give the minimum overall cost?

A	System 1
B	System 2
C	System 3
D	System 4

Circle your answer

A   B   C   D

13 A shop sells newspapers and books. Each customer buys either a newspaper or a book (but not both), and on average there are 45 customers buying newspapers and 20 customers buying books each hour. At present one server is employed. The server can on average serve 70 customers (of either type) an hour. An extra server could be employed, at £5 an hour. The extra server could also serve 70 customers (of either type) an hour on average, and if one is employed, one server would deal with all customers buying newspapers and the other would deal with all customers buying books.

What is the minimum cost of queueing time per customer per hour which would justify employing an extra server?

A	£0.41
B	£0.46
C	£0.77
D	£0.83

Circle your answer

A   B   C   D

14 On average, 20 customers arrive each hour in a queueing system. Each channel can serve 30 customers an hour, and the traffic intensity for the whole system is 0.1111. How many service channels are there?

A	6 channels
B	9 channels
C	10 channels
D	14 channels

Circle your answer

A   B   C   D

Data for questions 15 - 19

A queueing system comprises a single queue and three service channels. The customer at the head of the queue goes into whichever service channel first becomes free. On average, 30 customers arrive each hour. Each channel can serve 16 customers an hour on average.

15 What is the probability of a customer having to queue on arrival?

A	0.1322
B	0.375
C	0.625
D	0.8678

Circle your answer

A   B   C   D

16 What is the average number of customers in the system?

A   1.67 customers
B   2.22 customers
C   2.52 customers
D   3.60 customers

Circle your answer

A   B   C   D

17 What is the average length of time a customer spends in the system?

A   3.33 minutes
B   4.44 minutes
C   5.04 minutes
D   7.19 minutes

Circle your answer

A   B   C   D

18 What is the average number of customers in the queue?

A   0.35 customers
B   0.65 customers
C   1.04 customers
D   1.73 customers

Circle your answer

A   B   C   D

19 What is the average length of time a customer spends in the queue?

A   0.69 minutes
B   1.29 minutes
C   2.08 minutes
D   3.44 minutes

Circle your answer

A   B   C   D

20 The Monte Carlo method of simulation

A   cannot produce values for all output variables

B   is only applicable to continuous simulation models

C   uses random numbers to generate inputs to the simulation model

D   is the only way to take account of uncertainty

Circle your answer

A   B   C   D

21 Input variables in a simulation model

    A always represent factors which are under management's control

    B are always more numerous than the model's output variables

    C are the same thing as status variables

    D include parameters

Circle your answer

A	B	C	D

22 In a simulation of a stock control system with uncertain daily demand and uncertain lead time, which of the following would definitely *not* be a parameter?

    A The cost of holding one unit for one year

    B The cost of being unable to fulfil a customer's requirement immediately from stock

    C The number of units required by customers each year not supplied immediately from stock

    D The administrative cost of placing an order

Circle your answer

A	B	C	D

23 Arrivals in a queueing system are to be simulated using two-digit random numbers. The number of customers arriving each hour follows a Poisson distribution, with a mean of 0.7 arrivals per hour. Which of the following would be a suitable allocation of random numbers?

	\multicolumn{4}{c}{Arrivals per hour}
	0	1	2	≥ 3
A	00-49	50-84	85-96	97-99
B	01-37	38-74	75-92	93-99
C	00-39	40-69	70-89	90-99
D	01-50	51-85	86-97	98-99

Circle your answer

A	B	C	D

24 In a simulation of a tourist information service, it was assumed that the times taken to deal with queries followed a normal distribution, with a mean of 3 minutes and a standard deviation of 1 minute. The times taken for a series of queries to be answered are to be simulated using two-digit random numbers, starting with 00-01 for up to 1 minute, then 02-15 for 1 to 2 minutes, and so on. If the following sequence of numbers is used, how many queries will be treated as answered in 3 to 4 minutes?

Random numbers	52	71	07	75	74	92	80	98	66	54
	82	86	42	36	62	44	74	65	66	52

A   7 queries
B   9 queries
C   11 queries
D   13 queries

Circle your answer

A   B   C   D

25 In a stock control model, both demand per day and lead time are uncertain. Demand per day may be 5 units (probability 0.3) or 6 units. Lead time may be 2 days (probability 0.4) or 3 days. Daily demand and lead time are independent of one another. A single series of two-digit random numbers is to be used to simulate total demand in lead time. Which of the following would be a suitable allocation of random numbers to possible demands?

	Demand during lead time (units)			
	10	*12*	*15*	*18*
A	00-17	18-44	45-66	67-99
B	00-11	12-39	40-57	58-99
C	00-17	18-39	40-66	67-99
D	01-12	13-40	41-58	59-99

Circle your answer

A   B   C   D

26 A stock control system is to be simulated. Daily demand is uncertain. It can be 0, 1 or 2 units (probability of each level 0.1), 3 units (probability 0.3) or 4 units (probability 0.4). This demand is to be simulated using 1-digit random numbers, assigning low numbers to low demand and working left to right from the start of the following random number table:

07203   97798   98911   28745   92920   51446

What would the simulated total demand be for days 4-12 inclusive?

A   25 units
B   29 units
C   31 units
D   33 units

Circle your answer

A   B   C   D

27 A shop sells fresh cakes. Cakes not sold on the day of supply must be thrown away. Both the number of cakes supplied to the shop and the number demanded vary randomly (and independently of one another) in the range 300-399. Supply and demand are to be simulated using two-digit random numbers, using simulated quantity = 300 + random number. The random numbers to be used for 10 days are as follows:

Supply: 60 00 99 22 65 85 76 17 88 41
Demand: 45 63 03 45 04 24 31 95 88 25

On the basis of this 10-day simulation, on what proportion of days would there be unsatisfied demand?

A 30%
B 40%
C 50%
D 60%

Circle your answer

A   B   C   D

Data for questions 28 - 30

A company rates its customers entitled to credit on a scale of grade 1 (lowest credit rating) to grade 3. All new credit customers start at grade 1, and all gradings are reviewed monthly.

At each monthly review, the probability of a customer being moved from grade 1 to grade 2 is 0.3, and the probability of a customer being moved from grade 2 to grade 3 is 0.1. The probability of a customer being taken down a grade (grade 3 to grade 2, grade 2 to grade 1, or grade 1 to not entitled to credit) is 0.07. A customer can be moved from grade 1 to grade 2, or from grade 1 to not entitled to credit, at the end of his first month. All customers not changing grades in any of the above ways stay on the same grade.

At the start of month 3 the company had the following customers:

Grade	Number
1	150
2	40
3	10

Ten entirely new customers enter grade 1 each month.

28 How many customers are expected to be at grade 2 immediately after the review at the end of month 4?

A   78 customers
B   82 customers
C   103 customers
D   123 customers

Circle your answer

A   B   C   D

29 How many customers are expected to be at grade 3 immediately after the review at the end of month 5?

A   20 customers
B   24 customers
C   29 customers
D   32 customers

Circle your answer

A   B   C   D

30 The information given is insufficient to enable us to say exactly how long a specified new customer will take to reach grade 3 because:

A some customers might go straight from grade 1 to grade 3

B actual times to reach particular grades will vary about expected times

C new customers are joining the system each month

D some customers might revert to grade 1 a month after being moved to grade 2

Circle your answer

A B C D

SECTION 2
MARKING SCHEDULES
AND COMMENTS

1: MARKING SCHEDULE

Question	Correct answer	Marks for correct answer
1	C	1
2	B	1
3	A	1
4	B	1
5	C	1
6	B	1
7	B	1
8	A	1
9	C	1
10	B	1
11	C	1
12	A	1
13	B	1

Question	Correct answer	Marks for correct answer
14	C	2
15	C	1
16	C	1
17	D	1
18	A	2
19	C	1
20	B	1
21	B	1
22	B	1
23	B	1
24	B	1
25	C	1

YOUR MARKS

Total marks available   27   Your total mark

GUIDELINES - If your mark was:

0 - 9 Poor. The important techniques in this chapter are causing you difficulty. Go back to your study text and work through each relevant section carefully, before trying this chapter again.

10 - 14 Fair. Several of the questions have caught you out. If there are one or two particular techniques which have caused you problems go back to your study text and read through the relevant sections carefully.

15 - 21 Good. There may be a particular group of questions which has caused you difficulty. Check whether this is so, and refer to your study text if there is a clear gap in your knowledge.

22 - 27 Very good. You have a thorough understanding of the principles of probability.

COMMENTS

1

The ways of getting two heads are:

		Probability
HHT	$0.5 \times 0.5 \times 0.5$	0.125
HTH	$0.5 \times 0.5 \times 0.5$	0.125
THH	$0.5 \times 0.5 \times 0.5$	0.125
		$\overline{0.375}$

2

The order of selection is unimportant, so the combinations formula applies.

Three men from eight: $_8C_3 = \dfrac{8!}{(8-3)!\ 3!} = \dfrac{8 \times 7 \times 6}{3 \times 2} = 56$

Two women from nine: $_9C_2 = \dfrac{9}{(9-2)!\ 2!} = \dfrac{9 \times 8}{2} = 36$

Any combination of men may be combined with any combination of women:
$$56 \times 36 = 2{,}016$$

3

The number of possible allocations of prizes is:

$$_{11}C_6 = \dfrac{11!}{(11-6)!\ 6!} = \dfrac{11 \times 10 \times 9 \times 8 \times 7}{5 \times 4 \times 3 \times 2} = 462$$

The number of possible allocations of prizes without awarding any books is:

$$_8C_6 = \dfrac{8!}{(8-6)!\ 6!} = \dfrac{8 \times 7}{2} = 28$$

The probability is $28/462 = 0.061$

4

A's team may include any two from the six, D - I:

$$_6C_2 = \dfrac{6!}{(6-2)!\ 2!} = \dfrac{6 \times 5}{2} = 15$$

B's team may include any two from the remaining four:

$$_4C_2 = \dfrac{4!}{(4-2)!\ 2!} = \dfrac{4 \times 3}{2} = 6$$

C's team must include the remaining two.
The number of possible ways of making up the teams is therefore $15 \times 6 = 90$.

Question

5

Number of possible hands =

$$_{52}C_5 = \frac{52!}{(52-5)!\,5!} = \frac{52 \times 51 \times 50 \times 49 \times 48}{5 \times 4 \times 3 \times 2} = 2,598,960$$

Number of hands with all cards of the same suit (there are four possible suits) =

$$4 \times {}_{13}C_5 = \frac{13!}{(13-5)!\,5!} = 4 \times \frac{13 \times 12 \times 11 \times 10 \times 9}{5 \times 4 \times 3 \times 2} = 5,148$$

Probability = 5,148/2,598,960 = 0.001981

6

The first player gets four cards from sixteen, the second four cards from the remaining twelve and so on. Possible ways of dealing the four hands:

$$_{16}C_4 \times {}_{12}C_4 \times {}_8C_4 \times {}_4C_4 = 1,820 \times 495 \times 70 \times 1 = 63,063,000$$

There are $_4P_4 = 24$ ways of allocating suits to players assuming the four hands do each comprise four cards of the suit. So the condition will be satisfied in one game in 63,063,000/24 = 2,627,625.

7

The full multiplication rule is P(R and S) = P(R) $\times$ P(S|R). If the events of which R and S are outcomes are independent, P(S|R) = P(S) and we are left with P(R) $\times$ P(S).

8

Mutual exclusivity means that for two outcomes R and S, P(R and S) = 0. Independence of the two events of which R and S are outcomes means that P(R and S) = P(R) $\times$ P(S). So P(R) $\times$ P(S) = 0, hence at least one of P(R) and P(S) must be zero, representing an impossible outcome.

9

It will rain on at least one day if:

(i)   it rains on Sunday (probability 0.3); or
(ii)   it is dry on Sunday but it rains on Monday (probability 0.7 $\times$ 0.2 = 0.14).

Outcomes (i) and (ii) are mutually exclusive (since it cannot both rain and be dry on Sunday) so the answer is 0.3 + 0.14 = 0.44.

10

The probability of one student being a woman or a mathematician is (applying the addition rule) 0.52 + 0.08 - 0.52 $\times$ 0.08 = 0.5584. The probability of both students fitting this criterion is $(0.5584)^2 \simeq 0.31$.

Question

11 The possibilities are:

J only: $0.4 \times (1 - 0.6) \times (1 - 0.7)$ $=$ 0.048
K only: $(1 - 0.4) \times 0.3 \times (1 - 0.2)$ $=$ 0.144
L only: $(1 - 0.4) \times (1 - 0.3) \times 0.7$ $=$ 0.294
                                                                          0.486

12 The possible pairs of skills are:

			Probability
Counting and writing:	$0.4 \times 0.6 \times (1 - 0.7)$	$=$	0.072
Counting and telephoning:	$0.4 \times (1 - 0.6) \times 0.4$	$=$	0.064
Writing and telephoning:	$(1 - 0.4) \times 0.6 \times 0.4$	$=$	0.144
			0.280

13 Consider 10,000 plates (any number would do, but large round numbers generally make the arithmetic easier):

		Size Correct	Wrong	Total	*Workings*
	Correct	9,312	388	9,700	$10,000 \times 0.04 = 400$
Colour	Wrong	288	12	300	$10,000 \times 0.03 = 300$
	Total	9,600	400	10,000	$400 \times 0.03 = 12$

The total number of defective plates is $288 + 12 + 388 = 688$.
The numbers which will pass are:

288×0.03 $=$ 8.64
$12 \times 0.03 \times 0.06$ $=$ 0.0216
388×0.06 $=$ 23.28
                                          31.9416

The percentage is $\frac{31.9416}{688} \times 100\% = 4.64\%$

14 The probability of the company meeting its target is:

T and U meet their targets	0.7×0.8	$=$	0.56
S exceeds its target, T meets its target and U falls short	$0.4 \times 0.7 \times 0.2$	$=$	0.056
S exceeds its target, U meets its target and T falls short	$0.4 \times 0.8 \times 0.3$	$=$	0.096
			0.712

Question

15

The probability is:

3 days of 400:	$(0.2)^3$	= 0.008
2 days of 400 and 1 day of 300:	$3 \times (0.2)^2 \times 0.4$	= 0.048
2 days of 400 and 1 day of 200:	$3 \times (0.2)^2 \times 0.3$	= 0.036
1 day of 400 and 2 days of 300:	$3 \times 0.2 \times (0.4)^2$	= 0.096
		= $\overline{0.188}$

We multiply by 3 in all lines except the first because there are 3 ways of choosing the one odd day (eg in line 2, the day with 300 could be day 1, day 2 or day 3; we could have 300, 400, 400; 400, 300, 400; or 400, 400, 300).

16

Consider 10,000 mirrors:

		Test result			Workings
	Perfect	Second	Unsaleable	Total	
Perfect	8,200	-	-	8,200	$10,000 \times 0.82 = 8,200$
Actual Second	30	1,380	90	1,500	$10,000 \times 0.15 = 1,500$
Unsaleable	-	12	288	300	$1,500 \times 0.02 = 30$
Total	8,230	1,392	378	10,000	$1,500 \times 0.06 = 90$
					$300 \times 0.04 = 12$

The required probability is $\dfrac{30 + 12}{8,230 + 1,392}$ = 0.0044, since mirrors categorised as unsaleable will not be sent out.

17

A = Finance director ill
B = Meeting cancelled

$P(B) = P(A)P(B|A) + P(\text{not -}A) P(B|\text{not -}A)$

$P(A|B) = \dfrac{P(A) P(B|A)}{P(B)} = \dfrac{0.4 \times 0.8}{0.4 \times 0.8 + 0.6 \times 0.1} = \dfrac{0.32}{0.38} = 0.84$

If you used this formula approach in your answer, see if you can draw up a table to get the same result.

159

Question

18

Consider 12,000 pens, 9,000 made in factory X and 3,000 in factory Y.

Factory X

	Good	Defective	Total	Workings
Black	5,880	120	6,000	$9,000 \times 2/3 = 6,000$
Red	2,910	90	3,000	$6,000 \times 0.02 = 120$
Total	8,790	210	9,000	$3,000 \times 0.03 = 90$

Factory Y

	Good	Defective	Total	
Black	1,980	20	2,000	$3,000 \times 2/3 = 2,000$
Red	960	40	1,000	$2,000 \times 0.01 = 20$
Total	2,940	60	3,000	$1,000 \times 0.04 = 40$

The required probability is $\dfrac{60}{210 + 60} = 0.22$

19

By definition, independent events are those where the probability of any particular outcome of one event occurring is the same whatever the outcome of the other event. So if R and S were outcomes of independent events, $P(R|S) = P(R)$. But this is not so, hence the events concerned must be dependent. Note that dependence does not prove causation in either direction.

20

	Profit	No profit	Total	Workings
High cost	0.03	0.27	0.3	0.3 and 0.6 from question
Low cost	0.6	0.1	0.7	$0.3 \times 0.1 = 0.03$
Total	0.63	0.37	1.0	

The required probability is 0.37.

Alternatively, A = high cost
B = profit

Question

P (not B) = 1 - P(B)
= 1 - [P(B | A) P(A) + P(B | not-A) P(not -A)]
= 1 - [0.1 × 0.3 + 0.6]
= 1 - 0.63 = 0.37

21 Sensitivity analysis is easily performed, by computing expected values under various assumptions.

22

Amount £	Probability	EV £
-1	1	-1.00
+1	0.2	0.20
+4	0.5 × 0.3 = 0.15	0.60
		-0.20

Don't forget the stake money of £1.

23 Expected variable cost per pen = 60 × 0.4 + 80 × (1 - 0.4) = 72p.

Expected contribution per pen = £2 - 72p = £1.28

Expected weekly demand = 2,000 × 0.4 + 3,000 × (1 - 0.4) = 2,600 pens

Expected weekly profit = 2,600 × £1.28 - £900 = £2,428.

24 Each card has an equal chance of being selected, so

Average winnings
= 2 × average value of cards
= 2 × (1 + 2 + 3 + 4 + 5)/5 = 2 × 3 = £6

Expected value = £6 - £8 (stake money) = -£2.

25 The probability of Mary being right is 0.4 × 0.6 + (1 - 0.4) × 0.8 = 0.24 + 0.48 = 0.72

If she will pay Ken £x if she is wrong, then

0.72 × £10 - (1 - 0.72) × £x = £2

£7.20 - £2 = 0.28 × £x

£x = £5.20 ÷ 0.28 = £18.57

161

2: MARKING SCHEDULE

Question	Correct answer	Marks for correct answer	Question	Correct answer	Marks for correct answer
1	B	1	15	B	1
2	B	1	16	B	1
3	D	1	17	C	2
4	A	1	18	A	1
5	A	1	19	A	1
6	B	1	20	B	1
7	D	1	21	C	1
8	D	2	22	D	1
9	B	1	23	D	1
10	B	1	24	A	1
11	D	2	25	D	2
12	D	1	26	B	1
13	C	1	27	B	1
14	C	1	28	C	1

YOUR MARKS

Total marks available   32   Your total mark

GUIDELINES - If your mark was:

0 - 8
Poor. The important techniques in this chapter are causing you difficulty. Go back to your study text and work through each relevant section carefully, before trying this chapter again.

9 - 16
Fair. Several of the questions have caught you out. If there are one or two particular techniques which have caused you problems go back to your study text and read through the relevant sections carefully.

17 - 24
Good. There may be a particular group of questions which has caused you difficulty. Check whether this is so, and refer to your study text if there is a clear gap in your knowledge.

25 - 32
Very good. You have a thorough understanding of techniques for decision making under uncertainty.

Question	COMMENTS

1

If 1,000 copies are printed, profit will certainly be $1,000 \times £(4 - 1.50) = £2,500$.

If 2,000 copies are printed, expected profit will be:

$0.3 \times (1,000 \times £4 + 1,000 \times 10p) + 0.7 \times 2,000 \times £4 - 2,000 \times £1.50$

$= 0.3 \times £4,100 + 0.7 \times £8,000 - £3,000 = £3,830$

£3,830 is the higher expected profit.

2

	£
40 rooms	
Revenue	6,400
Loss of tourist lettings	(4,000)
Net	2,400
45 rooms	
Revenue $(40 \times 0.2 + 45 \times 0.8) \times 160$	7,040
Loss of tourist lettings	(4,500)
Net	2,540
50 rooms	
Revenue $(40 \times 0.2 + 45 \times 0.3 + 50 \times 0.5) \times 160$	7,440
Loss of tourist lettings	(5,000)
Net	2,440
55 rooms	
Revenue $(40 \times 0.2 + 45 \times 0.3 + 50 \times 0.4 + 55 \times 0.1) \times 160$	7,520
Loss of tourist lettings	(5,500)
Net	2,020

45 rooms gives the highest expected revenue.

3

Let the probability of 400 tickets being demanded be p; then the probability of 500 tickets being demanded is $1 - (0.2 + p) = 0.8 - p$.

We will first find the expected profit from hiring hall Y, and then set that amount equal to the expected profit from hiring hall Z so as to get an equation involving p.

Expected profit from hiring hall Y = $(300 \times 0.2 + 400 \times 0.8) \times £5 - £590 = £1,310$.

Expected profit from hiring hall Z
$= (300 \times 0.2 + 400 \times p + 500 \times (0.8 - p)) \times £5 - £670 = £1,310$

Question

$$60 + 400p + 400 - 500p = (1{,}310 + 670)/5 = 396$$

$$460 - 100p = 396$$

$$100p = 460 - 396 = 64$$

$$p = 0.64$$

4

Decision-making is always about the future. Perfect information is that which is guaranteed to predict accurately.

5

If one option would be the most profitable whatever the circumstances, knowledge of the circumstances will not affect the decision, so such knowledge has no value for decision making.

6

Without the information, the punter's expected gain per race is $0.4 \times £50 - 0.6 \times £10 = £14$.

With the information, his expected gain is £50 per race.

The expected value of perfect information is therefore $£(50 - 14) = £36$ per race.

7

Abandon product: EV = £0 (the costs of preliminary research have already been incurred, so are irrelevant).

Go ahead: EV = $0.7 \times £30{,}000 - 0.3 \times £10{,}000 = £18{,}000$

Have survey: EV = $-£4{,}000 + 0.7 \times £30{,}000 = £17{,}000$.

The best decision is therefore to go ahead without the survey, yielding an EV of £18,000.

8

High exposure: $-£4{,}000 + 0.6 \times £8{,}000 + 0.4 \times £3{,}000 = £2{,}000$ (television not worthwhile, as £50,000 > £49,500).

Low exposure: $-£1{,}500 + 0.7 \times (£2{,}000 - £50{,}000 + 0.5 \times £60{,}000 + 0.5 \times £46{,}000) + 0.3 \times £500 = £2{,}150$

Low radio exposure should be chosen, and television only proceeded with if the extra gross profit is £2,000.

The expected value is £2,150.

Question

9

Without information, the expected values of the products are:

X: £(20,000 × 0.2 + 15,000 × 0.5 + 6,000 × 0.3) = £13,300

Y: £(17,000 × 0.2 + 16,000 × 0.5 + 7,000 × 0.3) = £13,500

So without information, product Y would be selected.

With perfect information, product X would be selected if the market was good, and product Y in any other case. The expected value would then be:

£(20,000 × 0.2 + 16,000 × 0.5 + 7,000 × 0.3) = £14,100

The expected value of perfect information is therefore £(14,100 - 13,500) = £600.

10

Without the information, the expected value is 0.6 × £18,000 = £10,800. Business Q would not be selected even if it were certain to do well, as even then it would only have an expected value of £10,000. Similarly, once the information has been obtained, there is only an 0.4 probability that Q will even be considered, as if P will do well it will be selected.

If the required probability is q, we have:

18,000 × 0.6 + 10,000 × 0.4 × q - 10,800 = 1,500

4,000q = 1,500

q = 0.375

11

Without information:

	£
Expected revenue = £(25,000 × 0.55 + 19,000 × 0.45) =	22,300
Expected costs = £(18,000 × 0.2 + 22,000 × 0.8) =	(21,200)
Expected net profit =	1,100

With information on exchange rates only:

As expected costs are £21,200, the contract would only be accepted if revenues were to be £25,000. We therefore have:

	£
Expected gross profit = 0.55 × £(25,000 - 21,200) =	2,090
Cost of information =	(1,500)
Expected net profit =	590

With information on costs only:

As expected revenue exceeds even the higher cost figure, the contract would be accepted in any case, so it cannot be worth spending £50 on information.

Question

With information on both revenue and costs:

The contract would be accepted if costs are low (regardless of revenue), of if costs are high but so is revenue. We therefore have:

£

Expected gross profit
(i) Low costs: $0.2 \times £(22,300 - 18,000)$ 860
(ii) High costs and revenue: $0.8 \times 0.55 \times £(25,000 - 22,000)$ 1,320

2,180

Cost of information $£(1,500 + 50)$ .... (1,550)
Expected net profit = ... 630

The best choice is not to obtain any further information, because that gives the highest expected net profit.

12 Perfect information is certain to be right about the future. Imperfect information may predict wrongly.

13 As with some of the probability questions in the last chapter, it is often best to draw up a table.

| | | Prediction | | | |
		Heavy	Light	Total	Workings
	Heavy	0.21	0.14	0.35	0.35 from question
Actual	Light	0.195	0.455	0.65	$0.35 \times 0.6 = 0.21$
	Total	0.405	0.595	1.00	$0.65 \times 0.7 = 0.455$

The required probability is $0.21/0.405 = 0.519$.

14

| | | Prediction | | | |
		Rise	Fall	Total	Workings
	Rise	0.385	0.165	0.55	0.55 from question
Actual	Fall	0.045	0.405	0.45	$0.55 \times 0.7 = 0.385$
	Total	0.43	0.57	1.00	$0.45 \times 0.9 = 0.405$

The required probability is $0.385 + 0.405 = 0.79$.

Question

15 Expected value without information = expected value of buying (higher than that of selling) = $0.5 \times £2,000 + 0.5 \times £20,000 = £11,000$.

Expected value with information:

	£
Predict good: $0.5 \times (0.9 \times £12,000 + 0.1 \times £0)$	5,400
Predict poor: $0.5 \times (0.9 \times £20,000 + 0.1 \times £2,000)$	9,100
	14,500

In this calculation, each line starts with 0.5 for the probability of a particular prediction. The 0.9 and 0.1 correspond to the predictions being correct and incorrect respectively.

Expected value of information = £14,500 - £11,000 = £3,500.

16 Expected value without survey:

If increase production, $0.63 \times £25,000 + 0.37 \times £8,000 = £18,710$.

If do not increase production, $0.63 \times £16,000 + 0.37 \times £15,000 = £15,630$

Expected value = £18,710

Survey reliability:

		Prediction			Workings
		High	Low	Total	
	High	0.504	0.126	0.63	0.63 from question
Actual	Low	0.037	0.333	0.37	$0.63 \times 0.8 = 0.504$
	Total	0.541	0.459	1.00	$0.37 \times 0.9 = 0.333$

P (Actually high | predicted high) = 0.504/0.541 = 0.9316

P (Actually low | predicted low) = 0.333/0.459 = 0.7255

Expected value with survey:

	£
$0.541 \times (0.9316 \times £25,000 + 0.0684 \times £8,000)$	12,896
$0.459 \times (0.7255 \times £15,000 + 0.2745 \times £16,000)$	7,011
	19,907

Increase in expected value = £(19,907 - 18,710) = £1,197, or £1,200 to the nearest £100.

Question

17

Abandoning the purchase has an expected value of £0.

Buying the machine without an investigation has an expected value of 0.35 × £20,000 - 0.65 × £5,000 = £3,750.

Reliability of investigation:

		Prediction Gain	Loss	Total	Workings
	Gain	0.35	0.00	0.35	0.35, 0.65 from question
Actual	Loss	0.13	0.52	0.65	0.35 × 1 = 0.35
	Total	0.48	0.52	1.00	0.65 × 0.8 = 0.52

P (actual gain | predicted gain) = 0.35/0.48 = 0.7292

P (actual loss | predicted loss) = 0.52/0.52 = 1

Expected value with investigation:

	£
0.48 × (0.7292 × £20,000 - 0.2708 × £5,000)	6,350
0.52 × 1 × £0	0
	6,350

The expected value of the information is £(6,350 - 3,750) = £2,600, so the manufacturer should buy it for £2,000, but not for £4,000.

18

Attitudes to risk can be taken into account, so statement 1 is true. Reflecting this, a lower expected monetary value with lower risk of extreme monetary values may be preferred, so statement 2 is false. Computation of utilities is often difficult, so statement 3 is false.

19

Project A has the highest minimum profit (£28,000), so it should be chosen.

20

The worst possible outcomes are:

P only: 2 × -£500	=	-£1,000
Q only: 2 × £3,000	=	£6,000
P and Q: -£500 + £3,000	=	£2,500
R:	=	£2,000

Q only should therefore be chosen.

Question

21

Once the possible profits and losses are known, we merely have to rank the options by lowest profit/highest loss, and select the best of these undesirable outcomes, so statement 1 is true. 'Maximin' abbreviates 'maximum minimum profit', and 'minimax' abbreviates 'minimum maximum loss', which comes to the same thing, so statement 2 is true. No account is taken of any outcomes other than the worst, so probabilities are irrelevant, and statement 3 is false.

22

The minimum costs are:

A £185
B £160
C £100
D £ 50

Applying the minimin criterion, system D should be chosen.

23

The highest possible profits are:

A   £1,500
B   £1,400
C   £1,300
D   £1,600

On the basis of the maximax criterion, investment D should be chosen.

24

We must work out the regret for each option, defined as best outcome in the circumstances minus actual outcome. In this case, the circumstances are Y Ltd's choice. The regret figure for a cell in the table is (with circumstances as columns) highest figure in the column minus figure in the cell.

		I	*II*	*III*	Maximum regret
		Y Ltd's choice			
X Ltd's choice	A	5	0	3	5
	B	2	7	3	7
	C	0	8	0	8
	D	10	3	7	10

The option with the lowest maximum regret is A.

Question

25

Company J: Expected return $= 0.6 \times £80 + 0.4 \times £40 = £64$

Standard deviation

$$= \sqrt{0.6 \times (80 - 64)^2 + 0.4 \times (40 - 64)^2}$$

$$= \sqrt{384} = £20$$

Points $= 64 - 20/2 = 54$

Company K: Expected return $= £62$

Standard deviation $= £0$

Points $= 62$

Company L: Expected return $= 0.5 (90 + 30) = £60$

$$\text{Standard deviation} = \sqrt{0.5 \times (90 - 60)^2 + 0.5 \times (60 - 30)^2}$$

$$= \sqrt{900} = £30$$

Points $= 60 - 30/2 = 45$

Ranking is K, J, L

26 Risk aversion is a general policy to prefer lower variability of return. It does not entail taking no risks, nor does it entail ignoring other considerations, such as expected returns.

27

Return (x) £'000	Probability (p)	px	$p(x - \bar{x})^2$
50	0.1	5	40.401
68	0.75	51	3.3075
94	0.15	14.1	85.6815
		$\bar{x} = \overline{70.1}$	$\overline{129.39}$

Standard deviation $= \sqrt{129.39} = 11.375$

Coefficient of variation $= 11.375/70.1 = 0.16$

Question

28

The coefficient of variation is $\sigma/\bar{x} = \sqrt{\Sigma p\,(x - \bar{x})^2}\,/\,\bar{x}$.

All possible returns are taken into account, so statement 1 is false.

$\bar{x}$ is the expected return and σ measures the variation in returns, so statement 2 is true.

Both σ and $\bar{x}$ are in the currency unit, so their quotient is in no units, so statement 3 is false.

Variation is measured about the expected return, $\bar{x}$, which may well not equal the most likely return (it may not even equal any possible return), so statement 4 is false.

3: MARKING SCHEDULE

Question	Correct answer	Marks for correct answer	Question	Correct answer	Marks for correct answer
1	A	1	14	B	1
2	C	1	15	B	1
3	C	1	16	B	1
4	B	1	17	B	1
5	B	1	18	D	1
6	D	1	19	B	1
7	A	1	20	C	1
8	A	1	21	B	2
9	B	1	22	B	1
10	B	1	23	B	1
11	A	1	24	D	1
12	C	1	25	C	1
13	A	1	26	B	1

YOUR MARKS

Total marks available **27**   Your total mark

GUIDELINES - If your mark was:

0 - 7
Poor. The important techniques in this chapter are causing you difficulty. Go back to your study text and work through each relevant section carefully, before trying this chapter again.

8 - 14
Fair. Several of the questions have caught you out. If there are one or two particular techniques which have caused you problems go back to your study text and read through the relevant sections carefully.

15 - 21
Good. There may be a particular group of questions which has caused you difficulty. Check whether this is so, and refer to your study text if there is a clear gap in your knowledge.

22 - 27
Very good. You have a thorough understanding of probability distributions.

172

Question   COMMENTS

1

The binomial distribution considers two alternatives (often called 'success' and 'failure'), so statement 1 is true. The probability of a success must be constant, so uninfluenced by the outcomes of other trials, so statement 2 is true. Any probabilities and any number of trials can be handled, so statements 3 and 4 are false.

2

The binomial distribution formula tells us the probability of x successes in n trials. Any x trials will do. For example, if n = 3 and x = 2, the successes could be trials 1 and 2, 1 and 3 or 2 and 3. The combinations formula gives us the number of ways of selecting the x trials to be successes.

3

This question can be answered using the binomial distribution formula, which gives all the terms in the expansion of $(p + q)^n$.

The term we want is:

$$_{15}C_3 \, p^3 \, q^{12} = \frac{15!}{(15 - 3)!3!} \, p^3 \, q^{12}$$

$$= \frac{15 \times 14 \times 13}{3 \times 2} \, p^3 \, q^{12} = 455 \, p^3 \, q^{12}$$

4

This question can be answered using the binomial distribution formula. A 'success' is taking more than £2,000.

$$n = 6$$
$$x = 4$$
$$p = 0.3$$
$$q = 0.7$$

Probability $= \,_6C_4 \, (0.3)^4 \, (0.7)^2$

$$= \frac{6!}{(6-4)!4!} \, (0.3)^4 \, (0.7)^2$$

$$= 15 \times 0.0081 \times 0.49 = 0.0595$$

Question

5

$$P(0 \text{ days}) = {}_5C_0 \; (0.4)^0 \; (0.6)^5 =$$ 　　　　0.07776
$$P(1 \text{ day}) = {}_5C_1 \; (0.4)^1 \; (0.6)^4 =$$ 　　　　0.25920
　　　　　　　　　　　　　　　　　　　　0.33696

$$P(>1 \text{ day}) = 1 - 0.33696 = 0.66304$$

6

Costs will be £220 or more if there are:

(i) 3 faults of each type,
probability $= (0.4)^3 \; (0.35)^3 =$ 　　　　0.002744

(ii) 3 faults of type A and 2 of type B
probability $= (0.4)^3 \times {}_3C_2 \; (0.35)^2 \; (0.65)^1 =$ 　　　0.015288

(iii) 2 faults of type A and 3 of type B
probability $= {}_3C_2 \; (0.4)^2 \; (0.6)^1 \times (0.35)^3 =$ 　　0.012348
　　　　　　　　　　　　　　　　　　　　　　　　0.03038

7

$$P(0 \text{ employees sick}) = (0.65)^6 =$$ 　　　　0.07542
$$P(1 \text{ employee sick}) = {}_6C_1 \; (0.35)^1 \; (0.65)^5 =$$ 　　0.24366
$$P(6 \text{ employees sick}) = (0.35)^6 =$$ 　　　　0.00184
　　　　　　　　　　　　　　　　　　　　　0.32092

$$P(2 \text{ to } 5 \text{ employees sick}) = 1 - 0.32092 = 0.67908$$

8

We have a binomial distribution, as the probability (p) of any one calculator being defective is constant.

Mean $= 50 = np = 2,000p$, so $p = 50/2,000 = 0.025$

Standard deviation $= \sqrt{np\,(1-p)}$

$$= \sqrt{2,000 \times 0.025 \times 0.975} = \sqrt{48.75} = 6.98$$

9

We should apply the Poisson distribution (number of occurrences (errors) in a given span (an hour)), with m = 3.5. The probabilities are found from tables.

x	Probability
0	0.0302
1	0.1057
2	0.1850
	0.3209

Question

10 If mean per day = 1.2, mean per 3 days = 3 × 1.2 = 3.6.

From Poisson distribution tables for m = 3.6, x = 3, probability = 0.2125.

11 The tables provided only give values of m up to 4.1, so the Poisson formula must be used.

m = 5, x = 7
m^x = 5^7 = 78,125
x! = 5,040
e^{-m} = $1/(2.71828)^5$ = 1/148.413
$\dfrac{m^x}{x!} e^{-m}$ = $\dfrac{78,125}{5,040 \times 148.413}$ = 0.1044

12 From looking at Poisson tables under x = 5, we find 0.0735 on the line for a mean of 2.6.

For a Poisson distribution, $\sigma = \sqrt{m} = \sqrt{2.6} = 1.61$

13 The Poisson distribution is appropriate as an approximation to the binomial distribution when there is a small probability of a success. The approximation improves as the number of trials is increased.

14 Since n is large and p is small, the Poisson approximation to the binomial distribution should be used, with m = np = 60 × 0.03 = 1.8.

From tables:

P(0) =	0.1653
P(1) =	0.2975
P(2) =	0.2678
P(3) =	0.1607
	0.8913

P(4 or more) = 1-0.8913 = 0.1087.

Question

15 True probability = $_{12}C_2$ $(0.1)^2$ $(0.9)^{10}$ = 66 $(0.1)^2$ $(0.9)^{10}$ = 0.2301

Approximate probability (from tables), using m = np = 12 × 0.1 = 1.2 and x = 2, is 0.2169.

Error = $\dfrac{0.2301 - 0.2169}{0.2301}$ × 100% = 5.74%

This shows that moderate errors can be made when n is only just over 10 and p is as high as 0.1. The Poisson approximation should be used with caution in such circumstances.

16 This is a situation to which the binomial distribution applies. Each selection of a brick for inspection is a trial, and finding an inspected brick to be defective is a success. The Poisson approximation to the binomial distribution is appropriate, as n is large and p is small.

    p = 200/50,000 = 0.004
    n = 600
    m = np = 600 × 0.004 = 2.4

From tables:

P(0) =	0.0907
P(1) =	0.2177
P(2) =	0.2613
P(3) =	0.2090
	0.7787

P (more than 3) = 1 - 0.7787 = 0.2213

17 From tables, the probability of the value of the variable being over 1.52 standard deviations above the mean is 0.5 - 0.4357 = 0.0643. The question asked about the probability of being more than 1.52 standard deviations away from the mean (in either direction), so the answer is 0.0643 × 2 = 0.1286.

18 A search of normal distribution tables shows that a probability of 0.5 - 0.0314 = 0.4686 corresponds to values between the mean and 1.86 standard deviations above the mean.

Standard deviation = $\dfrac{6,000 - 5,200}{1.86}$ = 430 kg

Question

19 7,900 hours is $\dfrac{8,000 - 7,900}{330}$ = 0.30 standard deviations below the mean.

From tables, probability of lasting between 7,900 and 8,000 hours = 0.1179

8,200 hours is $\dfrac{8,200 - 8,000}{300}$ = 0.61 standard deviations above the mean

From tables, probability of lasting between 8,000 and 8,200 hours = 0.2291

Required probability = 0.1179 + 0.2291 = 0.347

20 From tables, a probability of 0.5 - 0.1 = 0.4 corresponds to values between the mean and 1.28 standard deviations above the mean, and a probability of 0.5 - 0.33 = 0.17 corresponds to values between the mean and 0.44 standard deviations below the mean.

$\mu + 1.28\,\sigma$ = 12   (1)

$\mu - 0.44\,\sigma$ = 4   (2)

1.72σ = 8   (1) - (2)

σ = 4.65

μ = 12 - 1.28 σ = 6.05 minutes

21 From tables, 1,480 words must represent a point 0.84 standard deviations below the mean (0.5 - 0.2 = 0.3 is found under 0.84 standard deviations). The probability of a speech exceeding 1,560 words is 1 - (0.2 + 0.4) = 0.4, so 1,560 words must represent a point 0.25 standard deviations above the mean (0.5 - 0.4 = 0.1 is found under 0.25 standard deviations).

$\mu - 0.84\,\sigma$ = 1,480   (1)

$\mu + 0.25\,\sigma$ = 1,560   (2)

$1.09\,\sigma$ = 80   (2) - (1)

σ = 73.4

μ = 1,480 + 0.84 σ = 1,542

1,600 words is $\dfrac{1,600 - 1,542}{73.4}$ = 0.79 standard deviations above the mean, so the

required probability is (from tables) 0.5 - 0.2852 = 0.2148, or approximately 0.215.

Question

22

The normal distribution is symmetrical. The binomial distribution is symmetrical when p = 0.5, and becomes more skewed the further p is from 0.5. When p = 1 - p, p = 0.5, so closeness of p and 1-p indicates a nearly symmetrical distribution. When n is large, the discrete binomial distribution can be approximated by a continuous distribution. The normal distribution is continuous.

23

The normal approximation to the binomial distribution is appropriate, as n is large and p is close to 0.5.
Mean = np = 1,000 × 0.45 = 450

Standard deviation = $\sqrt{np(1-p)}$ = $\sqrt{1,000 \times 0.45 \times 0.55}$ = $\sqrt{247.5}$ = 15.73

470 wins is $\dfrac{470 - 450}{15.73}$ = 1.27 standard deviation above the mean.

From tables, the required probability is 0.5 - 0.398 = 0.102.

24

np = 79.9

$\sqrt{npq}$ = 6.507

npq = 42.341

q = npq/np = 42.341/79.9 = 0.53

p = 1 - q = 0.47

n = 79.9/p = 170

25

The normal distribution is an appropriate approximation, as n is large and p is 0.5.

n = 250

p = 0.5

μ = np = 250 × 0.5 = 125

σ = $\sqrt{npq}$ = $\sqrt{250 \times 0.5 \times 0.5}$ = 7.906

The range to consider is 121.5 to 125.5 successes.

Question

121.5 successes is $\dfrac{125 - 121.5}{7.906}$ = 0.44 standard deviations below the mean.

125.5 is $\dfrac{125.5 - 125}{7.906}$ = 0.06 standard deviations above the mean.

P   (between mean and 0.44 standard deviations
below mean) =

P   (between mean and 0.06 standard deviations
above mean) =

Required probability

0.1700

0.0239

0.1939

26 The normal approximation is appropriate, as n is large and p is reasonably close to 0.5.

μ = np = 50 × (1 - 0.38) = 31

$\sigma = \sqrt{npq} = \sqrt{50 \times 0.62 \times 0.38}$ = 3.432

The relevant range is 38.5 to 39.5 successes.

38.5 successes is $\dfrac{38.5 - 31}{3.432}$ = 2.19 standard deviations above the mean.

39.5 successes is $\dfrac{39.5 - 31}{3.432}$ = 2.48 standard deviations above the mean.

The required probability is (from tables) 0.4934 - 0.4857 = 0.0077.

4: MARKING SCHEDULE

Question	Correct answer	Marks for correct answer	Question	Correct answer	Marks for correct answer
1	A	1	15	A	1
2	B	1	16	B	1
3	D	1	17	C	1
4	A	1	18	B	1
5	A	1	19	D	1
6	B	1	20	C	1
7	A	1	21	D	1
8	D	1	22	D	1
9	B	1	23	C	1
10	D	1	24	D	1
11	D	1	25	C	1
12	C	1	26	B	1
13	B	1	27	D	1
14	D	1	28	B	1

YOUR MARKS

Total marks available   28   Your total mark

GUIDELINES - If your mark was:

0 - 7   Poor. The important techniques in this chapter are causing you difficulty. Go back to your study text and work through each relevant section carefully, before trying this chapter again.

8 - 14   Fair. Several of the questions have caught you out. If there are one or two particular techniques which have caused you problems go back to your study text and read through the relevant sections carefully.

15 - 21   Good. There may be a particular group of questions which has caused you difficulty. Check whether this is so, and refer to your study text if there is a clear gap in your knowledge.

22 - 28   Very good. You have a thorough understanding of sampling theory.

Question

COMMENTS

1 A sampling frame is a list of every member of the population. We select our sample from this list.

2 Secondary data are data collected for another purpose. Thus a manufacturer trying to predict sales of his product might use Government statistics on consumer spending.

3 If there is no interviewer, bias cannot be introduced by interviewers presenting questions in particular ways, so 1 is an advantage. 2 is correspondingly a disadvantage, as uniform interpretation of questions is desirable. Completeness of response is sought, so 3 is not an advantage. Larger samples for the same expenditure are generally desirable, so 4 is an advantage.

4 Any interference with the product of random number tables, such as trying to ensure regular spacing of the results, or a balance between even and odd numbers, leads to a loss of randomness. On the other hand, any part of a table is as good as any other part, so there is nothing wrong with using the ends of rows.

5 Numbers must be selected according to a consistent plan (in A, take two digits then skip one), and digits should not be taken twice (as in B, and at the end in D). In C, the pattern of taking two digits then skipping three breaks down at the end.

6 The population has been broken down into strata (layers) and a sample taken within each stratum.

7 If a grid is drawn up, first putting in figures from the question, all the missing numbers can be filled in.

	Male	Female	Total
Sport, at least weekly	208	112	320
Less frequent sport	104	16	120
No sport	208	352	560
Total	520	480	1,000

The answer is therefore 104.

Question

8 Pilot surveys are tests of data collection methods, so that problems can be ironed out before substantial resources are invested in a full scale survey.

9 If one takes all possible samples of a given size and computes each sample's mean, those means themselves form a distribution, the standard deviation of which is called the standard error of the mean.

10 Standard error of the mean $= \dfrac{\sigma}{\sqrt{n}} = \dfrac{25}{\sqrt{70}} = 2.99$

11 Standard error $= \dfrac{\sigma}{\sqrt{n}}$

$30.22 = \dfrac{2,770}{\sqrt{n}}$

$n = (2,770/30.22)^2 = 8,402$

12 $\dfrac{\sigma}{\sqrt{100}} = 839,$

$\sigma = 839\sqrt{100}$

$\dfrac{\sigma}{\sqrt{500}} = \dfrac{839\sqrt{100}}{\sqrt{500}} = \dfrac{839 \times 10}{22.361} = 375$ units

13 95% confidence interval $=$ Sample mean $\pm\ 1.96 \times$ standard error

$= £18,000 \pm 1.96 \times \dfrac{£1,500}{\sqrt{75}} = £18,000 \pm £339.48$

$= £17,660.52$ to $£18,339.48.$

Question

14

Width of interval = 2 × 2.58 × standard error = $2 \times 2.58 \times \dfrac{£8.92}{\sqrt{150}}$ = £3.76

Thus we can be 99% confident that the mean size of a telephone bill lies within a range of values which is £3.76 wide.

15

The interval given is 1.65 standard errors either side of the population mean. This is the 90% confidence interval, within which 90% of all possible sample means lie, since from normal distribution tables about 0.45 of the total distribution lies between the mean and 1.65 standard deviations above the mean, so 2 × 0.45 = 0.9 lies in the range mean ± 1.65 standard deviations.

16

$$5.835 = 2 \times 1.96 \times \dfrac{12}{\sqrt{n}}$$

$$\sqrt{n} = 2 \times 1.96 \times \dfrac{12}{5.835} = 8.0617$$

$$n = 65$$

17

The 99% confidence interval is 2.58 standard errors either side of the mean:

$$10 = 2.58 \times \dfrac{46}{\sqrt{n}}$$

$$\sqrt{n} = 2.58 \times \dfrac{46}{10} = 11.868$$

$$n = 141$$

18

$$\dfrac{1.96\sigma}{\sqrt{65}} = 0.04$$

$$1.96\sigma = 0.04\sqrt{65}$$

For a sample of 195 packets,

$$\dfrac{1.96\sigma}{\sqrt{n}} = \dfrac{0.04\sqrt{65}}{\sqrt{195}} = 0.0231$$

The new confidence interval is 1.05kg ± 0.0231 kg.

Question

19

The sample size is less than 30, so the t distribution should be used. There are 20 - 1 = 19 degrees of freedom; t distribution tables give a factor of 2.86.

The 99% confidence interval is therefore $137 \pm 2.86 \times \dfrac{42}{\sqrt{20-1}}$ = 137 ± 27.56 months

= 109.44 months to 164.56 months

20

The sample proportion is 64/320 = 0.2. The 95% confidence interval is therefore

$$0.2 \pm 1.96 \sqrt{\frac{0.2 \times (1 - 0.2)}{320}} = 0.2 \pm 0.044$$

21

The t distribution with 25 - 1 = 24 degrees of freedom gives $t_{0.005}$ = 2.80. The 99% confidence interval is

$$0.4 \pm 2.80 \times \sqrt{\frac{0.4 \times 0.6}{25}} = 0.4 \pm 0.274.$$

The width of the interval is 2 × 0.274 = 0.55 = 55%.

22

$$0.05034 = 2.58 \sqrt{\frac{0.45 \times 0.55}{n}}$$

Squaring both sides:

$$0.002534 = \frac{6.6564 \times 0.45 \times 0.55}{n}$$

$$n = \frac{6.6564 \times 0.45 \times 0.55}{0.002534} = 650$$

23

For a given n, the standard error, and hence the confidence interval, is largest when the proportion is as near as it can be to 0.5. As the proportion must in this case be at least 0.7, the closest it can get to 0.5 is 0.7. We will assume this 'worst case', and find n on that basis, so that we will definitely get the required precision.

$$0.02 = 1.96 \sqrt{\frac{0.7 \times 0.3}{n}}$$

Question

Squaring both sides,

$$0.0004 = \frac{3.8416 \times 0.7 \times 0.3}{n}$$

$$n = \frac{3.8416 \times 0.7 \times 0.3}{0.0004}$$

$$= 2,017$$

24 For a given n, the standard error is largest when the proportion is 0.5.

$$0.016 = 2.58 \sqrt{\frac{0.5 \times 0.5}{n}}$$

Squaring both sides,

$$0.000256 = \frac{6.6564 \times 0.5 \times 0.5}{n}$$

$$n = \frac{6.6564 \times 0.5 \times 0.5}{0.000256}$$

$$= 6,501 \text{ (round up to ensure required narrowness of confidence interval)}$$

25 Applying Bessel's correction, the best estimate of the population standard deviation is:

$$£4.32 \times \sqrt{\frac{25}{25\text{-}1}} = £4.41$$

26 At the desired point,

$$1.01 = \sqrt{\frac{n}{n-1}}$$

$$1.01 \sqrt{n-1} = \sqrt{n}$$

$$1.0201(n-1) = n$$

$$0.0201n = 1.0201$$

$$n = 51$$

This shows how Bessel's correction can easily become insignificant as n is increased.

Question

27

$$\sqrt{\frac{12 \times 14^2 + 16 \times 11^2}{12 + 16 - 2}} = 12.84 \text{ units}$$

28

$$\frac{(26 \times 47) + (18 \times 44) + (37 \times 46)}{(26 + 18 + 37)} = 45.877 \text{ units}$$

We are thus effectively weighting the different sample means by the sizes of the samples.

5: MARKING SCHEDULE

Question	Correct answer	Marks for correct answer
1	D	1
2	B	1
3	C	1
4	C	1
5	D	1
6	B	1
7	D	1
8	A	1
9	C	1
10	D	1
11	B	1
12	C	1
13	C	1

Question	Correct answer	Marks for correct answer
14	A	1
15	D	1
16	B	1
17	C	1
18	C	1
19	B	1
20	B	1
21	C	1
22	B	2
23	D	2
24	D	2
25	B	1
26	C	2

YOUR MARKS

Total marks available   30   Your total mark   ☐

GUIDELINES - If your mark was:

0 - 8   Poor. The important techniques in this chapter are causing you difficulty. Go back to your study text and work through each relevant section carefully, before trying this chapter again.

9 - 15   Fair. Several of the questions have caught you out. If there are one or two particular techniques which have caused you problems go back to your study text and read through the relevant sections carefully.

16 - 22   Good. There may be a particular group of questions which has caused you difficulty. Check whether this is so, and refer to your study text if there is a clear gap in your knowledge.

23 - 30   Very good. You have a thorough understanding of methods of hypothesis testing.

Question	COMMENTS

1

This is a two-tailed large sample test at 1% significance, so the sample mean must lie within 2.58 standard errors of the hypothesised mean for the null hypothesis to be accepted.

2

This is a one-tailed test (H_1 is that μ > £13,000) at 5% significance with n > 30, so the critical value is 1.65. The test statistic is

$$\frac{£13,250 - £13,000}{£2,000/ \sqrt{200}} = 1.77$$

The null hypothesis, μ = £13,000, should be rejected because 1.77 exceeds 1.65. We conclude that the mean income in the UK exceeds £13,000.

3

The test statistic (test of one mean) is

$$\frac{192 - 180}{50/ \sqrt{55}} = 1.78$$

As this is a two-tailed test (H_1 is that $\mu \neq 180$), for which the critical values are 1.96 (5% significance) and 2.58 (1% significance), the null hypothesis that μ = 180 should be accepted at either level of significance.

4

The test statistic is

$$\frac{730 - 700}{141/ \sqrt{80}} = 1.90$$

The proportion of the normal distribution more than 1.90 standard deviations above the mean is (from tables) 0.5-0.4713 = 0.0287. This is a one-tailed test (H_1 is that μ > 700g), so the significance level is 2.87%.

5

H_0 is that π = 0.25, and H_1 is that $\pi \neq 0.25$. This is therefore a two-tailed test with n > 30. The acceptable sample proportion is 0.25 ± 2.58 × standard error of one proportion

$$= 0.25 \pm 2.58 \sqrt{\frac{0.25 \times 0.75}{80}} = 0.1251 \text{ to } 0.3749$$

Question

This corresponds to 80 × 0.1251 = 10.008 to 80 × 0.3749 = 29.992 people. The acceptance range must be rounded 'inwards', to 11-29 people.

6

The critical proportion of batteries is:

$$0.03 + 1.65 \sqrt{\frac{0.03 \times 0.97}{200}} = 0.0499$$

This corresponds to 200 × 0.0499 = 9.98 batteries. If 10 batteries are defective, the null hypothesis will be rejected.

7

This is a one-tailed test of the null hypothesis that $\pi = 0.4$, against the alternative hypothesis that $\pi > 0.4$. The test statistic is

$$\frac{0.4 - 99/300}{\sqrt{0.4 \times 0.6/300}} = 2.47$$

The null hypothesis should therefore be rejected both at 5% significance (critical level 1.65) and at 1% significance (critical level 2.33).

8

The value of the test statistic is

$$\frac{0.5 - 0.44}{\sqrt{0.5 \times 0.5/150}} = 1.47$$

Normal distribution tables show that the probability of a value of more than 1.47 standard deviations above the mean is 0.5 - 0.4292 = 0.0708. Bearing in mind that this is a two-tailed test, the significance level is 2 × 0.0708 = 0.1416 ≃ 14%.

9

The null hypothesis must be that the population means are equal.

$$\text{Test statistic} = \frac{£13,200 - £13,020}{\sqrt{\frac{700^2}{150} + \frac{900^2}{120}}} = 1.8$$

As 1.8 exceeds 1.65, the critical value for a one-tailed test at 5% significance, the null hypothesis should be rejected.

Question

10

Difference between means =

$$2.58 \sqrt{\frac{47^2}{80} + \frac{32^2}{130}} = 15 \text{ units}$$

11

Test statistic $= \dfrac{26.6}{\sqrt{\dfrac{75^2}{50} + \dfrac{45^2}{60}}} = 2.2$

From normal distribution tables, and bearing in mind that this is a two-tailed test, significance level = 2 × 0.0139 = 0.0278 = 2.78%

12

The two sets of data are not independent: the wearer's lifestyle affects the life of a jacket. A paired-data test should therefore be performed, using the differences between the lives of jackets for each wearer. Because there are only 8 (fewer than 30) pairs of data, the t distribution with 8 - 1 = 7 degrees of freedom should be used. The null hypothesis is that the mean lives are equal. Because the alternative hypothesis is that the mean lives are unequal (either way round), this is a two-tailed test, with critical values $t_{0.025} = \pm 2.36$ (5% significance) and $t_{0.005} = \pm 3.50$ (1% significance).

Wearer	Life (X) - Life (Y)	(Life (X) - Life (Y))²
P	-10	100
Q	-20	400
R	20	400
S	10	100
T	-10	100
U	0	0
V	-20	400
W	-10	100
	-40	1,600

Mean difference = -40/8 = -5
Estimated population standard deviation of differences:

$$\sqrt{\frac{8}{8-1}} \times \sqrt{\frac{1,600}{8} - (-5)^2} = 14.14$$

Test statistic $= \dfrac{-5}{14.14/\sqrt{8}} = -1$

As this is within the critical values at both significance levels, the null hypothesis should be accepted at either level.

Question

13

The critical levels for the test will be set at $148 \pm 1.96 \times 24/\sqrt{45} = 140.99$ and 155.01. We therefore require the probability of getting a sample mean between these limits, given a population mean of 162.

The upper limit is $\dfrac{162 - 155.01}{24/\sqrt{45}} = 1.95$ standard errors below the mean, and the

lower limit is $\dfrac{162 - 140.99}{24/\sqrt{45}} = 5.87$ standard errors below the mean.

The probability of getting a sample mean within this range is (from normal distribution tables, and ignoring the negligible probability of getting a mean of below 140.99), $0.5 - 0.4744 = 0.0256$.

14

$$p = \frac{0.6 \times 90 + 0.55 \times 80}{90 + 80} = 0.576$$

$$\text{Test statistic} = \frac{0.6 - 0.55}{\sqrt{0.576\,(1-0.576)\left(\dfrac{1}{90} + \dfrac{1}{80}\right)}} = 0.66$$

As the critical levels are 1.96 (5% significance) and 2.58 (1% significance), the null hypothesis should be accepted at either significance level.

15

$$p = \frac{0.4 \times n + 0.5 \times n}{n + n} = 0.45$$

$$2.58 = \frac{0.5 - 0.4}{\sqrt{0.45 \times 0.55 \left(\dfrac{1}{n} + \dfrac{1}{n}\right)}}$$

$$\frac{0.5 - 0.4}{2.58} = \sqrt{\frac{0.495}{n}}$$

$$\left(\frac{0.1}{2.58}\right)^2 = \frac{0.495}{n}$$

$$0.0015023 = \frac{0.495}{n}$$

$$n = \frac{0.495}{0.0015023} = 329$$

Question

16

Test statistic = $\dfrac{1,150 - 1,000}{235/\sqrt{14-1}}$ = 2.30

This is more than the critical level for a 1-tailed test (H_1 is $\mu > 1,000$) at 5% significance with 13 degrees of freedom (1.77) but less than the critical level at 1% significance (2.65). The null hypothesis that $\mu = 1,000$ should therefore be accepted at 1% significance but rejected at 5% significance.

17

Test statistic = $\dfrac{62,000 - 56,000}{6,000/\sqrt{6-1}}$ = 2.24

This is less than the critical level for a 2-tailed test with five degrees of freedom both at 5% significance (2.57) and at 1% significance (4.03). The null hypothesis should be accepted at either significance level.

18

F = the larger of $\quad \dfrac{s_1{}^2}{s_2{}^2} \quad$ and $\quad \dfrac{s_2{}^2}{s_1{}^2}$

$\qquad = \quad \dfrac{27^2}{12^2} \quad = 5.0625$

19

The F test should be used.

$F \quad = \quad \dfrac{\text{larger variance}}{\text{smaller variance}} \quad = \quad \dfrac{80^2}{35^2} \quad = 5.22$

The numbers of degrees of freedom are 7 - 1 = 6 for the numerator and 10 - 1 = 9 for the denominator. The critical values of F are then (from tables at the end of this book) 3.37 (10% significance) and 5.80 (2% significance). The null hypothesis should therefore be rejected at the 10% significance level and accepted at the 2% significance level.

20

O	E	O - E	$(O - E)^2 /E$
12	10	2	0.4
9	10	-1	0.1
8	8	0	0.0
2	5	-3	1.8
7	5	2	0.8
38	38		3.1

The value of χ^2 was 3.1.

Question

21

O	E	O - E	$(O - E)^2 / E$
47	51	-4	0.3137
50	45	5	0.5556
70	60	10	1.6667
37	30	7	1.6333
96	114	-18	2.8421
		χ^2 =	7.0114

The critical values for 5 - 1 = 4 degrees of freedom are 9.49 (5% significance) and 13.3 (1% significance). The hypothesis should therefore be accepted at either significance level, because the value of χ^2 in this case is less than both critical values.

22

We must first find a mean for the hypothesised Poisson distribution.

x	f	fx
0	32	0
1	40	40
2	14	28
3	14	42
	100	110

The mean is 110/100 = 1.1.

We can now find values of E from Poisson distribution tables for m = 1.1, multiplying each probability by the number of observations (100).

O	E	$(O-E)^2 / E$
32	33.29	0.05
40	36.62	0.31
14	20.14	1.87
14	9.95 *	1.65
100	100.00 $\quad \chi^2$	3.88

* Balancing figure

23

The expected proportions are derived from normal distribution tables. Thus the expected proportion for the range from 1 to 2 standard deviations below the mean is 0.4772 - 0.3413 = 0.1359. Each proportion is then multiplied by 1,000.

O	E	O - E	$(O - E)^2 / E$
40	22.8	17.2	12.98
150	135.9	14.1	1.46
300	341.3	-41.3	5.00
350	341.3	8.7	0.22
100	135.9	-35.9	9.48
60	22.8	37.2	60.69
			89.83

Question

The critical levels for 6 - 3 = 3 degrees of freedom are 6.25 (10% significance) and 11.3 (1% significance). The hypothesis should therefore be rejected at either level of significance.

24 The expected frequencies (no effect of choice of fertiliser) for each cell are

row total $\times$ column total/grand total

Thus for the top left cell, $E = 38 \times 30/100 = 11.4$

O	E	O - E	$(O - E)^2$ /E
5	11.4	-6.4	3.5930
8	11.4	-3.4	1.0140
25	15.2	9.8	6.3184
10	7.8	2.2	0.6205
6	7.8	-1.8	0.4154
10	10.4	-0.4	0.0154
15	10.8	4.2	1.6333
16	10.8	5.2	2.5037
5	14.4	-9.4	6.1361
		χ^2	22.2498

The critical values for (3 - 1) (3 -1) = 4 degrees of freedom are 7.78 (10% significance) and 9.49 (5% significance). The hypothesis of no effect should therefore be rejected at either level of significance because the value of χ^2 exceeds both critical values.

25 Yates' correction (bringing (O-E) closer to zero by 0.5 before squaring) applies to 2×2 contingency tables.

Expected values are found as:

row total $\times$ column total/grand total

O	E	O - E $\pm$ 0.5	$(O - E \pm 0.5)^2$ /E
25	28.4	-2.9	0.2961
46	42.6	2.9	0.1974
15	11.6	2.9	0.7250
14	17.4	-2.9	0.4833
			1.7018

The value of χ^2 is 1.7018.

Question

26

We have three samples.

Typeface	Sample size (n)	Sample total (T)	T^2/n
Normal	4	127	4,032.25
Bold	3	114	4,332.00
Italic	3	102	3,468.00
	10	343	11,832.25

The sum of the squares of all ten sales figures is 12,105.

Total sum of squares = $12,105 - 343^2/10 = 340.1$.

Treatment (ie effect of typeface) sum of squares = $11,832.25 - 343^2/10 = 67.35$.

Error (ie other factors) sum of squares = $340.1 - 67.35 = 272.75$.

There are three different typefaces, so the mean sum of treatment squares is $67.35/(3-1)$ = 33.675.

There are ten data items, and three typefaces, so the mean sum of error squares is $272.75/(10-3) = 38.96$.

The F statistic is therefore $33.675/38.96 = 0.86$. The critical values of F, with $3 - 1 = 2$ degrees of freedom for the numerator and $10 - 3 = 7$ degrees of freedom for the denominator, are 4.74 (5% significance) and 9.55 (1% significance). The null hypothesis should therefore be accepted at both levels of significance.

6: MARKING SCHEDULE

Question	Correct answer	Marks for correct answer	Question	Correct answer	Marks for correct answer
1	D	1	14	D	1
2	C	1	15	C	1
3	A	1	16	C	1
4	D	1	17	D	1
5	C	1	18	B	2
6	C	1	19	D	1
7	A	1	20	D	1
8	B	1	21	B	1
9	C	1	22	C	1
10	D	1	23	C	1
11	D	1	24	C	2
12	A	1	25	C	1
13	D	1			

YOUR MARKS

Total marks available   27   Your total mark

GUIDELINES - If your mark was:

0 - 7   Poor. The important techniques in this chapter are causing you difficulty. Go back to your study text and work through each relevant section carefully, before trying this chapter again.

8 - 15   Fair. Several of the questions have caught you out. If there are one or two particular techniques which have caused you problems go back to your study text and read through the relevant sections carefully.

16 - 21   Good. There may be a particular group of questions which has caused you difficulty. Check whether this is so, and refer to your study text if there is a clear gap in your knowledge.

22 - 27   Very good. You have a thorough understanding of correlation and regression.

Question

COMMENTS

1

The proportion of variation in the value of one variable explained by variation in the value of the other is the coefficient of determination = r^2 = $(-1)^2$ = 1 = 100%.

2

r can never exceed 1. Past correlation cannot be guaranteed to continue. Strong correlation is more significant when n is large, because it is less likely that this strong correlation is due to chance. It does not matter which is the independent variable (unlike regression).

3

When cold drinks sell well, so will suntan cream. Neither sales level causes the other; both are caused by the weather.

4

x	y	x^2	y^2	xy
1	6	1	36	6
2	5	4	25	10
3	3	9	9	9
4	8	16	64	32
$\overline{10}$	$\overline{22}$	$\overline{30}$	$\overline{134}$	$\overline{57}$

n = 4

$$r = \frac{n\Sigma xy - \Sigma x\, \Sigma y}{\sqrt{[n\Sigma x^2 - (\Sigma x)^2]\,[n\Sigma y^2 - (\Sigma y)^2]}}$$

$$= \frac{4 \times 57 - 10 \times 22}{\sqrt{[4 \times 30 - 10^2]\,[4 \times 134 - 22^2]}}$$

$$= \frac{8}{\sqrt{1{,}040}} = + 0.25$$

5

$$r = \frac{6 \times 7 - 1 \times 15}{\sqrt{[6 \times 15 - 1^2][6 \times 65 - 15^2]}} = \frac{42 - 15}{\sqrt{89 \times 165}}$$

$$= \frac{27}{121.18} = 0.22$$

This low figure suggests that there is little link between a company's sales and its net expenditure on office furniture.

Question

6

$$\bar{x} = \frac{10}{4} = 2.5$$

$$\bar{y} = \frac{9}{4} = 2.25$$

$$r = \frac{\Sigma xy - n\,\bar{x}\,\bar{y}}{n\sigma_x\,\sigma_y} = \frac{17 - 4 \times 2.5 \times 2.25}{4 \times 1.118 \times 1.299}$$

$$= \frac{-5.5}{5.809} = -0.95$$

This high negative correlation suggest that high average salaries are linked to low staff turnover.

7

The coefficient of determination is r^2, so statement 1 is true and statement 2 is false. r can reach 1 or -1, so r^2 can reach 1 and statement 3 is false. Correlation does not prove a causal link, so statement 4 is false.

8

$$r = \frac{\Sigma\,(x - \bar{x})\,(y - \bar{y})}{\sqrt{\Sigma(x - \bar{x})^2\;\Sigma(y - \bar{y})^2}} = \frac{-6}{\sqrt{10 \times 4}}$$

$$= \frac{-6}{6.3246} = -0.9487$$

$$r^2 = (-0.9487)^2 = 0.9$$

9

Skater	Rank		d	d²
	Technical	Artistic		
P	1	4	3	9
Q	5	3	2	4
R	4	5	1	1
S	3	2	1	1
T	2	1	1	1
				16

$$r_s = 1 - \frac{6\Sigma d^2}{n(n^2 - 1)} = 1 - \frac{6 \times 16}{5 \times (25 - 1)} = 0.2$$

This low value suggests that there is little connection between skaters' positions for technical merit and artistic impression.

Question

10

Competitor	Competition 1	Competition 2	d	d^2
U	1	4	3.0	9.00
V	2.5	2	0.5	0.25
W	2.5	1	1.5	2.25
X	4	4	0.0	0.00
Y	5	4	1.0	1.00
Z	6	6	0.0	0.00
				12.50

n = 6

Note that when there is a tie, an average rank is used. A tie for second/third place gives 2.5, and a tie for third/fourth/fifth place gives 4.

$$r_s = 1 - \frac{6\,\Sigma d^2}{n(n^2-1)} = 1 - \frac{6 \times 12.5}{6 \times (36-1)} = 0.64$$

11 The sum minimised is that of the squares of the vertical distances.

12

x	y	x^2	xy
1	2	1	2
2	3	4	6
3	5	9	15
4	5	16	20
10	15	30	43

n = 4

$$b = \frac{n\Sigma xy - \Sigma x\,\Sigma y}{n\Sigma x^2 - (\Sigma x)^2}$$

$$= \frac{4 \times 43 - 10 \times 15}{4 \times 30 - 10^2} = \frac{22}{20} = 1.1$$

$$a = \bar{y} - b\bar{x} = \frac{15}{4} - 1.1 \times \frac{10}{4} = 1$$

Thus we have y = 1 + 1.1x.

This indicates that each extra member of sales staff can generate an extra £1.1m of sales on average.

Question

13
Note that we are asked for the equation of the regression line of x on y; x and y must therefore be interchanged in the formulae

x	y	y^2	xy
4	1	1	4
7	2	4	14
9	3	9	27
8	3	9	24
9	3	9	27
37	12	32	96

$n = 5$

$$b = \frac{n\Sigma xy - \Sigma x \Sigma y}{n\Sigma y^2 - (\Sigma y)^2}$$

$$= \frac{5 \times 96 - 37 \times 12}{5 \times 32 - 12^2} = \frac{36}{16} = 2.25$$

$$a = \bar{x} - b\bar{y} = \frac{37}{5} - 2.25 \times \frac{12}{5} = 2$$

The equation is $x = 2 + 2.25y$

14
In the regression line $y = a + bx$,

$$b = \frac{\text{covariance (x,y)}}{\text{variance (x)}} = \frac{10}{4} = 2.5$$

$$a = \bar{y} - b\bar{x} = 6 - 2.5 \times 2 = 1$$

The line is therefore $y = 1 + 2.5x$

For $x = 5$, $y = 1 + 2.5 \times 5 = 13.5$

Thus if five employees are ill, we may expect 13,500 units of production to be lost.

15
The Pearsonian correlation coefficient is the square root of the product of the coefficients of y and x in the respective regression lines. As these coefficients are negative, the correlation coefficient must be negative.

$$r = -\sqrt{(-1.8)(-0.53)} = -\sqrt{0.954} = -0.977$$

If we drew the two regression lines on a graph, we would find that high correlation (as here) corresponded to a small angle between the lines. When $r = 1$ or $r = -1$, the two lines (y on x and x on y) coincide.

Question

16

y = $475 + 0.7 \times 7 + 3.2 \times 42 - 1.9 \times 0.9$

  = $475 + 4.9 + 134.4 - 1.71$

  = $\underline{612.59}$

17

Standard error = $\sqrt{\dfrac{\Sigma(y-y_e)^2}{n-2}}$

y	y_e	$y - y_e$	$(y - y_e)^2$
1	1.3	-0.3	0.09
4	3.8	0.2	0.04
7	6.5	0.5	0.25
2	2.0	0.0	0.00
6	6.4	-0.4	0.16
9	9.0	0.0	0.00
			$\overline{0.54}$

$n = 6$

Standard error = $\sqrt{\dfrac{0.54}{6-2}}$ = $\sqrt{0.135}$ = 0.367

18

$y = -1.03 + 1.66x$, giving a predicted value for y when x = 14.5 of

$-1.03 + 1.66 \times 14.5 = 23.04$

The standard error of the estimated regression line is:

S_e = $\sqrt{\dfrac{58,640 + 1.03 \times 1,320 - 1.66 \times 35,890}{40-2}}$ = 3.33

The required 95% confidence interval is therefore

$23.04 \pm 1.96 \times 3.33 \times \sqrt{1 + \dfrac{1}{40} + \dfrac{40(14.5 - 820/40)^2}{40 \times 22,140 - 820^2}}$

= 23.04 ± 6.63 = 16.41 to 29.67

Question

19
We must perform a test of the null hypothesis that $a = 0$ (so that $y = bx$, a purely variable cost) against the alternative hypothesis that $a \neq 0$. We use t tables with $15 - 2 = 13$ degrees of freedom. The critical values are ± 2.16 (5% significance) and ± 3.01 (1% significance).

We first find the factor by which the standard error must be multiplied. This is

$$\sqrt{\frac{1}{n} + \frac{n\bar{x}^2}{n\Sigma x^2 - (\Sigma x)^2}}$$

Since $\bar{x} = 120/15 = 8$, this is:

$$\sqrt{\frac{1}{15} + \frac{15 \times 8^2}{15 \times 1{,}240 - 120^2}} = \sqrt{0.2952} = 0.54$$

$6 \times 0.54 = 3.24$

Test statistic $= (12-0)/3.24 = 3.70$

As this exceeds both 2.16 and 3.01, the hypothesis should be rejected at both significance levels. We conclude that there is a fixed component in costs.

20
We must first work out $\sqrt{\dfrac{n\Sigma x^2 - (\Sigma x)^2}{n}}$

This is $\sqrt{\dfrac{12 \times 650 - 78^2}{12}} = 11.96$

$t_{0.025}$ for $12-2 = 10$ degrees of freedom is (from tables) 2.23

So the 95% confidence interval is

$$b \pm \frac{2.23 \times 27}{11.96} = b \pm 5.03$$

21
We must perform a two-tailed test of the hypothesis that $b = 0$ against the alternative that $b \neq 0$. This is because if $b = 0$, the value of x in $y = a + bx$ will have no influence on the value of y.

Test statistic $= \dfrac{0.25 - 0}{2.5} \sqrt{\dfrac{20 \times 2{,}870 - 210^2}{20}} = 2.58$

202

Question

The critical values from t distribution tables, with 20 - 2 = 18 degrees of freedom, are 2.10 (5% significance) and 2.88 (1% significance).

As the value of the test statistic lies between these two values, we should reject at 5% significance but accept at 1% significance that the slope is not different from zero, ie that daily sales are uninfluenced by the number of newspaper advertisements on the same day.

22 The test statistic we require is:

$$\sqrt{\frac{r^2(n-2)}{1-r^2}} = \sqrt{\frac{(-0.6)^2(7-2)}{1-(-0.6)^2}} = \sqrt{1.8/0.64} = 1.68$$

The critical values from t distribution tables for 7 - 2 = 5 degrees of freedom are 2.57 (5% significance) and 4.03 (1% significance).

As 1.68 is less than either value, the hypothesis should be accepted at both levels of significance.

23 $y = ax^b$

$\log y = \log a + b \log x$

x	y	log x	log y
2	32	0.3010	1.5051
3	108	0.4771	2.0334

We can now form two simultaneous equations, in log a and b.

1.5051	= log a + 0.3010b	(1)
2.0334	= log a + 0.4771b	(2)

Subtracting the first equation from the second gives

0.5283 = 0.1761 b
b = 0.5283/0.1761 = 3

Substituting in equation (1) gives

1.5051 = log a + 0.3010 × 3
log a = 1.5051 - 0.3010 × 3 = 0.6021

From antilogarithm tables, a = 4

Question

24

If $y = ax^b$, $\log y = \log a + b \log x$

x	y	log x	log y	(log x)^2	log x log y
1	2	0	0.3010	0	0
2	5	0.3010	0.6990	0.0906	0.2104
3	15	0.4771	1.1761	0.2276	0.5611
4	22	0.6021	1.3424	0.3625	0.8083
		1.3802	3.5185	0.6807	1.5798

n = 4

$$b = \frac{4 \times 1.5798 - 1.3802 \times 3.5185}{4 \times 0.6807 - 1.3802^2} = \frac{1.4630}{0.8178} = 1.79$$

25

If $y = ab^x$, then $\log y = \log a + x \log b$

x	y	log y	x^2	x log y
1	2	0.3010	1	0.3010
2	2	0.3010	4	0.6020
3	2.7	0.4314	9	1.2942
4	3.3	0.5185	16	2.0740
10		1.5519	30	4.2712

$$\log b = \frac{4 \times 4.2712 - 10 \times 1.5519}{4 \times 30 - 10^2} = 0.078$$

$$\log a = \frac{1.5519}{4} - 0.078 \times \frac{10}{4} = 0.193$$

b = antilog 0.078 = 1.197

a = antilog 0.193 = 1.560

For x = 6, the predicted value of y is $1.56 \times 1.197^6 = 4.59 \simeq 4.6$

7: MARKING SCHEDULE

Question	Correct answer	Marks for the correct answer	Question	Correct answer	Marks for the correct answer
1	A	1	13	B	2
2	C	1	14	B	1
3	D	1	15	D	1
4	D	1	16	B	1
5	C	1	17	D	1
6	B	1	18	D	1
7	C	1	19	B	1
8	A	1	20	C	1
9	D	1	21	A	1
10	C	1	22	A	1
11	C	1	23	A	1
12	B	2			

YOUR MARKS

Total marks available 25   Your total mark

GUIDELINES - If your mark was:

0 - 7 Poor. The important techniques in this chapter are causing you difficulty. Go back to your study text and work through each relevant section carefully, before trying this chapter again.

8 - 12 Fair. Several of the questions have caught you out. If there are one or two particular techniques which have caused you problems go back to your study text and read through the relevant sections carefully.

13 - 18 Good. There may be a particular group of questions which has caused you difficulty. Check whether this is so, and refer to your study text if there is a clear gap in your knowledge.

19 - 25 Very good. You have a thorough understanding of time series analysis.

Question

COMMENTS

1 The four components are:

  The trend
  Cyclical variations
  Seasonal variations
  Random variations

2 The components are:

  A - trend
  B - random
  C - seasonal
  D - cyclical

3 Cyclical variations are of longer period than seasonal variations, but otherwise need not be of any particular length, nor need their magnitude be constant. They need not be connected with the trade cycle, even if the time series is economic in nature, and many time series are unconnected with economics.

4 Three-month moving average for April = average of March, April and May data

$$= \frac{700 + 900 + 1,250}{3} = 950 \text{ houses}$$

As we have taken an odd number of months, this average is centred on April without the need to take a further total.

5

Year	Quarter	Data	4-quarter total	8-quarter total
1	2	54		
	3	56		
			222	
	4	55		450
			228	
2	1	57		
	2	60		

The required total is 450

Question

6

Year	Quarter	Data	4-quarter total	8-quarter total	8-quarter average
1	3	45			
	4	35			
			146		
2	1	36		280	35
			134		
	2	30			
	3	33			

The required figure is 280/8 = 35. Note that the data we use are those for the quarter we are interested in and the two quarters either side of it. If there are n seasons in a time period, and n is even, we will go n/2 seasons either side of the season we are interested in. Here n = 4.

7

Week	Day	Data	7-day total	7-day average
1	Wednesday	19		
	Thursday	22		
	Friday	18		
	Saturday	16	127	18.1
	Sunday	15		
2	Monday	17		
	Tuesday	20		

The required figure is 127/7 = 18.1. If there are n seasons in a time period and n is odd, we will take data from (n-1)/2 seasons either side of the season we are interested in. Here n = 7.

8

For week 9, the trend value is 84 + 0.7 × 9 = 90.3.

The seasonal variation is actual - trend = 88.7 - 90.3 = -1.6, indicating that the value for week 9 is below what one might expect from the trend.

9

Month	Data	Three-month total	Three-month average (trend)	Seasonal variation
March	8			
April	13	37	12.33	+0.67
May	16			

Question

10

Day	Data	Four-day totals	Eight-day total	Eight-day average (trend)	Seasonal variation (data-trend)
4	2				
5	6				
		25			
6	8		54	6.75	+ 1.25
		29			
7	9				
8	6				

11

		Spring	Summer	Season Autumn	Winter	Total
	1			+ 5	+ 6	
Year	2	-6	-4	+ 4	+ 7	
	3	-5	-5			
		‾-11	‾-9	‾+ 9	‾+ 13	
Average		-5.50	-4.50	+ 4.50	+ 6.50	+ 1
Adjustment		-0.25	-0.25	-0.25	-0.25	-1
		‾-5.75	‾-4.75	‾+ 4.25	‾+ 6.25	‾0

The average seasonal adjustment for summer is -4.75.

12

Year	Quarter	Data	Four-quarter total	Eight-quarter total	Trend	Seasonal variation
1	1	32				
	2	36				
			136			
	3	40		276	34.5	+ 5.5
			140			
	4	28		283	35.375	-7.375
			143			
2	1	36		288	36	0
			145			
	2	39		294	36.75	+ 2.25
			149			
	3	42		307	38.375	+ 3.625
			158			
	4	32		325	40.625	-8.625
			167			
3	1	45		342	42.75	+ 2.25
			175			
	2	48		357	44.625	+ 3.375
			182			
	3	50				
	4	39				

Question

		1	2	Quarter 3	4	Total
	1			+ 5.5	- 7.375	
Year	2	0	+ 2.25	+ 3.625	- 8.625	
	3	+ 2.25	+ 3.375			
		+ 2.25	+ 5.625	+ 9.125	-16	
Average		+ 1.125	+ 2.8125	+ 4.5625	-8	+ 0.5
Adjustment		-0.125	-0.125	-0.125	-0.125	-0.5
		+ 1	+ 2.6875	+ 4.4375	-8.125	0

The average seasonal variation for quarter 2 is + 2.6875.

13

Year	Quarter	Data	Four-quarter total	Eight-quarter total	Trend	Seasonal variation %
1	1	157				
	2	140				
			517			
	3	100		1,047	130.875	76.4
			530			
	4	120		1,075	134.375	89.3
			545			
2	1	170		1,100	137.5	123.6
			555			
	2	155		1,120	140	110.7
			565			
	3	110				
	4	130				

The seasonal variation for quarter 4 is 89.3%. It is calculated as

$$\frac{\text{Actual}}{\text{Trend}} \times 100\% = \frac{120}{134.375} \times 100\% = 89.3\%$$

14

The seasonal variations are found as $\frac{\text{Actual}}{\text{Trend}} \times 100\%$

		1	2	Day 3	4	5	Total
	1			93.1	111.1	144.5	
Week	2	65.5	79.3	97.4	120.0	135.1	
	3	62.9	90.2	103.3			
		128.4	169.5	293.8	231.1	279.6	
Average		64.2	84.8	97.9	115.6	139.8	502.3
		(0.5)	(0.5)	(0.5)	(0.4)	(0.4)	(2.3)
		63.7	84.3	97.4	115.2	139.4	500.0

The average seasonal variation for day 4 is 115.2%.

209

Question

15 The residual is the difference between the actual data and the figure predicted by the time series analysis. It is the unexplained element in the actual figure.

Actual		4,000
Trend (3,150 + 72 × 12)	4,014	
Seasonal variation	(47)	
		(3,967)
Residual		33

16 On the additive model,

    Trend + Seasonal variation = Actual

so   Trend = Actual - Seasonal variation

Seasonally adjusted (deseasonalised) data are meant to show the trend, so we must deduct positive seasonal variations from the data, and add negative ones.

	July	August
Actual	2,030,500	2,027,000
Adjustment	20,000	(40,000)
Deseasonalised	2,050,500	1,987,000

17 Under the multiplicative model, Actual = Trend × Seasonal variation.

Deseasonalised data are trend figures, so the actual sales figures are as follows.

Spring: £32,567 × 0.92 = £29,962

Summer: £44,098 × 1.15 = £50,713

18

Predicted trend 37 + 3 × 21	100
Seasonal variation	5
Prediction	105

19 The trend figures increased by 231 - 189 = 42 over the seven quarters from year 1, quarter 3 to year 3, quarter 2. This represents an average of 42/7 = 6 per quarter.

Trend for year 3, quarter 2	231
Expected increase in trend 6 × 5	30
Predicted trend for year 4, quarter 3	261
Seasonal variation	(8)
Predicted actual figure for year 4, quarter 3	253

Question

20

Trend for January 19X9	452
Increase to May 19X9: 4 × 16	64
Trend for May 19X9	$\overline{516}$

Predicted value for May 19X9
= Trend × Seasonal variation
= 516 × 103% = 531

21

The trend has fallen by 1,475 - 1,190 = 285 over the 15 quarters from year 1, quarter 3 to year 5, quarter 2. This is an average fall of 19 per quarter.

Trend for year 5, quarter 2	1,190
Fall to year 6, quarter 1: 3 × 19	(57)
Trend value for year 6, quarter 1	$\overline{1,133}$

Predicted value for year 6, quarter 1
= Trend × Seasonal variation
= 1,133 × 95% = 1,076

22

The exponential smoothing formula is

$$\text{Forecast}_{t+1} = \text{Forecast}_t + \text{Smoothing constant (Actual}_t - \text{Forecast}_t)$$

We therefore have:

Forecast absentees for Thursday = 470 + 0.3 (520 - 470) = 485.

23

The exponential smoothing formula is

$$\text{Forecast}_{t+1} = \text{Forecast}_t + \text{Smoothing constant (Actual}_t - \text{Forecast}_t)$$

We therefore have
  5 = 4 + Smoothing constant (8 - 4)
  1 = 4 × Smoothing constant

Smoothing constant = 1/4 = 0.25.

8: MARKING SCHEDULE

Question	Correct answer	Marks for the correct answer	Question	Correct answer	Marks for the correct answer
1	A	1	14	B	2
2	B	1	15	C	1
3	D	1	16	A	1
4	D	1	17	D	2
5	C	1	18	D	1
6	C	1	19	D	1
7	D	1	20	A	1
8	D	2	21	D	1
9	A	2	22	B	1
10	D	1	23	A	1
11	B	1	24	C	1
12	C	1	25	D	1
13	A	2			

YOUR MARKS

Total marks available   30   Your total mark

GUIDELINES - If your mark was:

0 - 9
Poor. The important techniques in this chapter are causing you difficulty. Go back to your study text and work through each relevant section carefully, before trying this chapter again.

10 - 15
Fair. Several of the questions have caught you out. If there are one or two particular techniques which have caused you problems go back to your study text and read through the relevant sections carefully.

16 - 23
Good. There may be a particular group of questions which has caused you difficulty. Check whether this is so, and refer to your study text if there is a clear gap in your knowledge.

24 - 30
Very good. You have a thorough understanding of linear programming.

Question

COMMENTS

1

The total labour usage per week in hours is 0.5x + 2y, since each unit of X uses 30 minutes (half an hour) of labour and each unit of Y uses 2 hours of labour. This must not exceed 5,000 hours, so the labour constraint is $0.5x + 2y \leqslant 5,000$.

The requirement to produce at least 50 units of X each week gives $x \geqslant 50$.

The requirement to produce at least twice as many units of Y as of X each week gives $y \geqslant 2x$.

2

The businessman has $6 \times 5 = 30$ hours available. The total time taken in hours is 2x + y. The time constraint is therefore $2x + y \leqslant 30$.

The requirement that at least three building societies are visited for every two banks gives

$$\tfrac{1}{3} y \geqslant \tfrac{1}{2} x, \text{ or } 2y \geqslant 3x.$$

The constraint on the number of banks visited is $x \geqslant 2$.

3

The minimum weight of 50kg of P per hectare gives $p \geqslant 50$.

The requirement that the weight of Q per hectare be between two and five times the weight of P per hectare gives

$$q \geqslant 2p$$
$$q \leqslant 5p.$$

The maximum total weight of 500 kg per hectare gives $p + q \leqslant 500$.

4

For product F, costs are 60% of selling price, so profit must be 40% of selling price. Profit per unit of F = £20 × 40% = £8.

For product G, profit is 40% of cost. Profit per unit of G = £15 × 40% = £6.

The objective is therefore: maximise 8f + 6g.

5

The expected value of order from a visit to a small company is £500 × 60% = £300. The expected value of order from a visit to a large company is £3,000 × (100 - 70)% = £3,000 × 30% = £900.

The objective is therefore to maximise 300s + 900l.

Question

6

The expected cost of a call in peak hours is 40% × £1 + 60% × £1.50 = £1.30 = 130p. The expected cost of a call at other times is 30% × 80p + 50% × 90p + 20% × £1 = 89p. The objective is therefore: Minimise 130x + 89y.

7

A sketch graph of the feasible region and a trial objective (3x + y = 450) is as follows:

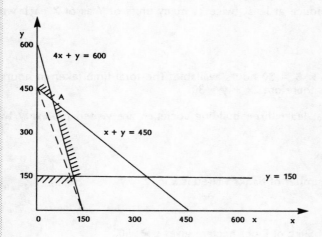

The optimum is at point A, the intersection of x + y = 450 and 4x + y = 600.

At this point,

$$4x + y = 600 \qquad (1)$$
$$x + y = 450 \qquad (2)$$
$$3x = 150 \qquad ((1) - (2))$$
$$x = 50$$

Substituting in (2)
$$50 + y = 450$$
$$y = 400$$

The value of the objective function is then 3 × 50 + 400 = 550.

8

We must first formulate the constraints and the objective function, then sketch a graph and identify the optimum point, then work out the total contribution at that point.

Let r = number of records made each day
     c = number of CDs made each day

The constraints are as follows.
Labour: r + 2c ⩽ 4,000
Machine time: 2r + 0.4c ⩽ 5,000
Administration time: r + c ⩽ 3,000

Question

The objective is to maximise $2r + 6c$

A sketch graph follows. A trial objective of $2r + 6c = 6,000$ has been included.

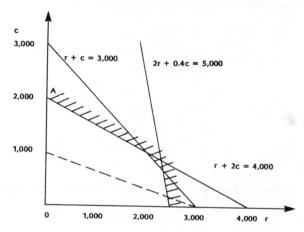

The optimum is at point A, where $r = 0$ and $c = 2,000$. The maximum daily contribution is therefore $0 \times £2 + 2,000 \times £6 = £12,000$.

9

We must formulate the constraints and the objective function, draw a sketch graph, identify the optimum point, and find the total cost at this point.

Let   l = number of large posters
      s = number of small posters.

The constraints are:

$$l \geqslant 0.5s$$
$$l \geqslant 50$$
$$l+s \geqslant 100$$
$$s \leqslant 150$$

The objective is to minimise $4l + 2s$.

A sketch graph follows. A trial objective ($4l + 2s = 400$) has been included.

Question

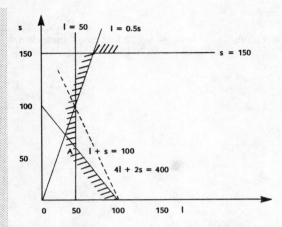

The optimum is at point A, at the intersection of the lines $l = 50$ and $l + s = 100$.

At this point,

$$l = 50$$
$$l + s = 100$$
$$50 + s = 100$$
$$s = 50$$

The cost at this point, which is the minimum total cost, is $50 \times £4 + 50 \times £2 = £300$.

10 If weekly purchases of H can be reduced by one unit, weekly purchases of G can be reduced by two units (because purchases of G must be at least twice those of H).

The saving to be made, and hence the maximum payment for a one unit reduction in the contractual obligation, is therefore $1 \times £8 + 2 \times £3 = £14$.

11 We must find the contribution at the actual optimum point and the contribution which would be obtainable, were one extra unit of electricity available. The difference between the two contributions is the dual price per unit of electricity.

At the actual optimum point,

Electricity	$2x + 5y = 10,000$	(1)
Machine time	$x + 2y = 4,300$	(2)
Multiply equation (2) by 2	$2x + 4y = 8,600$	(3)
Subtract equation (3) from equation (1)	$y = 1,400$	
Substitute in equation (2)	$x + 2,800 = 4,300$	
	$x = 1,500$	

At $x = 1,500$, $y = 1,400$, the total contribution is
$£2 \times 1,500 + £4.5 \times 1,400 = £9,300$.

Question

If one more unit of electricity were available, the new optimum would be at:

Electricity	$2x + 5y = 10,001$	(1)
Machine time	$x + 2y = 4,300$	(2)
Multiply equation (2) by 2	$2x + 4y = 8,600$	(3)
Subtract equation (3) from equation (1)	$y = 1,401$	
Substitute in equation (2)	$x + 2,802 = 4,300$	
	$x = 1,498$	

At $x = 1,498$, $y = 1,401$, the total contribution is £2 × 1,498 + £4.50 × 1,401 = £9,300.50

The dual price per unit of electricity is therefore £9,300.50 - £9,300 = £0.50.

12 We must first work out the number of hours of direct labour per unit of K, so we can find the normal hourly labour rate. The sum of this normal rate and the dual price per hour (£5.30) will be the maximum which should be paid per extra hour.

The labour constraint must be $2j + 3k \leqslant$ hours available, with j denoting the number of units of J per time period and k denoting the number of units of K per time period. This is so that the gradient on a graph would be -2/3.

Thus each unit of K takes 3 hours, and the normal hourly rate is £10.50/3 = £3.50.

The maximum hourly rate that should be paid for extra direct labour is therefore £3.50 + £5.30 = £8.80.

13 We must first work out the gradients of the constraints and of the objective function.

$x + 2y = 10,000$: gradient = -1/2 = -0.5

$3x + y = 18,000$: gradient = -3/1 = -3

$5x + 3y =$ contribution: gradient = -5/3 = -1.6667

Because the gradient of the objective function (-1.6667) lies between the gradients of the constraints (-0.5 and -3), the optimum is at the intersection of these constraints. There will be a shift to a new optimum when the contribution from a product changes to such an extent that the gradient of the contribution line reaches -0.5 or -3.

Question

Let c = contribution per unit of X. Then the contribution function is cx + 3y, which has a gradient of -c/3.

As the contribution from X increases, this gradient will become more negative, so we are looking for the point where

$$\frac{-c}{3} = -3$$

$$-c = -9$$
$$c = 9$$

Thus if the contribution per unit of X rises by £4 to £9, the optimum production mix will change.

14

If the price per unit of W is p, the objective is to minimise 17v + pw, which has a gradient of -17/p.

We will get a change in the optimum point if this gradient comes to equal either -0.6 or -1.2. For the first option,

$$\frac{-17}{p} = 0.6$$

$$p = \frac{-17}{-0.6} = 28.33$$

This represents a rise of £3.33, or $\frac{3.33}{25} \times 100\% = 13.3\%$

For the second option,

$$\frac{-17}{p} = -1.2$$

$$p = \frac{-17}{-1.2} = 14.16$$

This represents a fall of £10.83, or $\frac{10.83}{25} \times 100\% = 43.3\%$

15

To obtain the dual problem:

(i)   change 'maximise' to 'minimise' or vice versa;
(ii)   change '≤' to '≥' or vice versa in the constraints (except the non-negativity constraints);
(iii) change x and y to p and q (any letters different from x and y will do);
(iv)   Use 14 and 9 (from the objective) in the constraints and 10,000 and 12,000 (from the constraints) in the objective;

Question

(v) get values for the coefficients of p and q in the first constraint from the coefficients of x in the two primal problem constraints, and for the coefficients of p and q in the second constraint from the coefficients of y.

16 The value of p at the optimum in the dual problem will be the dual price per unit of the corresponding constraint in the original (primal) problem.

A sketch graph for the dual problem follows. A trial objective of 200p + 250q = 2,000 has been included.

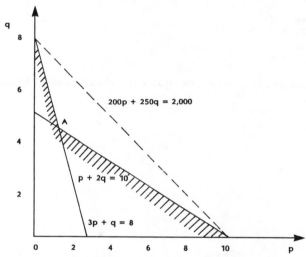

The optimum is at point A. At that point

3p + q = 8	(1)
p + 2q = 10	(2)

Multiply equation (1) by 2
Subtract equation (2) from equation (3)

$$6p + 2q = 16 \quad (3)$$
$$5p = 6$$
$$p = 1.2$$

The dual price per litre of oil is therefore £1.20.

Question

17 We will formulate the dual problem (which will have two variables and three constraints), and find the optimum value of the variable corresponding to the protein constraint in the primal problem.

Let x = dual problem variable corresponding to protein constraint
    y = dual problem variable corresponding to carbohydrate constraint

The dual problem is

Maximise $50x + 70y$

Subject to $0.2x + 0.4y \leqslant 1$
             $0.3x + 0.2y \leqslant 1$
             $0.1x + 0.5y \leqslant 1$
                  $x, y \geqslant 0$

A sketch graph follows. A trial objective of $50x + 70y = 140$ has been included.

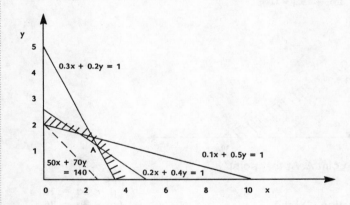

The optimum is at point A.

At this point,

$$0.3x + 0.2y = 1 \qquad (1)$$
$$0.2x + 0.4y = 1 \qquad (2)$$

Multiply equation (1) by 2 $0.6x + 0.4y = 2 \qquad (3)$
Subtract equation (2) from equation (3) $0.4x = 1$
                                      $x = 2.5$

The dual price of the protein constraint is therefore 2.5g. So for each 1g relaxation in the protein constraint, the total weight of the bar can be reduced by 2.5g.

Question

18 Each variable (x, y, z) in the primal problem will have a corresponding constraint in the dual problem. At least one of those constraints will not pass through the optimum point in the dual problem, and will therefore have a dual price of zero. The corresponding variable(s) will have a value of zero at the optimum point in the primal problem.

Let p and q be the dual problem variables corresponding to the first and second constraints respectively of the primal problem.

The dual problem is:

$$\text{Minimise} \quad 1{,}200 + 800q$$

$$\begin{array}{rl}
\text{Subject to} \quad & 2p + q \geqslant 3 \\
& 2p + 4q \geqslant 4 \\
& 3p + q \geqslant 1 \\
& p,q \geqslant 0
\end{array}$$

The first constraint, $2p + q \geqslant 3$, corresponds to x, the second to y, and the third to z.

A graph of the dual problem is as follows. A trial objective of $1{,}200p + 800q = 2{,}400$ has been included.

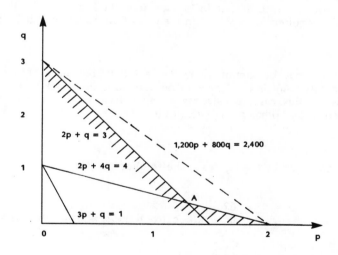

The optimum lies at point A, at the intersection of $2p + 4q = 4$ and $2p + q = 3$. The constraint $3p + q \geqslant 1$ is clearly non-critical, so at the optimum in the primal problem z = 0. The other two constraints are critical, so x and y will not equal zero.

Question

19
The simplex method can deal with any number of variables and any number of constraints, so statement 1 is false. There is a slack variable or a surplus variable corresponding to each constraint, so statement 3 is true. In the final solution, the values of slack variables indicate the dual prices of the corresponding constraints. These values will only be zero where the constraints are not critical, so statement 2 is false.

20
The numbers *above* the solution row in the columns corresponding to the variables in the original problem (x, y and z) and in the solution column are all taken directly from the constraints. Because z does not feature in the second constraint, 0 is put in the second row in the column for z.

The numbers in the solution row in the columns for x, y and z are the negatives of the corresponding coefficients in the objective function. All other numbers in the solution row are zero. The remaining numbers are in a square formed by the rows and columns corresponding to the slack variables, a and b. This square has ones on the diagonal from top left to bottom right and zeros everywhere else.

21
The steps are performed in the order 3, 1, 2. The variable to be introduced is identified by its column, the row to introduce it in is then identified, and finally the variable's column is got into the required form, with 1 in the row of introduction and 0 elsewhere.

22
Non-critical constraints may be identified by the fact that they have zero dual prices. The dual price for a constraint is the figure in the corresponding slack variable's column in the solution row. In this case, constraints a and c have dual prices of 3 and 0.25 respectively, while constraint b has a dual price of 0.

23
The units of output are given by the figures in the solution column.

Variable	kg	
x	62.5	
y	0	(because there is no row labelled 'y')
z	37.5	
	100.0	

Question

24 The effects of making available an extra unit of a resource are shown by the figures in the column of the corresponding slack variable. -0.25 in the row labelled 'x' shows that there would be a fall in the output per week of x of 0.25kg. +0.25 in the row labelled 'z' indicates the opposite: output per week of z would rise by 0.25 kg. +0.25 in the row labelled 'b' indicates a rise in the unused units of the resource which is the subject of constraint b. This resource has a dual price of 0 (see the comment on question 22), so this resource is already not fully used.

Although not required for this question, you might like to note that if one extra unit of the resource which is the subject of constraint c became available, weekly contribution would rise from 337.50 to 337.50 + 0.25 = 337.75. The dual price of this resource is the 0.25 in the solution row in the column labelled 'c'.

25 Constraint c will cease to be critical when 62.5/0.25 = 250 extra units become available. Further extra units will then have no influence on the optimum.

(We take, for each row where there is a negative figure in c's column,

$$\frac{\text{value in solution}}{\text{value in constraint column}} \quad \text{and take the lowest figure found in this way.)}$$

9: MARKING SCHEDULE

Question	Correct answer	Marks for the correct answer	Question	Correct answer	Marks for the correct answer
1	A	1	12	C	1
2	A	1	13	C	1
3	B	1	14	B	1
4	C	1	15	C	1
5	D	1	16	D	1
6	B	1	17	A	1
7	B	1	18	B	1
8	B	1	19	B	1
9	B	1	20	B	1
10	D	1	21	C	1
11	B	1			

YOUR MARKS

Total marks available   21   Your total mark

GUIDELINES - If your mark was:

0 - 5
Poor. The important techniques in this chapter are causing you difficulty. Go back to your study text and work through each relevant section carefully, before trying this chapter again.

6 - 10
Fair. Several of the questions have caught you out. If there are one or two particular techniques which have caused you problems go back to your study text and read through the relevant sections carefully.

11 - 16
Good. There may be a particular group of questions which has caused you difficulty. Check whether this is so, and refer to your study text if there is a clear gap in your knowledge.

17 - 21
Very good. You have a thorough understanding of the principles of transportation and assignment.

Question

COMMENTS

1

Note that once route JQ is used, no more units can be allocated to column Q, and once route KP is used, no more units can be allocated to row K.

2

Factory	Shop	Units	Unit cost	Total cost
			£	£
J	Q	300	1	300
J	R	200	5	1,000
K	P	400	3	1,200
L	P	400	4	1,600
L	R	200	5	1,000
M	R	500	7	3,500
				8,600

3 - 5

The shadow despatch cost of the first factory (F) is set to 0, and the other costs are worked out in the following order (taking all *used* routes) (* denotes a balancing figure).

Factory	Depot	Shadow costs Despatch	Receipt	Cost of route
		£	£	£
F	W	0	2 *	2
F	X	0	3 *	3
G	X	2 *	3	5
G	Y	2	2 *	4
H	Y	1 *	2	3
H	Z	1	1 *	2

The shadow despatch cost for factory H is therefore £1, and the shadow receipt cost for depot X is £3.

The cost of not using an unused route is the sum of the shadow despatch cost for its factory and the shadow receipt cost for its depot. Thus the cost of not using the route from G to Z is £2 + £1 = £3.

The shadow cost of an unused route is the cost of using the route less the cost of not using it. The shadow cost of the route from G to Z is therefore £5 - £3 = £2. This means that route GZ should not be used, as using it would increase costs.

Question

6

The shadow cost of an unused route is the cost of using it minus the cost of not using it. If the latter cost exceeds the former, then:

(i)   the shadow cost will be negative; and

(ii) it would be cheaper to use the route than to leave it unused.

(ii) shows that an optimum has not been reached. Thus it is only when there are no negative shadow costs that an optimum has been reached.

7

We want to select the route which will lead to the greatest cost saving. The shadow cost of an unused route is the cost of using it less the cost of not using it. A high negative shadow cost indicates a low cost of using a route compared to the cost of not using it, so that route is a good one to use. We therefore select the route with the highest negative shadow cost, in this case that from factory B to depot 1 (shadow cost = -£5).

8 - 11

Shadow despatch and receipt costs must be worked out, starting with a shadow despatch cost of 0 for factory P and then finding costs as follows (* denotes a balancing figure).

Factory	Depot	Shadow costs		Cost of route
		Despatch	Receipt	
P	X	0	8 *	8
Q	X	-6 *	8	2
Q	Y	-6	7 *	1
Q	Z	-6	10 *	4
R	Z	-7 *	10	3

The shadow costs of the unused routes are therefore as follows:

Route	Cost of using	Cost of not using	Shadow cost
	£	£	£
PY	7	7	0
PZ	5	10	-5
RX	7	1	6
RY	5	0	5

Route PZ has the highest negative shadow cost (as it happens, the only negative shadow cost), so it is to be introduced.

We now apply the stepping stone procedure. We look for a cycle of cells, such that we can add and subtract units without changing the row and column totals. The only other occupied cell in the same row as PZ is PX; the only other occupied cell in the same column as cell PX is cell QX; from cell QX we can to go cell QZ, and we are then back in the same column as cell PZ.

Question

The smallest quantity in any cell to lose units is 100, so that amount is subtracted from cells PX and QZ and added to cells PZ and QX. The feasible solution is therefore as follows (shadow despatch and receipt costs, and the shadow costs of unused routes, have been recomputed and put in on the solution).

Factories \ Depots	X	8	Y	7	Z	5	Available
P	0	200		0	100		300
Q	-6	200	150			5	350
R	-2		1	0	200		200
Required		400	150		300		850

As there are no unused routes with negative shadow prices, an optimum has been reached. The most expensive used route is PX, costing £8 a unit. This is the most expensive route of all, but it has to be used to allow use of other very cheap routes. The cost is:

Factory	Depot	Units	Unit cost £	Total cost £
P	X	200	8	1,600
P	Z	100	5	500
Q	X	200	2	400
Q	Y	150	1	150
R	Z	200	3	600
				3,250

12 Degeneracy is a condition which prevents the calculation of all the shadow despatch and receipt costs, so statement 2 is true. It occurs when fewer than m + n - 1 routes are used, so statement 1 is false. The reason why we need this number of used routes is that we have m + n - 1 shadow despatch and receipt costs to find (the first despatch cost is set at 0), so we need this many computations to find these costs as balancing figures.

The remedy is to treat an unused route as used, but so as not to make any change to allocations to routes in use, the route chosen is given an allocation of 0 units. Thus statement 3 is true and statement 4 is false.

Question

13

The term 'impossible route' is applied where there is no route between a particular factory and a particular depot, so statement 1 is true. The non-availability of a route can be dealt with by assigning a very high cost, so that the route is never used in the solution because it always has a positive shadow price, so statement 2 is true. The problem cannot be dealt with by removing a row and a column, as the factory concerned must be included to supply other depots and the depot concerned must be included to receive supplies from other factories, so statement 3 is false.

14

Dummy factories and depots are used when supply and demand are unequal. Dummy factories notionally produce units to make up a shortfall in supply (their 'output' represents the shortfall), and dummy depots absorb excess supply (their 'demand' represents units left at the factories or not produced at all). Statement 1 is therefore true of dummy factories, but not of dummy depots. Statement 3 is false, because dummy factories and dummy depots deal with opposite imbalances of supply and demand and so are not both used in the same problem.

Statement 2 is true, because units left at the factories which produce them (or not produced at all) do not incur any transport costs.

15

A profit maximisation problem is converted into a cost minimisation problem by taking as the 'cost' of each combination of machine and product the following:

| Highest profit on any | - | Profit on this machine/ |
| machine/product pair | | product pair |

Highly profitable choices will thus have low 'costs', and minimising total 'costs' will maximise profits.

The initial solution is as follows. The figures in the top left of the cells are the 'costs' (£12 - profit of that combination, as £12 is the maximum profit, from making product P on machine L), and the figures in the left hand column and the top row are the shadow despatch and receipt costs, computed exactly as for any other transportation problem.

Question

Machine \ Product	P -2	Q 6	R 5	Available
J (0)	4	6 — 20	5 — 30	50
K (-3)	2	3 — 25	10	25
L (2)	0 — 20	8 — 5	7	25
Required	20	50	30	100

The cost of using machine J to make product P is £4. The cost of not using it is 0-2 = - £2. The shadow cost is therefore £4 - -£2 = £6.

16 The steps in the Vogel approximation method are as follows.

(i) For each row and column, compute the penalty, equal to the difference between the lowest and the second lowest costs in the row or column, ignoring any dummy routes.

(ii) Select the row or column with the highest penalty, and allocate as many units as possible to the cheapest route in that row or column. (If there is a tie for highest penalty, one of the two or more rows or columns may be chosen arbitrarily.)

(iii) Repeat steps (i) and (ii), but ignore in computing penalties any routes no longer available because the units for the relevant row or column have all been allocated already.

(iv) Once steps (i) and (ii) have been repeated as often as possible, fill in the rest of the table, and check to see whether an optimum solution has been found. If it has not been the least cost method should be applied.

In this example, the construction of the solution proceeds as follows. At each stage, the selected row or column is marked with an asterisk. Route costs to be considered in finding penalties are entered in the top left corners of cells.

Question

Depots / Factories	X	Y	Z	Available	Row penalty
P	3	4	6	250	1
Q	2 _400_	8	5	400	3*
R	1	5	3	300	2
Required	400	350	200	950	
Column penalty	1	1	2		

Depots / Factories	X	Y	Z	Available	Row penalty
P		4	6	250	2
Q	400			400	
R		5	3 _200_	300	2
Required	400	350	200	950	
Column penalty		1	3*		

We can see that 200 units are allocated to the route from factory R to depot Z.
The remaining allocations must then be 250 to PY and 100 to RY, and this solution
would then be tested for optimality.

Question

17 The cost of a route from a factory to a shop is the lower of the costs of the two routes:

(i)   Factory-warehouse S - shop
(ii)   Factory-warehouse T - shop

We take the lower cost because we will always choose to take the cheaper of the two routes. We can never be forced to use the more expensive route, because the warehouses have unlimited capacity. For example, the cost of sending one unit from factory P to shop X is the lower of

(i)   3 + 2 = 5 (via S)
(ii)   2 + 1 = 3 (via T).
ie   £3

18 The assignment method is used when entities of one sort (people, machines etc) are to be paired with entities of another sort (tasks, products, cars etc). It deals only with *assigning* items from one list to items from another, not with allocating numbers of units (for example, units of output to routes). Thus A cannot be dealt with. C cannot be dealt with because it is possible for one machine to be given more than one product. D is ruled out because the method requires something quantifiable, for example number of minutes to minimise. B is the right answer. The fact that there are six people and five tasks does not matter, because a dummy task can be introduced.

19 An optimal solution can be identified by using horizontal and vertical lines to cover all the zeros in the solution. In an $n \times n$ (in this case, 4×4) problem, an optimal solution will be one where n lines are needed to cover all the zeros. Solution B is the only one which satisfies this criterion, as in the others three lines can cover all the zeros.

20 This is an assignment problem. The first step is to reduce each time figure by the lowest time figure in the same row:

	T	U	V	W
P	0	1	2	3
Q	4	3	2	0
R	2	0	1	0
S	2	3	1	0

Question

The second step is to reduce each time figure by the lowest time figure in the same column:

	T	U	V	W
P	0	1	1	3
Q	4	3	1	0
R	2	0	0	0
S	2	3	0	0

As it would not be possible to cover all the zeros with fewer than four horizontal and vertical lines, an optimum has been found. The assignments are indicated by the zeros, as follows:

T will do P;
U will do R;
V will do S;
W will do Q.

Total time = 3 + 8 + 5 + 4 = 20 hours

21

We must add a dummy programmer to give a square table. As each row already has a zero (in the dummy column), we first reduce the figures in each column by the smallest figure in the column.

	P	Q	R	Dummy
A	1	1	2	0
B	2	0	3	0
C	2	1	2	0
D	0	2	0	0

The zeros could be covered with three lines, as shown, so we must perform the following extra steps:

(i)   reduce each uncrossed amount by the smallest uncrossed amount (ie 1);

(ii)   add this amount (1) to every amount crossed by two lines.

Question

	P	Q	R	Dummy
A	0	0	1	0
B	2	0	3	1
C	1	0	1	0
D	0	2	0	1

We have now found an optimum, as the zeros cannot be covered with fewer than four lines. (If an optimum had not been found, we would repeat the usual steps: reduce each row by its smallest element, etc).

R will write D
P will write A
Dummy will write C (ie this program will not be written)
Q will write B

10: MARKING SCHEDULE

Question	Correct answer	Marks for the correct answer	Question	Correct answer	Marks for the correct answer
1	B	1	13	A	1
2	A	1	14	B	1
3	B	1	15	C	2
4	D	1	16	C	2
5	C	1	17	A	2
6	D	2	18	C	2
7	D	2	19	B	2
8	D	1	20	D	2
9	C	1	21	A	1
10	B	1	22	B	1
11	C	1	23	D	1
12	C	2			

YOUR MARKS

Total marks available   **32**   Your total mark

GUIDELINES - If your mark was:

0 - 8
Poor. The important techniques in this chapter are causing you difficulty. Go back to your study text and work through each relevant section carefully, before trying this chapter again.

9 - 16
Fair. Several of the questions have caught you out. If there are one or two particular techniques which have caused you problems go back to your study text and read through the relevant sections carefully.

17 - 24
Good. There may be a particular group of questions which has caused you difficulty. Check whether this is so, and refer to your study text if there is a clear gap in your knowledge.

25 - 32
Very good. You have a thorough understanding of networks.

Question

COMMENTS

1 V and W may be done together, and then all of X, Y and Z may be done together once V and W have been completed. Note the use of dummy activities, to avoid two activities running between the same two nodes.

2 Note that we need a dummy activity, because activity S must be preceded by both activity Q and activity R, while activity T need only be preceded by activity Q.

3 Activity O cannot be started until the second (right hand) dummy activity has been completed. That dummy activity cannot be started until activity J has been completed. Activity J cannot be started until activity H has been completed.

4 I must be preceded by both F and H (and also by E, but we do not need to state that because H must be preceded by E).

The effect of the dummy activity is to require K to be preceded by G as well as by I.

5 The critical path is the path with the longest total duration, so statement 1 is true and statement 2 is false. Statement 3 is false: the critical path could even comprise just one activity, if its duration was great enough. Statement 4 is true: if a project is to be completed in minimum total time, there must be no delay in starting and completing any activities on the critical path.

6 The network is as follows:

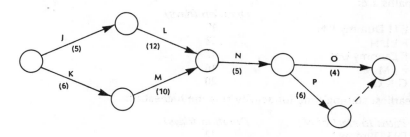

Question

The paths are:

	Duration (days)
J L N O	26
J L N P	28
K M N O	25
K M N P	27

The path with the longest duration, the critical path, is J L N P.

7

The network is as follows:

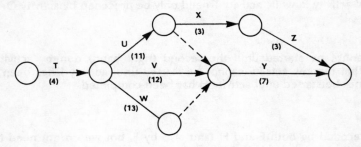

The paths are:

	Duration (days)
T U X Z	21
T U Dummy Y	22
T V Y	23
T W Dummy Y	24

The path with the longest duration, the critical path, is T W Dummy Y. The whole project cannot be completed in under 24 days.

8 - 11

The paths are:

	Duration (days)
E H Dummy L N	19
E I L N	18
F Dummy L N	17
F J M N	16
G K O	20

The earliest starting time for activity N is the highest of:

Paths to start of N	Duration (days)
E H Dummy L	13
E I L	12
F Dummy L	11
F J M	10

ie day 13

Question

The critical path is G K O, with duration 20 days. In order to complete the whole project within 20 days, activity O must be started by day 20 - 3 = 17.

Activity L could be finished by day 4 + 3 + 6 = 13 at the earliest.

In order to complete the whole project within 20 days, activity N must be started by day 20 - 6 = 14, so activity L must be started by day 14 - 6 = 8, and activity J by day 14 - 3 - 2 = 9. Activity F must therefore be finished by day 8 at the latest, and this is the latest finishing time required.

12 - 14

Total float of activity U

= latest finishing time - earliest starting time - duration
= 24 - 16 - 3 = 5 days

Activity U could be delayed by up to 5 days, but if it is, scope to delay other activities may be lost.

Free float of activity R

= earliest finishing time - earliest starting time - duration
= 15 - 9 - 6 = 0 days

Activity R may not be delayed at all without reducing the scope to delay later activities.

Independent float of activity W

= earliest finishing time - latest starting time - duration
= 26 - 12 - 5 = 9 days.

Activity W may be delayed by up to 9 days, without affecting scope to delay any other activities.

15 - 16

The network is as follows:

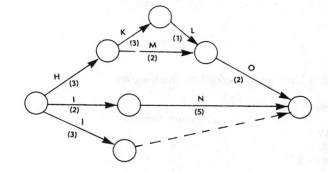

Question

Crash durations have been marked on the diagram.

The paths are:

	Duration (weeks)
H K L O	9
H M O	7
I N	7
J Dummy	

The minimum duration is therefore 9 weeks. This duration may be achieved even if activity M is extended to 4 weeks (so H M O = 9 weeks), activity I is extended to 4 weeks (so I N = 9 weeks; the savings per week from extending I are £40, and from extending N only £30), and activity J is extended to 4 weeks.

	£	£
Activities at crash durations		1,550
Savings from extending durations:		
M (£50 × 2)	100	
I (£40 × 2)	80	
J	10	
		(190)
		1,360
Overheads (£300 × 9)		2,700
Total cost		4,060

17 - 18

The network is as follows:

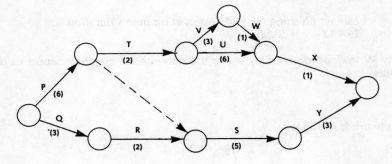

Crash durations have been marked on the diagram.

The paths are:

	Duration (weeks)
P T V W X	13
P T U X	15
P Dummy S Y	14
Q R S Y	13

Question

Activity durations should be increased to save money. Money will be saved if the total project duration is increased, so long as the saving from extending activities exceeds the additional overheads incurred (£80 per week).

Firstly, the non-critical paths should have their durations increased to 15 weeks, as follows:

P T V W X: Extend V to 4 weeks, saving £20, and W to 2 weeks, saving £20.
P Dummy S Y: Extend S to 6 weeks, saving £45.
Q R S Y: Cannot extend Q or R, and cannot extend S or Y because P Dummy S Y already lasts 15 weeks.

Possible further extensions, increasing the total duration, are:

Extend P to 7 weeks, saving £20 but permitting an extension of S to 7 weeks, saving another £45.

Extend U to 7 weeks, saving £30 but permitting an extension of S to 7 weeks, saving another £45.

Extend X to 2 weeks, saving £50 but permitting an extension of S to 7 weeks, saving another £45.

The best option is to extend X and S by a week each, saving £50 + £45 = £95 at an extra overhead cost of £80.

The best option after doing that is to extend U and Y by a week each, saving £30 + £35 = £65 at an extra overhead cost of £80. This would increase total costs, so should not be done.

	£	£
Cost of activities at crash times		1,285
Savings from extending activities:		
V	20	
W	20	
S (£45 × 2)	90	
X	50	
		(180)
		1,105
Overheads £80 × 16		1,280
Minimum total cost		2,385

The minimum time to achieve this minimum cost is 16 weeks.

Question

19 The network is as follows:

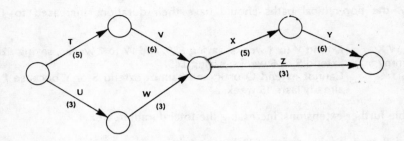

Activities U and W can both be performed at the same time as activity V, thus avoiding any overlap with activity T which uses 8 staff as against V's 6. The peak requirement in the first half of the network is then 6 + 7 = 13 staff.

Activity Z should be performed concurrently with activity X rather than with activity Y giving a peak requirement of 6 + 8 = 14 staff. The peak requirement over the whole project is therefore 14 staff.

20 - 21 The network is as follows:

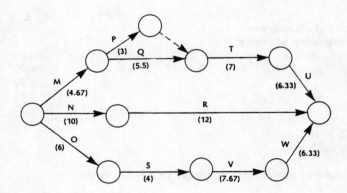

The expected durations have been marked on the network. They have been calculated as

$$\frac{\text{optimistic} + 4 \times \text{most likely} + \text{pessimistic}}{6}$$

Question

The expected duration of the path MQTU is $4.67 + 5.5 + 7 + 6.33 = 23.5$ days

The expected durations of the other paths are:

M P T U	21 days
N R	22 days
O S V W	24 days

On this basis, the critical path is O S V W. The standard deviations of the activities on this path are estimated as:

$$\frac{\text{pessimistic - optimistic}}{6}$$

Activity	Standard deviation	Variance
O	0	0
S	0.333	0.111
V	0.667	0.444
W	1	1
Variance of duration of critical path		$\overline{1.555}$

Standard deviation of duration of critical path = $\sqrt{1.555} = 1.25$ days.

A duration of 25 days is $\dfrac{25 - 24}{1.25} = 0.8$ standard deviations above the expected duration.

From normal distribution tables, the required probability is $0.5 - 0.2881 = 0.2119$.

22 In an activity-on-node diagram, an activity can be started when all the activities at the start of arrows leading into the activity have been completed.

23 Note that activity P can be started only when both activities O and M have been completed, and that we have two simple chains of activities, each activity on which can start when the preceding activity has been completed (H N Q and J L M).

11: MARKING SCHEDULE

Question	Correct answer	Marks for the correct answer	Question	Correct answer	Marks for the correct answer
1	B	1	11	B	1
2	D	1	12	D	2
3	C	1	13	B	1
4	A	1	14	B	1
5	D	1	15	B	1
6	C	1	16	D	1
7	C	1	17	B	1
8	C	1	18	B	2
9	A	2	19	B	1
10	D	1	20	B	2

YOUR MARKS

Total marks available   **24**   Your total mark

GUIDELINES - If your mark was:

0 - 6
Poor. The important techniques in this chapter are causing you difficulty. Go back to your study text and work through each relevant section carefully, before trying this chapter again.

7 - 12
Fair. Several of the questions have caught you out. If there are one or two particular techniques which have caused you problems go back to your study text and read through the relevant sections carefully.

13 - 18
Good. There may be a particular group of questions which has caused you difficulty. Check whether this is so, and refer to your study text if there is a clear gap in your knowledge.

19 - 24
Very good. You have a thorough understanding of the principles of stock control.

Question

COMMENTS

1

Only costs which vary with order size are relevant. Order size will affect the total number of orders per year, so costs 1 and 2 are relevant. Cost 3 is relevant, because the average quantity of stock held will vary with the order size. Costs 4 and 5 will not so vary, and are therefore irrelevant.

2

Statement 1 is correct. A stock out (statement 2) occurs when an order cannot be fulfilled, that is, when stocks have run out *before* new stocks arrive. Buffer stock (statement 3) is stock held to be used when actual requirements exceed average requirements, so it will sometimes be used. The re-order level (statement 4) is the level of stock held which leads to an order being placed, not the size of the order.

3

Holding cost per widget per year

$$= £2 + 10\% \times £50 = £7$$

Total holding cost =

$$\frac{900}{2} \times £7 = £3,150$$

4

Number of orders per year

$$= \frac{200 \times 250}{500} = 100.$$

Total ordering costs = 100 × £30 = £3,000.

5

At minimum total cost, T, the rate of change of T is zero, as at a minimum T is neither rising nor falling.

Hence $\quad \dfrac{dT}{dQ} = 0$

As Q moves from below the economic order quantity to above it, T first falls to its minimum then rises, so

$$\dfrac{dT}{dQ} \text{ is first negative then positive,}$$

ie $\quad \dfrac{dT}{dQ}$ is increasing.

Hence $\quad \dfrac{d^2 T}{dQ^2} > 0$

Question

6

The EOQ is where total costs, T, are at a minimum.

$$T = \frac{Qh}{2} + \frac{cd}{Q}$$

$$\frac{dT}{dQ} = \frac{h}{2} - \frac{cd}{Q^2} = 0 \text{ at minimum T}$$

ie $\quad \frac{h}{2} = \frac{cd}{Q^2}$

or $\quad h = \frac{2cd}{Q^2}$

7

c = £45
d = 300 × 52 = 15,600 wotsits
h = £2

$$EOQ = \sqrt{\frac{2 \times 45 \times 15,600}{2}} = 838 \text{ wotsits}$$

8

Only costs which vary with the order size should be considered:

Annual demand = 28,000 × 50 = 1,400,000 calculators.

Holding cost per calculator per year = £0.35.

Ordering cost per order = £22 + £14 = £36

$$EOQ = \sqrt{\frac{2 \times 36 \times 1,400,000}{0.35}} = 16,971 \text{ calculators}$$

9

c = £70
d = 12,000 sofas

	£
Lost rent 2m² × £1.30 × 2 (area not let reflects maximum stock)	5.20
Manager's bonus	1.00
Insurance £16 × 2 (average stock is half maximum)	32.00
h	38.20

$$EOQ = \sqrt{\frac{2 \times 70 \times 12,000}{38.20}} = 210 \text{ sofas}$$

Question

10   Average stock is $\dfrac{Q(1 - d/r)}{2}$

Total cost is therefore

$$T = \frac{Q(1 - d/r)h}{2} + \frac{cd}{Q}$$

At minimum total cost

$$\frac{dT}{dQ} = 0 = \frac{(1 - d/r)h}{2} - \frac{cd}{Q^2}$$

So $\dfrac{(1 - d/r)h}{2} = \dfrac{cd}{Q^2}$

or $\dfrac{Q^2\ (1 - d/r)h}{2} = cd$

11
$c = £230$
$d = 5{,}000 \times 50 = 250{,}000$ units
$h = £2$
$r = 1{,}000{,}000$ units

$$EBQ = \sqrt{\frac{2 \times 230 \times 250{,}000}{2(1 - 250{,}000/1{,}000{,}000)}} = 8{,}756 \text{ units}$$

12
$c = £135$
$d = 50{,}000$ units
$h = £1.50$

The economic order quantity ignoring discounts is:

$$\sqrt{\frac{2 \times 135 \times 50{,}000}{1.50}} = 3{,}000 \text{ units}$$

Thus the first level of discount will be obtained in any case.

At each level of order size, Q, we have:

     annual purchase costs $= 50{,}000 \times £3 \times (100 - \text{discount})\%$
     annual holding costs $= £1.50 \times Q/2$
     annnual ordering costs $= £135 \times 50{,}000/Q$

Question

	Q (units)		
	3,000	*4,000*	*5,000*
	£	£	£
Purchase	147,000	142,500	141,000
Holding	2,250	3,000	3,750
Ordering	2,250	1,688	1,350
	151,500	147,188	146,100

The cheapest option is Q = 5,000 units

13

$$c = £100$$
$$d = 40,000 \text{ units}$$
$$h = £3.50$$

The economic order quantity, ignoring any discount, is

$$\sqrt{\frac{2 \times 100 \times 40,000}{3.50}} = 1,512 \text{ units}$$

Annual cost $= \dfrac{1,512 \times £3.50}{2} + \dfrac{£100 \times 40,000}{1,512} = £5,292$

The annual cost of ordering 2,500 units at a time would be

$$\frac{2,500 \times £3.50}{2} + \frac{£100 \times 40,000}{2,500} = £5,975$$

This is an increase in costs of £683.

A net decrease in purchase cost of £683 would correspond to a discount of

$$\frac{£683}{40,000 \times £8} \times 100\% = 0.21\%$$

Note that only a very small discount is needed, reflecting the insensitivity of total stock related costs to order size.

14

The actual order quantity used will be

$$\sqrt{\frac{2 \times 85 \times 25,000}{4}} = 1,031 \text{ units}$$

If c is £85 × (100 + 10)% = £93.50, the economic order quantity is

$$\sqrt{\frac{2 \times 93.50 \times 25,000}{4}} = 1,081 \text{ units}$$

Question

Total annual costs with an order size of 1,081 units would be

$$1,081 \times 4/2 + 93.50 \times 25,000/1,081 = £4,324$$

Total annual costs with an order size of 1,031 units would be

$$1,031 \times 4/2 + 93.50 \times 25,000/1,031 = £4,329.$$

The percentage excess cost is:

$$\frac{4,329 - 4,324}{4,324} \times 100\% = 0.12\%$$

15 If the annual holding cost per unit is £4 × (100 - 25)% = £3, the economic order quantity is

$$\sqrt{\frac{2 \times 85 \times 25,000}{3}} = 1,190 \text{ units}$$

Total annual costs with an order size of 1,190 units would be

$$1,190 \times 3/2 + 85 \times 25,000/1,190 = £3,571$$

Total annual costs with an order size of 1,031 units would be

$$1,031 \times 3/2 + 85 \times 25,000/1,031 = £3,608$$

The percentage excess cost is

$$\frac{3,608 - 3,571}{3,571} \times 100\% = 1.04\%$$

Note (in both this question and the previous one) how insensitive total costs are to moderate errors in order quantity.

16
$$c = £220$$
$$d = 28,000 \text{ units}$$
$$h = £18$$
$$s = £7$$

Economic order quantity

$$= \sqrt{\frac{2 \times 220 \times 28,000}{18}} \times \sqrt{\frac{(7 + 18)}{7}} = 1,563 \text{ units}$$

Question

17 We can work down from the maximum possible demand in lead time, until we reach a level of demand which has a probability of 0.1 or more. Possible levels of demand over the three day lead time and associated probabilities are as follows:

			Probability
24 units			
8, 8, 8	$0.2 \times 0.2 \times 0.2$		0.008
23 units			
8, 8, 7			
8, 7, 8	$3 \times 0.2 \times 0.2 \times 0.3$		0.036
7, 8, 8			
			$\overline{0.044}$
22 units			
8, 8, 6			
8, 6, 8	$3 \times 0.2 \times 0.2 \times 0.5$		0.06
6, 8, 8			
7, 7, 8			
7, 8, 7	$3 \times 0.3 \times 0.3 \times 0.2$		0.054
8, 7, 7			
			$\underline{\overline{0.158}}$

A re-order level of 22 units will ensure that the probability of unfulfilled demand is only 0.044, while a re-order level of 21 units would give a probability of unfulfilled demand of 0.158.

18 We must weigh up the extra costs of holding stock (by setting a high re-order level) and the costs of running out of stock. Possible levels of demand in lead time are:

Demand (units)	Probability
60	0.2
80	0.5
100	0.2
120	0.1

Annual costs of stock outs are (multiply by 3 for the 3 orders each year):

Re-order level (units)	Costs
60	$(20 \times 0.5 + 40 \times 0.2 + 60 \times 0.1) \times £15 \times 3 = £1,080$
80	$(20 \times 0.2 + 40 \times 0.1) \times £15 \times 3 = £360$
100	$20 \times 0.1 \times £15 \times 3 = £90$
120	£0

Incremental annual stockholding costs are $20 \times £25 = £500$ for a re-order level of 80 units, $40 \times £25 = £1,000$ for 100 units, and $60 \times £25 = £1,500$ for 120 units. Final costs are therefore as follows:

Question

Re-order level (units)	Stock out costs £	Incremental holding costs £	Total relevant costs £
60	1,080	0	1,080
80	360	500	860
100	90	1,000	1,090
120	0	1,500	1,500

The cheapest re-order level is 80 units.

19

The probability of demand in lead time being more than 500 - 450 = 50 units above the mean is 0.1711. From normal distribution tables, 50 units above the mean must be 0.95 standard deviations above the mean. Also from tables, the probability of demand exceeding 1.65 standard deviations above the mean is 0.05. The required re-order level is therefore:

$$450 \; + \; \frac{50}{0.95} \times 1.65 = 537 \text{ units}$$

20

Possible levels of demand in lead time are as follows:

Demand	Probability
0	0.6065
1	0.3033
2	0.0758
3	0.0144 *
	1.0000

* Balancing figure: the probability of demand exceeding 3 units is negligible.

Annual stock out costs are as follows:

Re-order level (units)	Costs
0	$(1 \times 0.3033 + 2 \times 0.0758 + 3 \times 0.0144) \times £70 \times 4 = £139$
1	$(1 \times 0.0758 + 2 \times 0.0144) \times £70 \times 4 = £29$
2	$(1 \times 0.0144) \times £70 \times 4 = £4$
3	£0

The excess annual holding costs (over those with a re-order level of 0) are £80 per unit.

Total relevant costs are as follows:

Re-order level (units)	Stock out costs £	Incremental holding costs £	Total relevant costs £
0	139	0	139
1	29	80	109
2	4	160	164
3	0	240	240

The cheapest option is a re-order level of 1 unit.

12: MARKING SCHEDULE

Question	Correct answer	Marks for the correct answer	Question	Correct answer	Marks for the correct answer
1	D	1	16	C	1
2	A	1	17	C	1
3	C	1	18	B	1
4	B	1	19	B	1
5	B	1	20	C	1
6	D	1	21	D	1
7	D	1	22	C	1
8	D	1	23	A	1
9	C	1	24	D	2
10	A	1	25	B	1
11	B	1	26	C	2
12	B	2	27	A	1
13	B	2	28	C	2
14	A	1	29	C	1
15	D	1	30	B	1

YOUR MARKS

Total marks available   35   Your total mark

GUIDELINES - If your mark was:

0 - 9
Poor. The important techniques in this chapter are causing you difficulty. Go back to your study text and work through each relevant section carefully, before trying this chapter again.

10 - 17
Fair. Several of the questions have caught you out. If there are one or two particular techniques which have caused you problems go back to your study text and read through the relevant sections carefully.

18 - 26
Good. There may be a particular group of questions which has caused you difficulty. Check whether this is so, and refer to your study text if there is a clear gap in your knowledge.

27 - 35
Very good. You have a thorough understanding of queueing theory and simulation.

Question

COMMENTS

1 The calling population (statement 1) is all actual *and potential* customers. The service pattern (statement 2) is the way in which customers are served (eg first come, first served), not the number of queues. In a multiple channel system (statement 3), there are several service points, but there may be a single queue (with the person at the head of the queue going to the first free service point) or several queues (eg one for each service point).

2 Traffic intensity and queue discipline are correctly defined in statements 1 and 2. The system (statement 3) comprises both the queue and customers being served. When a system is in a steady state (statement 4) the length of the queue may still fluctuate, but queue length is not correlated with time.

3 Using Poisson distribution tables (at the end of this book), we find in the column x = 5 a probability of 0.1377 in the row for mean = 3.6.

If mean per hour = 3.6, mean per 40 minutes = 3.6 × 40/60 = 2.4.
For mean = 2.4, the tables give P(3) = 0.2090.

4 A system is in a transient state when its state is a function of time (so that what we would expect the queue size to be would depend on what time it was). For example, a post office's queueing system may be in a transient state just after the office opens, when there is an initial rush of customers, but after a certain time the system will settle down to a steady state. Once it is in a steady state, knowing the exact time does not help us to predict the size of the queue.

5

Average arrival rate $= \lambda = \dfrac{60}{14} = 4.2857$ per hour

Average service rate $= \mu = 7$ per hour

Traffic intensity $= \rho = \dfrac{\lambda}{\mu} = \dfrac{4.2857}{7} = 0.61$

6 It is assumed that there is no limit on the length of the queue, that the calling population is infinite, that the system is always in a steady state and that the number of customers arriving in a given period of time follows a Poisson distribution. These (and other) assumptions are made because they greatly simplify the mathematics required.

Question

7 - 11

From the question, $\lambda = 20$ and $\mu = 28.5$. Then $\rho = \lambda/\mu = 20/28.5 = 0.702$.

The probability that a customer has to queue on arrival $= \rho = 0.702$.

The average number of customers in the system

$$= \frac{\rho}{1-\rho} = \frac{0.702}{1-0.702} = 2.36$$

The average time spent in the system

$$= \frac{1}{\mu-\lambda} = \frac{1}{28.5-20} = 0.1176 \text{ hours} = 7.06 \text{ minutes}$$

The average number of customers in the queue

$$= \frac{\lambda\rho}{\mu-\lambda} = \frac{20 \times 0.702}{28.5 - 20} = 1.65$$

The average time spent in the queue

$$= \frac{\rho}{\mu-\lambda} = \frac{0.702}{28.5-20} = 0.0826 \text{ hours} = 4.96 \text{ minutes}$$

12

In each case, the average number of people in the system is $\lambda/(\mu-\lambda)$. The total hourly cost is therefore £4 × $\lambda/(\mu-\lambda)$ + direct cost of system.

The costs are

System 1:	£4 × 17/(20 - 17) + £12	= £34.67
System 2:	£4 × 17/(25 - 17) + £14	= £22.50
System 3:	£4 × 17/(32 - 17) + £18	= £22.53
System 4:	£4 × 17/(40 - 17) + £20	= £22.96

The cheapest option is system 2.

13

With one server, the total queueing time per hour is

$$(45 + 20) \times \frac{45 + 20}{70(70 -(45 + 20))} = 12.07 \text{ hours}$$

With two servers, the total queueing time per hour for newspaper purchases is

$$45 \times \frac{45}{70 (70-45)} = 1.16 \text{ hours}$$

Question

and the total queueing time per hour for book purchases is

$$20 \times \frac{20}{70 \, (70-20)} = 0.11 \text{ hours}$$

giving a total queueing time per hour for all purchases of 1.27 hours, a saving of 12.07 - 1.27 = 10.8 hours.

The minimum cost per customer per hour of queueing time to justify an extra server is therefore £5/10.8 = £0.46.

14

We have $\lambda = 20$, $\mu = 30$, $\rho = 0.1111$

If c is the number of channels, $\rho = \dfrac{\lambda}{\mu c}$

$$c = \frac{\lambda}{\mu \rho} = \frac{20}{30 \times 0.1111} = 6$$

15

-

19

We are given $\lambda = 30$, $\mu = 16$, $c = 3$, so

$$\rho = \frac{\lambda}{\mu c} = \frac{30}{16 \times 3} = 0.625$$

The probability that there are no customers in the system is

$$P_o = \frac{c!(1-\rho)}{(\rho c)^c + c!(1-\rho) \left[\displaystyle\sum_{n=o}^{c-1} \frac{1}{n!}(\rho c)^n \right]}$$

The sum on the bottom line is

$$\frac{1}{0!}(0.625 \times 3)^0 + \frac{1}{1!}(0.625 \times 3)^1 + \frac{1}{2!}(0.625 \times 3)^2 = 4.6328125$$

$$P_o = \frac{3! \, (1 - 0.625)}{(0.625 \times 3)^3 + 3!(1 - 0.625)4.6328125} = 0.1322$$

The probability of a customer having to queue on arrival is therefore 1 - 0.1322 = 0.8678.

253

Question

The average number of customers in the system is $\dfrac{\rho(\rho c)^c \, P_o}{c!\,(1-\rho)^2} + \rho c$

$= \dfrac{0.625(0.625 \times 3)^3 \times 0.1322}{3!\,(1-0.625)^2} + 0.625 \times 3 = 2.52 \text{ customers}$

The average time a customer spends in the system is

$\dfrac{(\rho c)^c \, P_o}{c!\,(1-\rho)^2 \, c\mu} + \dfrac{1}{\mu}$

$= \dfrac{(0.625 \times 3)^3 \times 0.1322}{3!\,(1-0.625)^2 \times 3 \times 16} + \dfrac{1}{16} = 0.084 \text{ hours} = 5.04 \text{ minutes}$

The average number of customers in the queue is

$\dfrac{\rho(\rho c)^c \, P_o}{c!\,(1-\rho)^2} = \dfrac{0.625\,(0.625 \times 3)^3 \times 0.1322}{3!\,(1-0.625)^2} = 0.65 \text{ customers}$

The average time a customer spends in the queue is:

$\dfrac{(\rho c)^c \, P_o}{c!\,(1-\rho)^2 \, c\mu} = \dfrac{(0.625 \times 3)^3 \times 0.1322}{3!\,(1-0.625)^2 \times 3 \times 16} = 0.0215 \text{ hours} = 1.29 \text{ minutes}$

20

The Monte Carlo method uses random numbers to generate inputs (for example, people joining a queue). It can be applied to discrete or continuous simulation models, and can produce values for all output variables. There are other ways of taking account of uncertainty, for example sensitivity analysis.

21

Input variables are the variables which the user of the model puts into the simulation. They include parameters (constants set for the simulation) and other variables for which a series of values may be input. Some of the factors represented by them will be outside management's control. There is no necessary link between the number of input variables and the number of output variables. Status variables describe the state of the system at any time, and are not the same thing as input variables.

22

Parameters are input variables set at some constant value in advance. The number of units required by customers each year not supplied immediately from stock would be an output variable, not a parameter.

Question

23

Relevant probabilities are found from Poisson distribution tables with m = 0.7, and rounded to two decimal places.

Arrivals	Probability	Number of numbers	Allocation of numbers
0	0.50	50	00 - 49
1	0.35	35	50 - 84
2	0.12	12	85 - 96
> 3	0.03	3	97 - 99
	1.00	100	

24

The allocation of random numbers is as follows (using normal distribution tables to find probabilities):

Time (minutes)	Standard deviations from mean	Probability to 2 decimal places	Random numbers
0-1	Below -2	0.02	00 - 01
1-2	-2 to -1	0.14	02 - 15
2-3	-1 to 0	0.34	16 - 49
3-4	0 to +1	0.34	50 - 83
4-5	+1 to +2	0.14	84 - 97
>5	Above 2	0.02	98 - 99

Of the 20 random numbers given, 13 fall in the range 50 - 83.

25

We must work out the probability of each possible level of demand in the lead time, and allocate random numbers on that basis.

Demand (units)	Probability	Allocation
10	0.3 × 0.4 = 0.12	00 - 11
12	0.7 × 0.4 = 0.28	12 - 39
15	0.3 × 0.6 = 0.18	40 - 57
18	0.7 × 0.6 = 0.42	58 - 99

26

The allocation of numbers will be as follows:

Demand	Probability	Random numbers
0	0.1	0
1	0.1	1
2	0.1	2
3	0.3	3-5
4	0.4	6-9

Total demand for days 4 - 12 is then 0 + 3 + 4 + 4 + 4 + 4 + 4 + 4 + 4 = 31 units

Question

27

There will be unsatisfied demand when demand exceeds supply. This occurs on the second, fourth and eighth days, ie on 30% of the days simulated.

28

-

30

A simulation can be set out as follows

	Grade 1	Grade 2	Grade 3
Start of month 3	150	40	10
Month 3 intake	10		
	160		
Month 3 review			
0.3 × 160	(48)	48	
0.1 × 40		(4)	4
0.07 × 10		1	(1)
0.07 × 40	3	(3)	
0.07 × 160	(11)		
Start of month 4	104	82	13
Month 4 intake	10		
	114		
Month 4 review			
0.3 × 114	(34)	34	
0.1 × 82		(8)	8
0.07 × 13		1	(1)
0.07 × 82	6	(6)	
0.07 × 114	(8)		
Start of month 5	78	103	20
Month 5 intake	10		
	88		
0.3 × 88	(26)	26	
0.1 × 103		(10)	10
0.07 × 20		1	(1)
0.07 × 103	7	(7)	
0.07 × 88	(6)		
Start of month 6	63	113	29

Thus after the month 4 review we may expect 103 customers to be at grade 2, and after the month 5 review we may expect 29 customers to be at grade 3.

We cannot say exactly how long a specified new customer will take to reach grade 3 because we are given only probabilities, so we can only work out the probabilities of different times to reach grade 3. We cannot tell whether or not a specified customer will be average without further information.

POISSON DISTRIBUTION

Mean m	x								
	0	1	2	3	4	5	6	7	8
0.1	0.9048	0.0905	0.0045	0.0002	0.0000	0.0000	0.0000	0.0000	0.0000
0.2	0.8187	0.1637	0.0164	0.0011	0.0001	0.0000	0.0000	0.0000	0.0000
0.3	0.7408	0.2222	0.0333	0.0033	0.0003	0.0000	0.0000	0.0000	0.0000
0.4	0.6703	0.2681	0.0536	0.0072	0.0007	0.0001	0.0000	0.0000	0.0000
0.5	0.6065	0.3033	0.0758	0.0126	0.0016	0.0002	0.0000	0.0000	0.0000
0.6	0.5488	0.3293	0.0988	0.0198	0.0030	0.0004	0.0000	0.0000	0.0000
0.7	0.4966	0.3476	0.1217	0.0284	0.0050	0.0007	0.0001	0.0000	0.0000
0.8	0.4493	0.3595	0.1438	0.0383	0.0077	0.0012	0.0002	0.0000	0.0000
0.9	0.4066	0.3659	0.1647	0.0494	0.0111	0.0020	0.0003	0.0000	0.0000
1.0	0.3679	0.3679	0.1839	0.0613	0.0153	0.0031	0.0005	0.0001	0.0000
1.1	0.3329	0.3662	0.2014	0.0738	0.0203	0.0045	0.0008	0.0001	0.0000
1.2	0.3012	0.3614	0.2169	0.0867	0.0260	0.0062	0.0012	0.0002	0.0000
1.3	0.2725	0.3543	0.2303	0.0998	0.0324	0.0084	0.0018	0.0003	0.0001
1.4	0.2466	0.3452	0.2471	0.1128	0.0395	0.0111	0.0026	0.0005	0.0001
1.5	0.2231	0.3347	0.2510	0.1255	0.0471	0.0141	0.0035	0.0008	0.0001
1.6	0.2019	0.3230	0.2584	0.1378	0.0551	0.0176	0.0047	0.0011	0.0002
1.7	0.1827	0.3106	0.2640	0.1496	0.0636	0.0216	0.0061	0.0015	0.0003
1.8	0.1653	0.2975	0.2678	0.1607	0.0723	0.0260	0.0078	0.0020	0.0005
1.9	0.1496	0.2842	0.2700	0.1710	0.0812	0.0309	0.0098	0.0027	0.0006
2.0	0.1353	0.2707	0.2707	0.1804	0.0902	0.0361	0.0120	0.0034	0.0009
2.1	0.1225	0.2572	0.2700	0.1890	0.0992	0.0417	0.0146	0.0044	0.0011
2.2	0.1108	0.2438	0.2681	0.1966	0.1082	0.0476	0.0174	0.0055	0.0015
2.3	0.1003	0.2306	0.2652	0.2033	0.1169	0.0538	0.0206	0.0068	0.0019
2.4	0.0907	0.2177	0.2613	0.2090	0.1254	0.0602	0.0241	0.0083	0.0025
2.5	0.0821	0.2052	0.2565	0.2138	0.1336	0.0668	0.0278	0.0099	0.0031
2.6	0.0743	0.1931	0.2510	0.2176	0.1414	0.0735	0.0319	0.0118	0.0038
2.7	0.0672	0.1815	0.2450	0.2205	0.1488	0.0804	0.0362	0.0139	0.0047
2.8	0.0608	0.1703	0.2384	0.2225	0.1557	0.0872	0.0407	0.0163	0.0057
2.9	0.0550	0.1596	0.2314	0.2237	0.1622	0.0940	0.0455	0.0188	0.0068
3.0	0.0498	0.1494	0.2240	0.2240	0.1680	0.1008	0.0504	0.0216	0.0081
3.1	0.0450	0.1397	0.2165	0.2237	0.1733	0.1075	0.0555	0.0246	0.0095
3.2	0.0408	0.1304	0.2087	0.2226	0.1781	0.1140	0.0608	0.0278	0.0111
3.3	0.0369	0.1217	0.2008	0.2209	0.1823	0.1203	0.0662	0.0312	0.0129
3.4	0.0334	0.1135	0.1929	0.2186	0.1858	0.1264	0.0716	0.0348	0.0148
3.5	0.0302	0.1057	0.1850	0.2158	0.1888	0.1322	0.0771	0.0385	0.0169
3.6	0.0273	0.0984	0.1771	0.2125	0.1912	0.1377	0.0826	0.0425	0.0191
3.7	0.0247	0.0915	0.1692	0.2087	0.1931	0.1429	0.0881	0.0466	0.0215
3.8	0.0224	0.0850	0.1615	0.2046	0.1944	0.1477	0.0936	0.0508	0.0241
3.9	0.0202	0.0789	0.1539	0.2001	0.1951	0.1522	0.0989	0.0551	0.0269
4.0	0.0183	0.0733	0.1465	0.1954	0.1954	0.1563	0.1042	0.0595	0.0298
4.1	0.0166	0.0679	0.1393	0.1904	0.1951	0.1600	0.1093	0.0640	0.0328

NORMAL DISTRIBUTION

	0.00	0.01	0.02	0.03	0.04	0.05	0.06	0.07	0.08	0.09
0.0	.0000	.0040	.0080	.0120	.0159	.0199	.0239	.0279	.0319	.0359
0.1	.0398	.0438	.0478	.0517	.0557	.1596	.0636	.0675	.0714	.0753
0.2	.0893	.0832	.0871	.0910	.1948	.1987	.1026	.1064	.1103	.1141
0.3	.1179	.1217	.1255	.1293	.1331	.1368	.1406	.1443	.1480	.1517
0.4	.1554	.1591	.1628	.1664	.1700	.1736	.1772	.1808	.1844	.1879
0.5	.1915	.1950	.1985	.2019	.2054	.2088	.2123	.2157	.2190	.2224
0.6	.2257	.2291	.2324	.2357	.2389	.2422	.2454	.2486	.2518	.2549
0.7	.2580	.2611	.2642	.2673	.2704	.2734	.2764	.2794	.2823	.2852
0.8	.2881	.2910	.2939	.2967	.2995	.3023	.3041	.3078	.3106	.3133
0.9	.3159	.3186	.3212	.3238	.3264	.3289	.3315	.3340	.3365	.3389
1.0	.3413	.3438	.3461	.3485	.3508	.3531	.3554	.3577	.3599	.3621
1.1	.3643	.3665	.3686	.3708	.3729	.3749	.3770	.3790	.3810	.3830
1.2	.3849	.3869	.3888	.3907	.3925	.3944	.3962	.3980	.3997	.4015
1.3	.4032	.4049	.4066	.4082	.4099	.4115	.4131	.4147	.4162	.4177
1.4	.4192	.4207	.4222	.4236	.4251	.4265	.4279	.4292	.4306	.4319
1.5	.4332	.4345	.4357	.4370	.4382	.4394	.4406	.4418	.4430	.4441
1.6	.4452	.4463	.4474	.4485	.4495	.4505	.4515	.4525	.4535	.4545
1.7	.4554	.4564	.4573	.4582	.4591	.4599	.4608	.4616	.4625	.4633
1.8	.4641	.4649	.4656	.4664	.4671	.4678	.4686	.4693	.4699	.4706
1.9	.4713	.4719	.4726	.4732	.4738	.4744	.4750	.4756	.4762	.4767
2.0	.4772	.4778	.4783	.4788	.4793	.4798	.4803	.4808	.4812	.4817
2.1	.4821	.4826	.4830	.4834	.4838	.4842	.4846	.4850	.4854	.4857
2.2	.4861	.4865	.4868	.4871	.4875	.4878	.4881	.4884	.4887	.4980
2.3	.4893	.4896	.4898	.4901	.4904	.4906	.4909	.4911	.4913	.4916
2.4	.4918	.4920	.4922	.4925	.4927	.4929	.4931	.4932	.4934	.4936
2.5	.4938	.4940	.4941	.4943	.4945	.4946	.4948	.4949	.4951	.4952
2.6	.4953	.4955	.4956	.4957	.4959	.4960	.4961	.4962	.4963	.4964
2.7	.4965	.4966	.4967	.4968	.4969	.4970	.4971	.4972	.4973	.4974
2.8	.4974	.4975	.4976	.4977	.4977	.4978	.4979	.4980	.4980	.4981
2.9	.4981	.4982	.4983	.4983	.4984	.4984	.4985	.4985	.4986	.4986
3.0	.49865	.4987	.4987	.4988	.4988	.4989	.4989	.4989	.4990	.4990
3.1	.49903	.4991	.4991	.4997	.4992	.4992	.4992	.4992	.4993	.4993
3.2	.49931	.4993	.4994	.4994	.4994	.4994	.4994	.4995	.4995	.4995
3.3	.49952	.4995	.4995	.4996	.4996	.4996	.4996	.4996	.4996	.4997
3.4	.49966	.4997	.4997	.4997	.4997	.4997	.4997	.4997	.4997	.4998
3.5	.49977									

T DISTRIBUTION

Degrees of freedom	$t_{0.05}$	$t_{0.025}$	$t_{0.01}$	$t_{0.005}$
1	6.31	12.7	31.8	63.7
2	2.92	4.30	6.96	9.92
3	2.35	3.18	4.54	5.84
4	2.13	2.78	3.75	4.60
5	2.01	2.57	3.36	4.03
6	1.94	2.45	3.14	3.71
7	1.89	2.36	3.00	3.50
8	1.86	2.31	2.90	3.36
9	1.83	2.26	2.82	3.25
10	1.81	2.23	2.76	3.17
11	1.80	2.20	2.72	3.11
12	1.78	2.18	2.68	3.05
13	1.77	2.16	2.65	3.01
14	1.76	2.14	2.62	2.98
15	1.75	2.13	2.60	2.95
16	1.75	2.12	2.58	2.92
17	1.74	2.11	2.57	2.90
18	1.73	2.10	2.55	2.88
19	1.73	2.09	2.54	2.86
20	1.72	2.09	2.53	2.85
21	1.72	2.08	2.52	2.83
22	1.72	2.07	2.51	2.82
23	1.71	2.07	2.50	2.81
24	1.71	2.06	2.49	2.80
25	1.71	2.06	2.48	2.79
26	1.71	2.06	2.48	2.78
27	1.70	2.05	2.47	2.77
28	1.70	2.05	2.47	2.76
29	1.70	2.05	2.46	2.76
∞	1.65	1.96	2.33	2.58

259

CHI-SQUARED DISTRIBUTION

Degrees of freedom	$\chi^2_{0.1}$	$\chi^2_{0.05}$	$\chi^2_{0.025}$	$\chi^2_{0.01}$	$\chi^2_{0.005}$
1	2.71	3.84	5.02	6.63	7.88
2	4.61	5.99	7.38	9.21	10.6
3	6.25	7.81	9.35	11.3	12.8
4	7.78	9.49	11.1	13.3	14.9
5	9.24	11.1	12.8	15.1	16.7
6	10.6	12.6	14.4	16.8	18.5
7	12.0	14.1	16.0	18.5	20.3
8	13.4	15.5	17.5	20.1	22.0
9	14.7	16.9	19.0	21.7	23.6
10	16.0	18.3	20.5	23.2	25.2

F DISTRIBUTION

$F_{0.05}$	D F for numerator									
	1	2	3	4	5	6	7	8	9	10
D.F. for denominator 1	161	200	216	225	230	234	237	239	241	242
2	18.5	19.0	19.2	19.2	19.3	19.3	19.4	19.4	19.4	19.4
3	10.1	9.55	9.28	9.12	9.01	8.94	8.89	8.85	8.81	8.79
4	7.71	6.94	6.59	6.39	6.26	6.16	6.09	6.04	6.00	5.96
5	6.61	5.79	5.41	5.19	5.05	4.95	4.88	4.82	4.77	4.74
6	5.99	5.14	4.76	4.53	4.39	4.28	4.21	4.15	4.10	4.06
7	5.59	4.74	4.35	4.12	3.97	3.87	3.79	3.73	3.68	3.64
8	5.32	4.46	4.07	3.84	3.69	3.58	3.50	3.44	3.39	3.35
9	5.12	4.26	3.86	3.63	3.48	3.37	3.29	3.23	3.18	3.14
10	4.96	4.10	3.71	3.48	3.33	3.22	3.14	3.07	3.02	2.98

$F_{0.01}$	D F for numerator									
	1	2	3	4	5	6	7	8	9	10
D.F. for denominator 1	4,052	5,000	5,403	5,625	5,764	5,859	5,928	5,982	6,023	6,056
2	98.5	99.0	99.2	99.2	99.3	99.3	99.4	99.4	99.4	99.4
3	34.1	30.8	29.5	28.7	28.2	27.9	27.7	27.5	27.3	27.2
4	21.2	18.0	16.7	16.0	15.5	15.2	15.0	14.8	14.7	14.5
5	16.3	13.3	12.1	11.4	11.0	10.7	10.5	10.3	10.2	10.1
6	13.7	10.9	9.78	9.15	8.75	8.47	8.26	8.10	7.98	7.87
7	12.2	9.55	8.45	7.85	7.46	7.19	6.99	6.84	6.72	6.62
8	11.3	8.65	7.59	7.01	6.63	6.37	6.18	6.03	5.91	5.81
9	10.6	8.02	6.99	6.42	6.06	5.80	5.61	5.47	5.35	5.26
10	10.0	7.56	6.55	5.99	5.64	5.39	5.20	5.06	4.94	4.85

LOGARITHMS

	0	1	2	3	4	5	6	7	8	9
10	·0000	0043	0086	0128	0170	0212	0253	0294	0334	0374
11	·0414	0453	0492	0531	0569	0607	0645	0682	0719	0755
12	·0792	0828	0864	0899	0934	0969	1004	1038	1072	1106
13	·1139	1173	1206	1239	1271	1303	1335	1367	1399	1430
14	·1461	1492	1523	1553	1584	1614	1644	1673	1703	1732
15	·1761	1790	1818	1847	1875	1903	1931	1959	1987	2014
16	·2041	2068	2095	2122	2148	2175	2201	2227	2253	2279
17	·2304	2330	2355	2380	2405	2430	2455	2480	2504	2529
18	·2553	2577	2601	2625	2648	2672	2695	2718	2742	2765
19	·2788	2810	2833	2856	2878	2900	2923	2945	2967	2989
20	·3010	3032	3054	3075	3096	3118	3139	3160	3181	3201
21	·3222	3243	3263	3284	3304	3324	3345	3365	3385	3404
22	·3424	3444	3464	3483	3502	3522	3541	3560	3579	3598
23	·3617	3636	3655	3674	3692	3711	3729	3747	3766	3784
24	·3802	3820	3838	3856	3874	3892	3909	3927	3945	3962
25	·3979	3997	4014	4031	4048	4065	4082	4099	4116	4133
26	·4150	4166	4183	4200	4216	4232	4249	4265	4281	4298
27	·4314	4330	4346	4362	4378	4393	4409	4425	4440	4456
28	·4472	4487	4502	4518	4533	4548	4564	4579	4594	4609
29	·4624	4639	4654	4669	4683	4698	4713	4728	4742	4757
30	·4771	4786	4800	4814	4829	4843	4857	4871	4886	4900
31	·4914	4928	4942	4955	4969	4983	4997	5011	5024	5038
32	·5051	5065	5079	5092	5105	5119	5132	5145	5159	5172
33	·5185	5198	5211	5224	5237	5250	5263	5276	5289	5302
34	·5315	5328	5340	5353	5366	5378	5391	5403	5416	5428
35	·5441	5453	5465	5478	5490	5502	5514	5527	5539	5551
36	·5563	5575	5587	5599	5611	5623	5635	5647	5658	5670
37	·5682	5694	5705	5717	5729	5740	5752	5763	5775	5786
38	·5798	5809	5821	5832	5843	5855	5866	5877	5888	5899
39	·5911	5922	5933	5944	5955	5966	5977	5988	5999	6010
40	·6021	6031	6042	6053	6064	6075	6085	6096	6107	6117
41	·6128	6138	6149	6160	6170	6180	6191	6201	6212	6222
42	·6232	6243	6253	6263	6274	6284	6294	6304	6314	6325
43	·6335	6345	6355	6365	6375	6385	6395	6405	6415	6425
44	·6435	6444	6454	6464	6474	6484	6493	6503	6513	6522
45	·6532	6542	6551	6561	6571	6580	6590	6599	6609	6618
46	·6628	6637	6646	6656	6665	6675	6684	6693	6702	6712
47	·6721	6730	6739	6749	6758	6767	6776	6785	6794	6803
48	·6812	6821	6830	6839	6848	6857	6866	6875	6884	6893
49	·6902	6911	6920	6928	6937	6946	6955	6964	6972	6981
50	·6990	6998	7007	7016	7024	7033	7042	7050	7059	7067
51	·7076	7084	7093	7101	7110	7118	7126	7135	7143	7152
52	·7160	7168	7177	7185	7193	7202	7210	7218	7226	7235
53	·7243	7251	7259	7267	7275	7284	7292	7300	7308	7316
54	·7324	7332	7340	7348	7356	7364	7372	7380	7388	7396

	0	1	2	3	4	5	6	7	8	9
55	·7404	7412	7419	7427	7435	7443	7451	7459	7466	7474
56	·7482	7490	7497	7505	7513	7520	7528	7536	7543	7551
57	·7559	7566	7574	7582	7589	7597	7604	7612	7619	7627
58	·7634	7642	7649	7657	7664	7672	7679	7686	7694	7701
59	·7709	7716	7723	7731	7738	7745	7752	7760	7767	7774
60	·7782	7789	7796	7803	7810	7818	7825	7832	7839	7846
61	·7853	7860	7868	7875	7882	7889	7896	7903	7910	7917
62	·7924	7931	7938	7945	7952	7959	7966	7973	7980	7987
63	·7993	8000	8007	8014	8021	8028	8035	8041	8048	8055
64	·8062	8069	8075	8082	8089	8096	8102	8109	8116	8122
65	·8129	8136	8142	8149	8156	8162	8169	8176	8182	8189
66	·8195	8202	8209	8215	8222	8228	8235	8241	8248	8254
67	·8261	8267	8274	8280	8287	8293	8299	8306	8312	8319
68	·8325	8331	8338	8344	8351	8357	8363	8370	8376	8382
69	·8388	8395	8401	8407	8414	8420	8426	8432	8439	8445
70	·8451	8457	8463	8470	8476	8482	8488	8494	8500	8506
71	·8513	8519	8525	8531	8537	8543	8549	8555	8561	8567
72	·8573	8579	8585	8591	8597	8603	8609	8615	8621	8627
73	·8633	8639	8645	8651	8657	8663	8669	8675	8681	8686
74	·8692	8698	8704	8710	8716	8722	8727	8733	8739	8745
75	·8751	8756	8762	8768	8774	8779	8785	8791	8797	8802
76	·8808	8814	8820	8825	8831	8837	8842	8848	8854	8859
77	·8865	8871	8876	8882	8887	8893	8899	8904	8910	8915
78	·8921	8927	8932	8938	8943	8949	8954	8960	8965	8971
79	·8976	8982	8987	8993	8998	9004	9009	9015	9020	9025
80	·9031	9036	9042	9047	9053	9058	9063	9069	9074	9079
81	·9085	9090	9096	9101	9106	9112	9117	9122	9128	9133
82	·9138	9143	9149	9154	9159	9165	9170	9175	9180	9186
83	·9191	9196	9201	9206	9212	9217	9222	9227	9232	9238
84	·9243	9248	9253	9258	9263	9269	9274	9279	9284	9289
85	·9294	9299	9304	9309	9315	9320	9325	9330	9335	9340
86	·9345	9350	9355	9360	9365	9370	9375	9380	9385	9390
87	·9395	9400	9405	9410	9415	9420	9425	9430	9435	9440
88	·9445	9450	9455	9460	9465	9469	9474	9479	9484	9489
89	·9494	9499	9504	9509	9513	9518	9523	9528	9533	9538
90	·9542	9647	9552	9557	9562	9566	9571	9576	9581	9586
91	·9590	9595	9600	9605	9609	9614	9619	9624	9628	9633
92	·9638	9643	9647	9652	9657	9661	9666	9671	9675	9680
93	·9685	9689	9694	9699	9703	9708	9713	9717	9722	9727
94	·9731	9736	9741	9745	9750	9754	9759	9763	9768	9773
95	·9777	9782	9786	9791	9795	9800	9805	9809	9814	9818
96	·9823	9827	9832	9836	9841	9845	9850	9854	9859	9863
97	·9868	9872	9877	9881	9886	9890	9894	9899	9903	9908
98	·9912	9917	9921	9926	9930	9934	9939	9943	9948	9952
99	·9956	9961	9965	9969	9974	9978	9983	9987	9991	9996

ANTI-LOGARITHMS

	0	1	2	3	4	5	6	7	8	9
·00	1000	1002	1005	1007	1009	1012	1014	1016	1019	1021
·01	1023	1026	1028	1030	1033	1035	1038	1040	1042	1045
·02	1047	1050	1052	1054	1057	1059	1062	1064	1067	1069
·03	1072	1074	1076	1079	1081	1084	1086	1089	1091	1094
·04	1096	1099	1102	1104	1107	1109	1112	1114	1117	1119
·05	1122	1125	1127	1130	1132	1135	1138	1140	1143	1146
·06	1148	1151	1153	1156	1159	1161	1164	1167	1169	1172
·07	1175	1178	1180	1183	1186	1189	1191	1194	1197	1199
·08	1202	1205	1208	1211	1213	1216	1219	1222	1225	1227
·09	1230	1233	1236	1239	1242	1245	1247	1250	1253	1256
·10	1259	1262	1265	1268	1271	1274	1276	1279	1282	1285
·11	1288	1291	1294	1297	1300	1303	1306	1309	1312	1315
·12	1318	1321	1324	1327	1330	1334	1337	1340	1343	1346
·13	1349	1352	1355	1358	1361	1365	1368	1371	1374	1377
·14	1380	1384	1387	1390	1393	1396	1400	1403	1406	1409
·15	1413	1416	1419	1422	1426	1429	1432	1435	1439	1442
·16	1445	1449	1452	1455	1459	1462	1466	1469	1472	1476
·17	1479	1483	1486	1489	1493	1496	1500	1503	1507	1510
·18	1514	1517	1521	1524	1528	1531	1535	1538	1542	1545
·19	1549	1552	1556	1560	1563	1567	1570	1574	1578	1581
·20	1585	1589	1592	1596	1600	1603	1607	1611	1614	1618
·21	1622	1626	1629	1633	1637	1641	1644	1648	1652	1656
·22	1660	1663	1667	1671	1675	1679	1683	1687	1690	1694
·23	1698	1702	1706	1710	1714	1718	1722	1726	1730	1734
·24	1738	1742	1746	1750	1754	1758	1762	1766	1770	1774
·25	1778	1782	1786	1791	1795	1799	1803	1807	1811	1816
·26	1820	1824	1828	1832	1837	1841	1845	1849	1854	1858
·27	1862	1866	1871	1875	1879	1884	1888	1892	1897	1901
·28	1905	1910	1914	1919	1923	1928	1932	1936	1941	1945
·29	1950	1954	1959	1963	1968	1972	1977	1982	1986	1991
·30	1995	2000	2004	2009	2014	2018	2023	2028	2032	2037
·31	2042	2046	2051	2056	2061	2065	2070	2075	2080	2084
·32	2089	2094	2099	2104	2109	2113	2118	2123	2128	2133
·33	2138	2143	2148	2153	2158	2163	2168	2173	2178	2183
·34	2188	2193	2198	2203	2208	2213	2218	2223	2228	2234
·35	2239	2244	2249	2254	2259	2265	2270	2275	2280	2286
·36	2291	2296	2301	2307	2312	2317	2323	2328	2333	2339
·37	2344	2350	2355	2360	2366	2371	2377	2382	2388	2393
·38	2399	2404	2410	2415	2421	2427	2432	2438	2443	2449
·39	2455	2460	2466	2472	2477	2483	2489	2495	2500	2506
·40	2512	2518	2523	2529	2535	2541	2547	2553	2559	2564
·41	2570	2576	2582	2588	2594	2600	2606	2612	2618	2624
·42	2630	2636	2642	2649	2655	2661	2667	2673	2679	2685
·43	2692	2698	2704	2710	2716	2723	2729	2735	2742	2748
·44	2754	2761	2767	2773	2780	2786	2793	2799	2805	2812
·45	2818	2825	2831	2838	2844	2851	2858	2864	2871	2877
·46	2884	2891	2897	2904	2911	2917	2924	2931	2938	2944
·47	2951	2958	2965	2972	2979	2985	2992	2999	3006	3013
·48	3020	3027	3034	3041	3048	3055	3062	3069	3076	3083
·49	3090	3097	3105	3112	3119	3126	3133	3141	3148	3155

	0	1	2	3	4	5	6	7	8	9
·50	3162	3170	3177	3184	3192	3199	3206	3214	3221	3228
·51	3236	3243	3251	3258	3266	3273	3281	3289	3296	3304
·52	3311	3319	3327	3334	3342	3350	3357	3365	3373	3381
·53	3388	3396	3404	3412	3420	3428	3436	3443	3451	3459
·54	3467	3475	3483	3491	3499	3508	3516	3524	3532	3540
·55	3548	3556	3565	3573	3581	3589	3597	3606	3614	3622
·56	3631	3639	3648	3656	3664	3673	3681	3690	3698	3707
·57	3715	3724	3733	3741	3750	3758	3767	3776	3784	3793
·58	3802	3811	3819	3828	3837	3846	3855	3864	3873	3882
·59	3890	3899	3908	3917	3926	3936	3945	3954	3963	3972
·60	3981	3990	3999	4009	4018	4027	4036	4046	4055	4064
·61	4074	4083	4093	4102	4111	4121	4130	4140	4150	4159
·62	4169	4178	4188	4198	4207	4217	4227	4236	4246	4256
·63	4266	4276	4285	4295	4305	4315	4325	4335	4345	4355
·64	4365	4375	4385	4395	4406	4416	4426	4436	4446	4457
·65	4467	4477	4487	4498	4508	4519	4529	4539	4550	4560
·66	4571	4581	4592	4603	4613	4624	4634	4645	4656	4667
·67	4677	4688	4699	4710	4721	4732	4742	4753	4764	4775
·68	4786	4797	4808	4819	4831	4842	4853	4864	4875	4887
·69	4898	4909	4920	4932	4943	4955	4966	4977	4989	5000
·70	5012	5023	5035	5047	5058	5070	5082	5093	5105	5117
·71	5129	5140	5152	5164	5176	5188	5200	5212	5224	5236
·72	5248	5260	5272	5284	5297	5309	5321	5333	5346	5358
·73	5370	5383	5395	5408	5420	5433	5445	5458	5470	5483
·74	5495	5508	5521	5534	5546	5559	5572	5585	5598	5610
·75	5623	5636	5649	5662	5675	5689	5702	5715	5728	5741
·76	5754	5768	5781	5794	5808	5821	5834	5848	5861	5875
·77	5888	5902	5916	5929	5943	5957	5970	5984	5998	6012
·78	6026	6039	6053	6067	6081	6095	6109	6124	6138	6152
·79	6166	6180	6194	6209	6223	6237	6252	6266	6281	6295
·80	6310	6324	6339	6353	6368	6383	6397	6412	6427	6442
·81	6457	6471	6486	6501	6516	6531	6546	6561	6577	6592
·82	6607	6622	6637	6653	6668	6683	6699	6714	6730	6745
·83	6761	6776	6792	6808	6823	6839	6855	6871	6887	6902
·84	6918	6934	6950	6966	6982	6998	7015	7031	7047	7063
·85	7079	7096	7112	7129	7145	7161	7178	7194	7211	7228
·86	7244	7261	7278	7295	7311	7328	7345	7362	7379	7396
·87	7413	7430	7447	7464	7482	7499	7516	7534	7551	7568
·88	7586	7603	7621	7638	7656	7674	7691	7709	7727	7745
·89	7762	7780	7798	7816	7834	7852	7870	7889	7907	7925
·90	7943	7962	7980	7998	8017	8035	8054	8072	8091	8110
·91	8128	8147	8166	8185	8204	8222	8241	8260	8279	8299
·92	8318	8337	8356	8375	8395	8414	8433	8453	8472	8492
·93	8511	8531	8551	8570	8590	8610	8630	8650	8670	8690
·94	8710	8730	8750	8770	8790	8810	8831	8851	8872	8892
·95	8913	8933	8954	8974	8995	9016	9036	9057	9078	9099
·96	9120	9141	9162	9183	9204	9226	9247	9268	9290	9311
·97	9333	9354	9376	9397	9419	9441	9462	9484	9506	9528
·98	9550	9572	9594	9616	9638	9661	9683	9705	9727	9750
·99	9772	9795	9817	9840	9863	9886	9908	9931	9954	9977

Further information

The Password series includes the following titles:

	Order code	
Economics	P01X	EC
Basic accounting	P028	BA
Financial accounting	P036	FA
Costing	P044	CO
Foundation business mathematics	P052	FB
Business law	P060	BL
Auditing	P079	AU
Organisation and management	P087	OM
Advanced business mathematics	P095	AB
Taxation	P109	TX
Management accounting	P117	MA
Interpretation of accounts	P125	IA
Financial management	P133	FM
Company law	P141	CL
Information technology	P15X	IT

Password is available from most major bookshops. If you have any difficulty obtaining them, please contact BPP directly, quoting the above order codes.

BPP Publishing Limited
Aldine Place
142/144 Uxbridge Road,
London, W12 8AW

Tel: 081-740 1111
Fax: 081-740 1184
Telex: 2665871 (MONREF G) - quoting '76:SJJ098'